TRANSFORMING THE PAST

Tradition and Kinship Among Japanese Americans

SYLVIA JUNKO YANAGISAKO

Transforming the Past

TRADITION AND KINSHIP AMONG JAPANESE AMERICANS

Stanford University Press, Stanford, California

For my parents,
Howard Kaoru Yanagisako and Sumiko Matsuda Yanagisako

Stanford University Press
Stanford, California
© 1985 by the Board of Trustees of the
Leland Stanford Junior University
Printed in the United States of America
Original printing 1985

Last figure below indicates year of this printing:
01   00   99   98   97   96   95   94   93   92

CIP data appear at the end of the book

Preface

A BOOK ABOUT JAPANESE AMERICANS cannot help but immediately hint of the particular cultural and historical context in which it was written. This is perhaps nowhere more succinctly displayed than in the decisions its author has made about a couple of editorial issues. The first issue was whether or not to place a hyphen between "Japanese American." I have chosen not to because hyphenated ethnic categories continue to be associated in some minds with divided national identities and loyalties. The absence of the hyphen, on the other hand, leaves no ambiguity that the subject of my book is Americans of Japanese ancestry. In citing or quoting from published works in which "Japanese-American" is hyphenated, however, I have been true to the original. The second issue was whether to state Japanese names in American order (surname last) or Japanese order (surname first). I have chosen to consistently use an American order because, although the first generation of Japanese Americans uses both orders (which one depends on the cultural context), the second generation uses an American order almost exclusively. To avoid any confusion, I use an American order even when giving the names of Japanese nationals who have never emigrated to the United States.

All the names of the persons interviewed, however, are pseudonyms, and in a few instances I have altered minor details about their individual or family characteristics that might have revealed their identities. My hope has always been that the people I interviewed would read this book; if they do they will have no difficulty recognizing themselves. In assigning pseudonyms, I have tried to convey the time period and cultural context in which people were born, while concealing their personal identities. Thus, persons with a Japanese surname and an American given name have similar pseudonyms, and when Japanese given names are used they are appropriate to the time period in which those so designated were born. To help readers keep track of the individuals, married couples, and families who appear in the case materials set off from the main text throughout the book, I have assigned each married couple an identifying number. Each number begins with a generation marker (I for the first generation and N for the second generation), followed by the couple's case number (1 through 24 for the first generation and 1 through 48 for the second generation), and finally a lowercase letter that indicates whether this is the first instance (a), second instance (b), and so on, on which the case has been cited.

I began the research for this book as the fieldwork for my dissertation in 1973-74 and continued it as postdoctoral fieldwork in 1974-75. The writing of my dissertation was supported by a grant from the University of Washington Graduate School, and my postdoctoral research was funded by a grant from the Rockefeller and Ford foundations' Program for Population Policy Research in the Social Sciences. I am grateful to the members of my dissertation committee who guided my fieldwork and the writing of my dissertation. I am particularly indebted to Professor Michael Lieber for introducing me to David M. Schneider's writings on American kinship, which inspired in me an interest in kinship studies that I had not thought possible, and to Professor Laura Newell-Morris for suggesting that I study Japanese Americans rather than a more conventional, exotic Other. Professors James A. Watson and Jay Miller also provided helpful comments on my dissertation, which pushed me toward some of the different tacks I have taken in this book.

My research benefited greatly from my association with Donna Leonetti, who conducted her dissertation research on fertility change in the same community, and with whom I later collaborated on a study of the interrelationship between kinship change and demographic change. I am also grateful to the many people who worked with us during different phases of our projects. In particular, I thank Mary Aoki for her invaluable work as an interpreter and interviewer, and Jeffrey Dann and Anne Roda for their skillful interviewing and the insights I acquired from our many discussions.

The writing of this manuscript was supported by a Mellon Junior Faculty Leave and a sabbatical leave from Stanford University. I am most grateful to the colleagues and friends who made extensive comments on the manuscript at different stages, including George Collier, Jane Collier, Renato Rosaldo, David M. Schneider, G. William Skinner,

Margery Wolf, and the late Michelle Z. Rosaldo. The manuscript has also benefited from comments by Harumi Befu, Theodore Bestor, Rainier Bauer, Keith Brown, Roger Rouse, and Raymond T. Smith. I thank my father, Howard Kaoru Yanagisako, for creating all the pseudonyms for the manuscript. J. M. B. Edwards's editorial queries were both delightful and demanding, and the manuscript has benefited greatly from his editing. John Sullivan neither typed this manuscript nor corrected its punctuation, but nonetheless he contributed greatly to its production.

Finally, I am most indebted to the people who welcomed me into their homes and spoke to me of their lives and their families.

S.J.Y.

Contents

Figures

Tables

APPENDIX TABLES

TRANSFORMING THE PAST

Tradition and Kinship Among Japanese Americans

CHAPTER 1

The Analysis of Kinship Change

THIS BOOK IS AT ONCE a cultural history of Japanese American kinship and a contribution to the study of the contemporary kinship system of the United States. It brings to the analysis of American kinship a theoretical perspective that attends to the historically situated, symbolic processes through which people interpret and thereby transform their kinship relations. By examining kinship change among Japanese Americans, I elucidate a particular case of a general process I take as having been central to the development of contemporary American kinship. For, while Japanese Americans have a unique and rich cultural heritage and a distinctive and troubled social history, the process of kinship change they have undergone since the turn of the century has been shared by many other Americans.

I begin with the premise that kinship relations are structured by symbolic relations and serve symbolic functions as well as social ones. It follows from this that kinship change involves symbolic processes, and that a study of it must attend to the manner in which relations among symbols, meanings, and actions have shaped relations among people. My second premise is that we can comprehend the system of symbols and meanings structuring people's kinship relations in the present only if we know their kinship relations in the past. If symbolic systems help people answer the questions and cope with the problems of meaning they confront in their everyday lives, symbolic analysis can only be enriched by a knowledge of the social history that has given rise to these questions and problems. Conversely, we can comprehend that social history only if we comprehend the system of symbols and meanings through which people interpret and thereby transform the past.

In this study I treat the oral kinship autobiographies I elicited from first- and second-generation Japanese Americans in Seattle, Washington, both as cultural tales and as accounts with a good degree of historical veracity. Because people's recollections of the past are reasonably accurate and do not obliterate facts so much as reinterpret them, they can be mined to reconstruct a social history of events and actions. At the same time they can be used, along with what people say about the present, as material for a symbolic analysis.[1] Unlike most Japanese Americans, and most of those who have studied them, I do not uncritically assume a timeless past of "Japanese tradition" in which stem-family households were endlessly reproduced by people who obeyed the "rules of the Japanese family system." Instead, on the one hand, I reconstruct kinship relations in Japan from immigrants' accounts of their kinship biographies and, on the other, regard the Japanese past and the American present that figure so centrally in these accounts as complex symbols whose meanings must be explicated.

The analytic strategy I have formulated for this study is one I think can be usefully applied to groups besides Japanese Americans and other ethnic groups whose conceptions of their particular cultural traditions and experiences as immigrants are similarly prominent in their discourse on kinship relations. It can help us better understand the social and symbolic processes shaping kinship even among those sectors of our society whose ethnicity has been made invisible by hegemonic processes that cast a particular cultural system as a generalized American one. For whether they view themselves as having an ethnic past that is Polish, Italian, African, English, or, in the case of "just plain American," one supposedly unmarked by ethnicity, all these folk commonly speak of a "traditional" past in opposition to the "modern" present. Like Japanese Americans, they too construct tradition by reconceptualizing the past in relation to the meaning of their actions in the present, thereby transforming past and present in a dialectic of interpretation.

TWO GENERATIONS OF JAPANESE AMERICANS IN SEATTLE

There are two reasons why Japanese Americans are uniquely suited for an intergenerational study of kinship change: their well-recorded history and their demographic characteristics as a population. This study is concerned with the first two generations of Japanese Ameri-

---

[1] As Rosaldo explains of his use of Ilongot stories of the past: "Although Ilongot recollections often are used as a political idiom, they retain a specific historical value.... What is contestable is less [their] veracity than the choice of historical incidents to be used as a guide for projected action. Even the most partisan of Ilongot narratives can be used in reconstructing a wider sense of their historical past" (R. Rosaldo 1980, 31).

cans in Seattle, Washington, which is among the most thoroughly documented of all Japanese American communities for the period before
World War II. Like others of its kind on the West Coast, the Seattle
community originated in the 1890's with the immigration of young and
for the most part unmarried men who came primarily from the prefectures of southwestern Japan. Whether they came from farms or small-
town, entrepreneurial households, these men emigrated from the area
of Japan that in the late nineteenth century was most integrated into
the rapidly expanding market economy.[2] For immigrants they were
well educated. The men had completed an average of eight years of
schooling in Japan.[3]

The Japanese community in Seattle passed quickly from an initial
"frontier period" characterized by a highly unbalanced sex ratio (5
males to every female) and few families to a "settling period" marked
by a more balanced sex ratio (153 males per 100 females) and an abundance of new marriages and births. During this frontier period (1890–
1910), the men worked primarily as wage laborers. Between 1910 and
1920 the number of males actually decreased as a result of the so-called
Gentlemen's Agreement between the United States and Japan, which
was intended to halt any further immigration of Japanese laborers. In
a historical irony of unintended consequence, however, the decrease in
the male population was more than compensated for by the arrival of
wives and brides and, shortly thereafter, high birth rates.

The period of marriage and family building among the first generation coincided with the economic boom accompanying U.S. entry into
World War I. In Seattle, the Japanese moved quickly to provide small
retail businesses and services that catered to the large influx of white
workers as well as to Japanese farmers in the surrounding rural areas.
Whether, for any individual, marriage preceded or followed the movement out of wage labor, marriage for the Seattle Japanese in general
was historically coincident with the shift to entrepreneurship. But the
expansion of the community was short-lived. The growing anti-Japa-

[2] Over two-thirds of the immigrant parents of the second-generation (Nisei) survey
sample (see Appendix) came from the area Richard K. Beardsley, John W. Hall, and Robert F. Ward (1959, 15) label the "core zone" of Japan, which constitutes the most economically developed area of the nation. Sixteen percent of the parents of that sample came
from the "frontier zone," which was poorer and more self-sufficient in production, and
13 percent came from the "peripheral zone," an intermediate area.

[3] The UCLA Japanese American Research Project survey of 1,047 Issei in the continental United States found that 64 percent of the combined male and female respondents had completed 8 or fewer years of schooling in Japan and 36 percent had gone
beyond 8 years (Levine and Montero 1973, 7).

nese sentiment that had already led to the passage of discriminatory laws in California brought about similar restrictions in Washington. In 1921 the State of Washington passed its version of an Alien Land Law denying foreign-born Japanese the right to lease or own land. A year later, in *Takao Ozawa* v. *United States*, the U.S. Supreme Court upheld the ineligibility of Japanese immigrants to citizenship through naturalization. Two years later the Immigration Act of 1924 halted immigration from Japan and further crippled the Seattle community's economy. After 1924 the growth of the Seattle Japanese population was due entirely to the births of the second generation.

Until World War II the Seattle Japanese presented a collective tale of small business in early twentieth-century America. In the 1930's, two-thirds of first-generation Japanese men and women were classified by the sociologist Frank Miyamoto as being self-employed entrepreneurs in "trades" or "domestic and personal services" (Miyamoto 1939, 71). Their businesses were restricted to a narrow range of service-oriented enterprises such as hotels, groceries, grocery stands, produce houses, restaurants, greenhouses, laundries, and peddling routes. Less than twenty percent of Seattle Japanese were wage-earners. Whether or not the predominance of entrepreneurship was responsible for creating what Miyamoto has called a strongly "solidary" community with a "lack of class distinctions" (Miyamoto 1939, 71), the community was without a doubt well organized and quite capable of lobbying for its economic and social welfare.

The events that followed the outbreak of World War II destroyed the community's entrepreneurial character at the same time that they ensured the continued documentation of its history. The imprisonment of the Japanese West Coast population, immigrant Japanese citizens and second-generation U.S. citizens alike, resulted in the forced sale or abandonment of their businesses. It also made the Japanese one of the most thoroughly studied, or at least exhaustively surveyed, immigrant populations in American history.[4] From studies of the "evacuation" of Japanese Americans into "relocation camps" in the interior of the western states, of the "relocation" program that attempted to place the American-born, second-generation in midwestern and eastern states, and the follow-up studies of the resettlement period that began with

---

[4] For descriptions of camp life see D. Kitagawa 1967, Kikuchi 1973, Thomas and Nishimoto 1946, Bloom 1943, Spicer 1969, and Daniels 1971. For studies of the resettlement period, see Bloom 1947, Broom and Riemer 1949, Broom and Kitsuse 1973, Thomas 1952, Thomas and Nishimoto 1946, Miyamoto and O'Brien 1947.

the closing of the camps in 1945, we know of the disruptions in family life, the decline in the first generation's parental and political control, and the financial and social hardships Japanese Americans faced trying to rebuild their communities. We know too that the two-thirds of the Seattle Japanese American population who returned to that city after the war did not reestablish its entrepreneurial character (Miyamoto and O'Brien 1947). By 1945 the majority of first-generation men were over forty-five years old; the majority of first-generation women were in their late forties and early fifties. Most of the couples who had small family businesses before the war were forced back into the unskilled, low-paying jobs in which they had started out in America, while their children moved predominantly into wage-earning and salaried occupations. After the war less than a third of second-generation men were self-employed businessmen, and second-generation women had even lower rates of self-employment.

In the 1970's Seattle Japanese Americans evidenced the high educational, occupational, and income levels that have made Japanese Americans a favorite tale of American social mobility. As of 1940, second-generation Japanese Americans in Seattle had surpassed the white population in median school years completed. Seventy-four percent of second-generation Japanese Americans over twenty-five years of age had completed high school compared with 48 percent of the Seattle native-born whites over the same age (U.S. Bureau of the Census 1943a, 1943b). In 1970, the percentage of Seattle Japanese American males over that age who had graduated from college was 29 percent compared to 16 percent among white males, and white-collar employment among them was 52 percent compared to 41 percent among white males (U.S. Bureau of the Census 1972, 1973). Third-generation Japanese Americans, who were coming of age in the 1960's and 1970's, showed every indication of surpassing the educational and occupational achievements of their parents (Bonacich and Modell 1980, 238).

This brief history of the community reveals a further reason for making Japanese Americans the focus of an intergenerational study of kinship change. Japanese Americans are one of those rare populations in which, for historical reasons, generations defined in terms of kinship coincide with cohorts defined in terms of birth date. The political history that shaped the character of Japanese immigration to the United States created relatively discrete, nonoverlapping generations (Thomas 1950). The concentration of first-generation marriages during the period from 1907 to 1924 in turn concentrated the births of the

second generation (see Table 9, page 65), and created a distinct bi-
modality in the age structure of the pre–World War II population.[5]
Second-generation marriages were similarly concentrated (see Table
10, ibid.), and produced a third generation that was mostly under the
age of thirty in 1970.

That Japanese Americans themselves label these generations—the
first Issei, the second Nisei, the third Sansei—and attribute to them different cultural and social characters as well as historical experiences,
explains the convention of generational comparison that pervades
studies of Japanese Americans, whether they focus on values (Kiefer
1974), personality structure (DeVos 1955, Connor 1977), "identity dilemmas" (Maykovich 1972), or the relationship between changing occupations and forms of ethnic solidarity (Bonacich and Modell 1980).
A most powerful differentiator, in addition, has from the start structured the relations between Issei and Nisei: although the Issei were denied U.S. citizenship until the late 1950's, by the principle of *jus soli* the
Nisei were American citizens from birth.[6] This difference in their political statuses generated for Issei and Nisei dilemmas about family goals
and strategies that influenced the course of change in Japanese American kinship.

By the time I initiated my research in 1973, the Japanese American
population in Seattle consisted of more than the Issei and their descendants whose history I have just described. Among the 10,557 Japanese
enumerated for Seattle by the 1970 U.S. Census were individuals who
had emigrated to the United States after the revision of the immigration laws in the 1950's.[7] These included war brides who had entered
after marrying men (the vast majority of them white) in the armed ser-

    [5] Although a small number of Japanese immigrants to Seattle married before 1900,
the overwhelming majority of Issei marriages were concentrated within the following
thirty-five years. I estimate, moreover, that between 70 and 80 percent of Seattle Issei
marriages occurred within the period from 1907 through 1924. This estimate excludes
Issei who married in Seattle but returned to Japan leaving no descendants. It is based on
the marriage dates of the Issei parents of the Nisei survey sample.

    [6] Because Japan, like many European nations, defined nationality by the principle of
jus sanguinis, the Nisei initially held dual citizenship. Japan revised its laws in 1916, however, to allow Nisei (except those between the ages of 17 and 28, who were eligible for
military service) to renounce their allegiance to Japan (Petersen 1971, 50). After 1924, by
Japanese law, American Nisei automatically lost their Japanese citizenship unless they
were registered as Japanese subjects with a consulate within fourteen days of their birth.
The exact proportion of Nisei who were so registered by their parents is unknown (ibid.).

    [7] After the U.S. Immigration Act of 1924, twenty-eight years passed before the Mc-
Carran-Walter Immigration Act allowed a token quota of Japanese to immigrate.

vices. Also enumerated were Japanese Americans who had moved to Seattle from other areas of the continental United States and Hawaii. All these more recent arrivals, in particular the postwar immigrants from Japan, do not share the historical experience of the prewar residents.

For the sake of historical coherence, this study focuses on those Seattle Japanese Americans whose families share a history that includes pre-1925 immigration from Japan, residence in Seattle prior to World War II, confinement in prison camps during the war, and postwar resettlement in Seattle. This nuclear population, which is defined in terms of a shared historical experience rather than solely in terms of racial or ethnic criteria, includes an estimated 56 percent of the approximately ten thousand Japanese in Seattle in 1970 (Leonetti 1976). The nuclear population, however, constitutes the core of a larger community into which other Japanese Americans are integrated through ties of marriage, kinship, and friendship. Most of the recent immigrants from Japan do not identify themselves as members of the same Japanese American community as the nuclear population, nor do they participate in the voluntary associations or kinship and friendship networks of the latter. But many Japanese Americans, who moved to Seattle after the war from other areas of the United States in which their parents or grandparents had settled before 1925, do consider themselves at least marginal members of the community. The history of the nuclear population, moreover, represents for those both at the core and at the margins of the community *the* history of Japanese Americans in Seattle. To the extent that they participate in the densely connected network of social relationships that constitute the community, I would expect other Japanese Americans in Seattle to share in the same kinship system as their kin and friends who have lived there longer.

The extent to which my analysis holds for Japanese Americans in other areas of the country is another issue. The great majority of Japanese Americans in the continental United States are concentrated in urban West Coast communities with social histories and contemporary socioeconomic characteristics that resemble the Seattle community's. These communities, if they existed before the war, likewise have nuclear populations that share a common history of pre-1925 immigration from Japan, imprisonment during World War II, and postwar resettlement in their former locale. Furthermore, today they constitute the cores of larger Japanese American communities into which more recently arrived Japanese Americans are integrated. Whether their populations today are larger than that of the Japanese American population in Seattle (as is the case of the Los Angeles and San Francisco communities) or smaller (as is the case of the Portland community), they were founded by immigrants who came at the turn of the century from the same prefectures of southwestern Japan, with the same occupational and educational backgrounds, and—most importantly—with the same goals and resources as the Seattle Issei.

One notable difference among these West Coast, urban Japanese American communities is in the predominance of entrepreneurship in their prewar economies. For example, before the war the San Francisco Japanese American community was characterized by a lower rate of entrepreneurship and a higher rate of wage work, including domestic service by women (Glenn 1980). In Los Angeles, although the proportion of self-employed Issei was comparable to that in Seattle (Broom and Reimer 1949, 17), a large number were in contract gardening, a field into which the Seattle Issei never entered in significant numbers. Yet these differences are small and, I suspect, of much less significance than the shared political and social history of urban Japanese Americans on the West Coast, a history that argues strongly for common social and cultural processes of kinship change. I make no claim that my analysis extends to Japanese Americans who live in rural communities or in other regions of the United States, in particular in Hawaii.[8] The radically different structural position of Japanese Americans in Hawaii, who until recently were the largest ethnic group in the islands, and of Japanese Americans in Seattle, who never comprised more than two percent of the population, would seem prima facie evidence of divergent political and social histories and cultural transformations.[9]

This difference is relevant here for other reasons besides the applicability of my analysis to all Japanese Americans. For what is shared and not shared by these two groups locates me in relation to those I studied. That I am not a member of the Seattle Japanese American community was as apparent to the "natives" as it was to me. My paternal and maternal grandparents had, like the Issei I interviewed, emigrated

[8] See the studies of kinship among Japanese Americans in Honolulu by Colleen L. Johnson (1973, 1974).

[9] It is not, as is often claimed (for instance, in Kitano 1969, 8), that the Japanese Americans in Hawaii have retained more "Japanese ways" than those in the continental United States because of a "larger and more cohesive ethnic culture." Rather, the particular social history that has led to Hawaii's present ethnically stratified class system has engendered cultural processes that have elaborated somewhat different "Japanese traditions" and imbued them with somewhat different meanings. It has also created somewhat different conceptions of what it means to be "Japanese American."

from southwestern Japan at the turn of the century. But the circumstances that brought them to work in the sugar and pineapple plantations of Hawaii rather than in the lumber camps and farms of the Northwest led their children and grandchildren to grow up in a social world quite different from that of the Seattle Nisei and Sansei. Such grandparents gave me not only a Japanese American identity but a generational status, as a Sansei, in relation to those I interviewed. However, my lack of kinship connections with Seattle Japanese Americans and, until I began my research, any friendships with them, placed me outside the community. Whether my ambiguous status as, in the words of one Nisei, "one of us," or, in the words of another, "you Hawaiians," or, in the words of yet another, "you social scientists" endowed me with what I then thought was the best of all possible social identities is something of which I am now less certain. Nevertheless, the people I interviewed frequently voiced their assumption that as "Japanese Americans" we shared experiences, knowledge, attitudes, and vocabularies. At times we did.

THEORETICAL ISSUES

The majority of the population in the United States today does not define itself as the biological progeny of English ancestors nor as the cultural heirs to an Anglo-American family "tradition." The social history of the family in colonial or even Victorian America, therefore, while essential to an understanding of present-day American kinship, is greatly misconstrued if portrayed as unearthing its traditional past. For families in eighteenth- and nineteenth-century America are no more the source of families in late twentieth-century America than are families in eighteenth- and nineteenth-century Ireland, Italy, and Japan. Nevertheless, the study of kinship change among immigrant groups is too often placed at the margins of the history of American kinship. This tendency can be attributed in good part to the theoretical perspectives that have guided our thinking about family and kinship organization among both recent immigrants and early founders, ethnic minorities and the supposedly nonethnic majority. The regnant sociological theory of American kinship since World War II has been the structural-functional one espoused by Talcott Parsons, which both asserts and explains the predominance of the "structurally isolated conjugal family" in capitalist-industrial society (Parsons 1943; Parsons and Bales 1955). In spite of the early recognition of strains and contradictions within the American family system—for example, the strain between the sexual asymmetry of the conjugal relationship and the ideology of romantic love—the conjugal family is thought to approximate the best of all possible kinship structures in an "open-class" society. Such a structure, it is argued, requires that child-care and socialization functions and the psychosocial needs of individuals be fulfilled in a way that interferes least with the occupational demands of an advanced, industrial society.

The image of individuals and kin groups fashioning families that best suit their needs and that at the same time facilitate the maintenance of the society's core institutions represents a particular version of a general functionalist theory of kinship in which people everywhere are portrayed as fashioning kinship systems to fit their material and social circumstances.[10] Immigrants coming from "old worlds" and "old traditions" could easily be accommodated within this functionalist scheme if one posited an initial period of cultural conservatism that in the long run would yield to some combination of economic and ideological forces. So long as an immigrant group remained unabsorbed into the core of American society—the core being commonly construed as the middle class—it might retain so-called traditional kinship structures and values. But once its social and economic circumstances came to resemble those of the middle class, so would its families. Moreover, given the Anglo-American heritage claimed by those at the upper levels of an ethnically stratified class society, the acculturation process begun by public education would be reinforced by the anticipation of social mobility. As a result of the combined processes of functional integration and cultural assimilation, therefore, the bulk of the American population would converge on the functionally adaptive version of an Anglo-American family tradition.

Aside from the trouncing that structural-functional theory in general has received over the past two decades, the mounting evidence from historical and sociological research has generated a healthy skepticism about this evolutionary tale of American kinship.[11] On one side, the sheer mass of ethnographic facts now documenting variations in kinship relations among ethnic groups, social classes, and regions in

[10] I include within this category of functionalist theories of kinship both the ones that emphasize material (whether ecological, biological, or economic) functions (for instance, Malinowski 1963; Forde 1934; Eggan 1966; Netting 1968; Nimkoff and Middleton 1960; Pasternak, Ember, and Ember 1976; Fox 1967) and the ones that emphasize social structural functions (for instance, Radcliffe-Brown 1950, 1952; Fortes 1949, 1969; Parsons and Bales 1955; Goody 1972, 1976).

[11] Among the most compelling critiques of structural-functional explanations are A. Smith 1973, Geertz 1957, Leach 1954, and Barth 1966.

the United States seems sufficient to deflate any uniformist theory of the family in industrial-capitalist society.[12] On the other, the more recent discovery of small households (Laslett 1972) and "modern" marriage and inheritance practices (Macfarlane 1978) in preindustrial England has severely undermined the hypothesized causal relationship between family system and occupational system.

Neither of these growing bodies of findings, however, has generated a more useful theoretical framework for analyzing change in American kinship or for ordering its diverse forms. Nor has either suggested a way to analytically integrate historical process and synchronic variation. The discovery of familiar features of household size and composition and familiar norms of property and inheritance in preindustrial England has contributed little to our understanding of change, because a fascination with the similarities between past and present predisposes researchers to assume that small households in the sixteenth century entailed the same social relationships and systems of meanings as small households in the twentieth. Equally fallacious is the inclination to equate a concept of individualism extracted from marriage and inheritance practices of thirteenth-century England with the individualism that underlies these institutions in English society today (Macfarlane 1978).

Likewise, the discovery of differences in the kinship relations of contemporary Americans has failed to push us beyond static cultural and functional theories. Here the current approaches are limited to a cultural pluralist perspective that attributes the present diversity to the maintenance of a variety of family "traditions" brought to America by immigrants, and a recycled functionalist model that explains it as the product of multiple adaptations to a variety of environmental "niches" in American society. The cultural pluralist model employs the same static concept of culture as the above-mentioned interpretation of the origins of the English family, and hence is inclined to discover sameness in surface similarity. If something labeled "filial piety" was once a core Japanese value, then any present commitments by Japanese Americans toward their parents are glossed, without benefit of a systematic analysis of the content and meaning of these commitments, as the perpetua-

---

[12] Many anthropological studies of contemporary American kinship have been published in recent years (see, for example, Chock 1974, 1976; DiLeonardo 1984; Stack 1974; Batteau 1978; Kennedy 1980; Mitchell 1978; Yanagisako 1977, 1978). There is also an extensive sociological literature (Bott 1957; Sussman and Burchinal 1962; Litwak 1960; Young and Willmott 1957) and a growing historical literature (for example, Anderson 1971; Hareven 1978; Tilly and Scott 1980; Gutman 1976).

tion of "Japanese family tradition." And so, for example, we read not only of Japanese American families who continue to manifest Japanese cultural norms and ideals of filial piety (Kitano and Kikumura 1976), but also of Greek American families who continue to manifest Greek cultural norms and ideals of filial piety (Kourvetaris 1976), though we cannot tell from these accounts whether they are the same or different norms and ideals in past and present. Similarly, we are told that Italian American marriages tend toward a "traditional Italian segregated conjugal pattern" in which husbands and wives have distinctly separate roles and activities (Gans 1962) while Japanese American marriages tend toward a "traditional Japanese" segregated conjugal pattern (Johnson 1978). The vague character of these purported cultural traditions renders them unsatisfactory for explaining the diversity in American kinship. The second alternative—the model of sundry "adaptations" to sundry "niches" in society—merely multiplies Parsons's functionalist model to accommodate a variety of family structures supposedly well integrated with a variety of structural positions. And so we have poor urban Blacks whose fluid consensual unions, flexible households, and extensive "domestic networks" are "survival strategies" and "adaptive mechanisms" in a situation of economic insecurity and racial discrimination (Stack 1974), just as the stable conjugal bonds and structural isolation of conjugal families are said to have been adjusted to the occupational circumstances of the middle class.

Both these attempted explanations succeed no better than their earlier versions because they share the same inadequate model of culture. Models of functional adaptation no longer predict the movement toward a uniform family form, but rather the movement toward several different forms adjusted to different structural positions in industrial-capitalist society, yet they continue to treat concepts, values, and ideals as either the ad hoc rationalization of strategic individuals or the epiphenomenal by-products of functional requirements—by-products that at the same time provide ideological support for the social system. The functional integration of ideological concepts with norms and institutional structures has long been emphasized (see, for instance, Parsons 1943), but the meaningful relations among concepts and the symbolic processes through which they change continue to be slighted.

Because they focus on what they call cultural traditions—whether these are said to be learned from parents or from agents of the dominant culture—cultural pluralist and acculturation frameworks might be expected to employ a more refined concept of culture. Yet the preoccupation with identifying elements of family structure and value systems as continuations of English, Italian, or Japanese "tradition" betrays a bits-and-pieces concept of culture. To be told that Japanese Americans have adopted white, middle-class concepts of "independence," but have retained Japanese concepts of "filial piety" is to be handed a two-column laundry list in place of a coherent model. The labeling of this value as "American" and that as "Japanese," this interactional pattern as "modern" and that as "traditional," is no substitute for analyzing the symbolic structures on which their meaning depends. These shortsighted perspectives predispose us to jump ahead to explanations of why this element from one "tradition" and that from the other have been adopted before we have adequately examined their meaning and their relations with other elements in a kinship system.

Progress in understanding both diversity and change would appear to require the reconceptualization of kinship as a domain of anthropological inquiry. For an academic discipline that for decades has been convinced that kinship lies at its theoretical center, anthropology has seen a surprising number of challenges to its conventions of kinship analysis in recent years. Having rejected the elegant formalism of French structuralists (Lévi-Strauss 1969) as well as the "jural" principles of British structuralists (for example, Fortes 1969), some theorists now insist that we treat kinship relations "as something people *make*, and with which they *do* something" (Bourdieu 1977, 35). Thus, a general concern on the part of such theorists as Raymond Firth (1951), Frederick Barth (1966), and Bruce Kapferer (1976) has been further elaborated within a Marxist model of conflicting interest within particular social formations.[13] The danger of this, however, is that it may lead us back to a conception of kinship as driven mainly by rational, utilitarian calculation. As Clifford Geertz (1973, 202) elegantly put it, the main defects of a Marxist interest theory are that "its psychology is too anemic and its sociology too muscular." In other words, we may simply replace functions of biological reproduction and social integration with functions of the reproduction of the social relations of production and of social inequality as the culturally unmediated determinants of kinship. The most promising way to avoid these theoretical problems lies in a symbolic approach to kinship.

Kinship as a Symbolic System

Although symbolic analysis has long proven productive in anthropology, it was not until David M. Schneider's (1968) exegesis of American kinship that it was brought to bear on what had been construed as

[13] See also Bloch 1975, Meillasoux 1972, and Godelier 1975.

a fundamentally utilitarian domain. As Schneider (1976, 207) notes, anthropologists have tended to limit symbolic analysis to spheres such as religion, ritual, magic, and myth that we construe as fulfilling expressive functions. Because kinship, on the other hand, appears to be rooted in the objective realities of birth, copulation, death, property, goods, and services, ethnographers have been content to describe the behavioral patterns and norms that organize these activities. In contrast, Schneider chooses to focus on the symbolic and meaningful structures underlying the normative and behavioral systems of kinship. The goal of his account of American kinship is to identify the cultural units and rules as these are defined and differentiated by the natives themselves, and to explicate the system of symbols and meanings these units form. He insists, moreover, on analyzing culture as a symbolic system "purely in its own terms rather than by systematically relating the symbols to the social and psychological systems" (1968, 1).

The analytic strategy Schneider advocates entails, first, taking into account the whole kinship system rather than treating kin classification as a distinct, autonomous part of the system; and second, asking what the definition of the domain of kinship is in every culture rather than assuming it is defined "by the biogenetic premises of the genealogically defined grid," an assumption he attributes to Lewis Henry Morgan and his followers. Third, he abstracts from "concrete observable patterns of behavior" the normative system consisting in "the rules and regulations which an actor should follow if his behavior is to be accepted by his community or his society as proper." Schneider's final step is to abstract the cultural system from the normative system (1972, 37).

Since the publication of Schneider's *American Kinship* in 1968, a growing number of anthropologists have produced symbolic analyses of kinship in other societies, as well as in different sectors of American society.[14] Others have brought symbolic analysis usefully to bear on issues in social structure and kinship organization.[15] In their monograph on Balinese kinship, Hildred and Clifford Geertz (1975) also employ a symbolic approach to extract the common ideational themes underlying the diversity of kinship practices within a single but complex society. Like Schneider, they draw an analytic distinction between the "cultural" and the "social structural" dimensions of kinship. The "cultural dimension" refers to "those Balinese ideas, beliefs and values which are

[14] Among them are Alexander 1976, Chock 1974, Drummond 1978, Inden and Nicholas 1977, Silverman 1971, and Witherspoon 1975.

[15] See, for example, A. Strathern 1973, Carroll 1970, and M. Strathern 1981.

relevant to their behavior as kinsmen—ideas, beliefs, and values that are abstracted from and distinguished from the concrete interpersonal relationships which obtain 'on the ground' among particular kinsmen" (ibid., 2). Unlike Schneider, however, Geertz and Geertz do not abstract "kinship symbols" from the normative system but directly from kinship institutions and the "vocabulary and practices" of domestic life (ibid., 158). Their analysis of the Balinese "idiom" of kinship (which they liken to E. E. Evans-Pritchard's (1940) analysis of the "idiom" of Nuer kinship) as part of a more inclusive "culture pattern" is a convincing illustration of Schneider's contention that kinship is not an autonomous domain of meaning (1972, 59-60).

Schneider insists that the limitations of kinship theory in anthropology derive from a history of assumptions about the genealogical basis of kinship. Here, too, he makes a radical break with that history, a break with theoretical consequences that are only beginning to be fully appreciated. In an ironic example of the dialectic between the knowing of other cultures and the knowing of our own, Schneider (1972) argues persuasively that the dominant anthropological view of kinship as grounded in the biological facts of sexual reproduction is a specific cultural one. That anthropologists who are members of a society in which the transmission of biogenetic substance defines "real" or "true" parenthood would begin their research on kinship in other societies by constructing genealogies has now been rendered understandable in a new way.

As powerful as are Schneider's insights, his method of analysis and concomitant theory of culture are not without faults (see Scheffler 1976 and Yanagisako 1978). The most serious of these is his insistence on isolating the analysis of cultural systems from the analysis of patterns of action. This insistence derives from a theory of culture that is a functional one, but that is very different from a Radcliffe-Brownian or a Malinowskian functional theory of culture. For Schneider the functions of symbols and meanings are "coping and adapting . . . with the problems of meaning and with the maintenance of solidarity and of particular patterns of solidarity. They provide a meaningful social order and social life in this sense. It is this that is the distinctly cultural question and the distinctly cultural problem" (1972, 47). This cultural problem is, for Schneider, very different from the "sociological or social system or social organizational question" of how people "cope with the facts of human reproduction" or of "how roles are defined and articulated into a set of patterns for action which adapt man to the facts of his environment" (ibid., 46). Hence the danger of carrying out a cultural and a sociological analysis simultaneously is that the former may be contaminated by the latter.

My objections to a cultural analysis oriented toward the isolation of "pure" symbolic systems need not be fully rehearsed here.[16] Above all, however, there is the puzzle of what gives shape to "the distinctly cultural question" and the "distinctly cultural problem" of which Schneider speaks. For unless we adhere to a Lévi-Straussian scheme in which *the* question and *the* problem of meaning are cast by a universal cultural template, then there must be *particular* cultural questions and *particular* cultural problems. These in turn must arise from people's particular social experiences within particular historical circumstances. Just because we should, as Schneider rightly argues, avoid miscasting cultural systems as the answers to social and psychological problems, we do not have to isolate the analysis of meaning from the analysis of a history of action.

Closely linked with this problem is the absence of a temporal dimension to Schneider's method of analysis and its implicit theory of culture. In analyzing American kinship, Schneider (1968) and Schneider and Smith (1973) assume we can understand the meanings underlying kinship relations in isolation from both present and past actions and without knowing the historical process through which both patterns of action and systems of meaning have evolved. It follows that their method of cultural analysis perpetuates the suspect sociological practice of separating statics from dynamics. But such an attempt to "reach an understanding or explanation of [a social phenomenon] which is different from and independent of any historical explanation of how it came into existence" (Radcliffe-Brown 1950, 3), however much called for at a time when evolutionary theories of society hampered the analysis of its systemic character, is less productive than an attempt to integrate history and social structure.

Modified to overcome the above limitations, Schneider's analysis of kinship as a system of symbols and meanings can be productively extended to the study of kinship change. If the function of symbolic systems is to cope with what he calls the "distinctly cultural problem" of meaning and to provide "a meaningful social order," neither the problem nor the order need be a static one. The "cultural question" to which kinship as a symbolic system responds may be the question of how to conceptually organize and make meaningful changing patterns of sol-

[16] See Yanagisako 1978. Such objections have also been raised by Geertz (1973, 17-18) and by Smith and Lomnitz (1980).

idarity rather than unchanging ones. In other words, we should seek an understanding of the way in which kinship as a symbolic system provides conceptual order by connecting the past with the present.

TOWARD A CULTURAL ANALYSIS OF KINSHIP CHANGE

To bring together the cultural analysis of kinship and the study of kinship change, I situate my analysis of kinship as a system of symbols and meanings in the context of a social history of kinship relations. I begin with the premise that one cannot comprehend what people are saying about their kinship relations in the present without knowing their past. The social history of Japanese American kinship in this book is reconstructed primarily from my informants' accounts. Although I occasionally cite published sources, including censuses and earlier sociological studies of Japanese Americans, I rely on them only for quantitative data on the demographic, economic, and political history of Japanese American communities. The material from which I extract the cultural system of Japanese American kinship includes both normative statements, that is, statements about what people should do or are expected to do, and a broader range of interpretive statements through which people describe, categorize, and only sometimes explicitly evaluate people's actions in the past and present. So, for example, when I examine the symbols and meanings structuring the conjugal relation, rather than identify the norms that define the proper roles and modes of interaction between husbands and wives and then extracting from the normative system the underlying cultural system, I extract the cultural system directly from the broad range of descriptive and evaluative statements that people make about their marital histories. My concern, then, is with the terms in which people talk about particular events, decisions, and actions in the history of their own kinship relations.

In assessing kinship change among Japanese Americans, I do not assume a static baseline of traditional Japanese kinship set within a premodern, agricultural Japan or even a modernizing, industrializing Japan. Indeed, a grave error of most studies of so-called ethnic families in America is their assumption of a timeless past of "family tradition." Yet the Japan in which the Issei grew up at the end of the nineteenth century was as dynamic as the United States in which their children, the Nisei, grew up in the twentieth century. At the end of the nineteenth century, Japan was a rapidly transforming nation characterized by great population growth, industrialization, a spreading market economy, and increasing rates of tenancy, urban migration, and emigration.

The leaders of the Meiji Restoration were not only intent on transforming Japan into an industrial-capitalist nation, they were also convinced that the best way to protect Japan from penetration by Western powers was to modernize it along Western lines. That entailed more than acquiring Western technology and military organization; it also meant adopting Western political theory, legal concepts, and legal codes. As part of its modernization program, the Meiji government incorporated Western European notions about the family into its Civil Code in the 1890's.

At the same time that ideas from the West were finding their way to Japan, the ideology of the ruling warrior class, including its marriage and family practices, was spreading to the peasantry in a process of "samuraization" (Befu 1971, 50). For example, the samurai (*bushi*) practice by which the head of the household selected a child's spouse was written into the Civil Code and began to replace the former peasant practice of selecting one's own spouse. Hence, in the context of the late nineteenth century, parentally arranged marriage can be construed as either a modern or a traditional practice. The same was true of the *bushi* standard of primogenitural succession and inheritance that was legislated by the Civil Code among a peasantry evincing a variety of local customs (Nakane 1967). The "rules of the Japanese family"—including the authority of the household head—taught to the Issei as part of their "moral training" in the state-controlled educational system were a blend of Western European and elite Japanese ideologies of family and polity. If today, therefore, those rules are viewed by Japanese Americans as quintessentially Japanese, this can only demonstrate how quickly a seemingly timeless tradition can be created.

For the same reason that I treat tradition as a cultural construct whose meaning must be discovered in present words no less than past acts, I deliberately eschew the practice of identifying and labeling aspects of Japanese American kinship—whether these are actions, norms, ideals, or values—as elements or modified versions of "Japanese culture" or "the Japanese family." For such a practice, which is rife in the literature on ethnic and immigrant families, is rooted in uncritical assumptions about the mechanical transmission of culture from one generation to the next through a near-mystical process of socialization within families. It leads, moreover, to the unwarranted conclusion that having identified an element of kinship structure as "Japanese" or "Polish" or "Italian," we have not only disclosed its origins but explained its present existence. Such a practice subverts cultural analysis by leading us away from systematic investigation of what elements mean and how they relate to each other.

Because a cultural system is not merely the sum of its elements of meaning, the relations between those elements must be explicated. To identify as Japanese the concept of *giri* (roughly translated as "duty") that emerges in both Issei and Nisei discussions of filial relations, and to elucidate its meaning in Japanese culture, for example, is only to seem to explain its meaning for Japanese Americans. For not until we have examined closely the usage of *giri* by Issei and Nisei in a range of contexts and explored its relation to other constructs can we understand its meaning and why it is so central to their discourse on filial relations. Just as people are selective in their accounts of the past, so they are selective in their claims to a "traditional" culture. To identify a concept, a norm, or a structure of obligations as "Japanese" is to raise questions about it rather than to answer them. The same is true of the identification of elements as "American." As shall soon be seen, Japanese Americans themselves label many aspects of their kinship relationships, values, norms, personal characteristics, and interactional styles as "Japanese" and "American." I treat these categories as key symbols in their culture system, and as material for my cultural analysis.

Neither the social history of kinship relationships nor the systems of symbols and meanings I extract from people's accounts should be considered more "real" or "concrete" than the other. Both are abstractions, that is, both reduce complex histories to simpler stories. Only a naive empiricism would lead one to claim that abstracted systems of relationships—labeled as social organization or social structure—are more "real" than abstracted systems of meaning. To arrive at either kind of abstraction, the anthropologist must sift through mounds of data, choose among them, and connect the chosen pieces into patterns that make analytic sense. To claim that a social structure is more empirically verifiable than a cultural system, therefore, is to confuse the source of the data with the level of abstraction.

A good deal of this confusion can be traced to the mistaken notion that a cultural analysis explicates the system of symbols and meanings that exist inside people's heads. Because meaning is extracted from things people say rather than things people do, and because symbolic relations are mental phenomena, they are commonly thought to have a psychic reality only for individuals and, therefore, are said to be impossible to verify. A cultural analysis of kinship or of any domain, however, is not extracted from what exists inside people's heads but from what is said between people. It is through the statements the "natives" make to each other and to the anthropologist that we come to know their norms, expectations, categories, and assumptions. Thus, the material of cultural analysis is not the mental stuff through which individuals alone make sense of the world. Because it is an abstraction of discourse among people, a cultural system of symbols and meanings is no more located inside people's heads than a social structure is located inside people's bodies.

RESEARCH PROCEDURES

The data for this study were collected primarily through interviews conducted with Japanese Americans from June 1973 to July 1975. I collaborated initially with Donna Lockwood Leonetti, who was then a graduate student in physical anthropology at the University of Washington, to collect demographic, socioeconomic, genealogical, and residential information on 102 Nisei, hereafter referred to as the Nisei survey sample (see Appendix for a description of sampling procedures and an assessment of the representativeness of the sample).[17] I then interviewed more intensively 31 of these Nisei (2 widows, 8 married couples in which both spouses were interviewed, 8 married men, and 5 married women) about their kinship relationships and histories. These interviews, along with those from the earlier survey, yielded the marital histories of the 48 Nisei couples whom I refer to as the Nisei marriage sample. Finally, I interviewed 30 Issei (17 widows, 6 married couples in which both spouses were interviewed, and one widower) which gave me an Issei marriage sample of 24 couples. Nine of these Issei couples were parents of members of the Nisei marriage sample.

All the Nisei and a third of the Issei were interviewed in English, with the exception of the use of key Japanese terms and phrases. Another third of the Issei were interviewed in a roughly equal mix of English and Japanese, and a third were interviewed in Japanese, with the exception of the use of key English terms and phrases. My Japanese-language skills were adequate to see me through the bilingual interviews, but inadequate for the interviews conducted primarily in Japanese. For these, I hired as an interpreter a Nisei woman who had spent her child-

[17] These interviews were conducted as part of the Seattle Japanese American Community Study (JACS). A complete description of the study is contained in a pamphlet (Watanabe 1977) that was distributed to all informants as well as interested community leaders, organizations, and public agencies. Leonetti's research (1976) focused on changing patterns of fertility and Jay McGough studied changing patterns of morbidity and mortality.

hood in the community, but who had attended high school and college in Japan. She had been one of my first informants, and she proved invaluable not only as an interpreter but as a research assistant. In the Japanese-language interviews I relied heavily upon her interpreting. While she was also present during many of the bilingual interviews, on these occasions she acted more as a research assistant because the Issei usually tired of waiting to hear themselves and me translated and would speak more and more in English. Or they would answer her in Japanese, and then turn to me and translate the answer themselves.

The mixture of English and Japanese used by the Issei and the use of Japanese phrases and terms by the Nisei underscore the importance of heeding a cardinal dictum of cultural analysis. The goal of a cultural analysis of kinship is to extract the system of symbols and meanings through which people interpret and act upon their relationships. To this end, the researcher must explicate her informants' context-specific usages of words and phrases rather than the definitions attached to these words and phrases by either informants or "experts." Hence, my analysis of the meanings of words and phrases, whether Japanese, English, or a mixture of Japanese and English, is *not* derived from the sum of the dictionary definitions and the definitions of these words and phrases offered by my interpreter or by the informants themselves. Rather, it is my analysis of the sum of the usages of these words and phrases by my informants. For example, when I analyze the Issei's conceptions of the gender domains of husbands and wives in Chapter 4, I am concerned with explicating the common meanings underlying their statements in *both* English and Japanese about the domains of husbands. (For a discussion of this procedure in relation to a specific set of phrases, see Chapter 4.) Similarly, my explication of the term *kazoku* (translated by the Issei, as well as by Japanese-English dictionaries, as "family") in Chapter 7, like my explication of the term "family" in Chapter 8, is derived from my analysis of people's usage of these terms, which may be inconsistent with their formal definition of them.

This book is limited to an analysis of kinship change in the first two generations of Japanese Americans. My decision to exclude the third generation (Sansei) from my analysis, despite the fact that I interviewed a good number of them, stemmed from two considerations. The first was simply that in order to bring them into the analysis I would have had to write a longer book or shorten my analysis of the Issei and Nisei, neither of which I found desirable. The second has to do with the life cycle. An informant's age and his or her stage in a family developmental cycle quite obviously shape his or her conceptions and attitudes about kinship relationships; they also constrain his or her kinship experiences. In comparing generations, therefore, one must recognize differences that reflect people's different phases in the life cycle. In the case of Issei and Nisei, the differences resulting from life cycle position are at least mitigated by the fact that both generations have by now been both child and parent and so have had complementary experiences in their natal and procreative families. This was not yet true of the Sansei, the great majority of whom had not married or had children at the time of this study.[18]

SOCIAL HISTORY AND CULTURAL INTERPRETATION: THE SCHEME OF THE BOOK

Like social scientists' accounts of what has changed in a kinship system, Japanese Americans' accounts of what has changed in their kinship relations are structured by an implicit theory of how that change occurred. This folk model of kinship change, in turn, is part of an encompassing system of symbols and meanings that has shaped people's actions at the same time that it has guided their interpretation of those actions. Explication of the Issei and Nisei ethnotheory of culture change is therefore central to my analysis of how Japanese American kinship has changed. The Issei and Nisei see themselves as a group of people who have experienced great change in the face of radically altered circumstances. They conceptualize this change as the outcome of choices they have made between fundamentally different cultures entailing different hierarchies of values, goals, relationships, and styles of action. Neither Issei nor Nisei have been engaged in the "reinvigoration of custom" or the "ideological retraditionalization" said to often accompany rapid social change (Geertz 1973, 219), for neither generation argues for a return to tradition. Rather, each has constructed a model of and for Japanese American kinship by constructing models of what it understands by "Japanese" kinship and "American" kinship.

In the chapters to follow we shall see how both generations conceptualize their kinship relations in terms of a symbolic opposition between "Japanese" and "American," and how they have formulated a "Japanese American" synthesis. We shall see too that these are the core categories used by Issei and Nisei to order and interpret their social history. The organizational scheme I have followed in this book is to focus in turn on each of three key relations: marriage, filial relations, and sib-

---

[18] Leonetti (1976, 29) estimates that 69 percent of the Sansei in the nuclear population of Japanese Americans in Seattle were under 20 years of age in 1970.

linghood. In each part of the book I begin by reconstructing the Issei history and then the Nisei history of that relationship. I then explicate the system of symbols and meanings through which each generation interprets and orders the commonalities and differences in their experiences—in short, how the generation aggregates individual biographies into a collective macrobiography. In Part I, which deals with marriage, I first establish a connection between conjugal power relations and kinship contexts in Issei marriage, and then explain it in terms of Issei conceptions of marriage and gender domains. Likewise, employment patterns among Nisei wives in four different marriage cohorts are explained in terms of Nisei conceptions of marriage and gender domains. In Part II, which focuses on filial relations, close attention is paid to the filial biographies of individual Issei and the filial macrobiographies of Nisei marriage cohorts. The Issei's relations with parents in Japan are found to have been just as fraught with ambiguity and their outcomes just as indeterminate as are their relations with children in America. My explication of the meanings underlying the Issei and Nisei normative dialogue about filial relations reveals that, in addition, Issei and Nisei have different ideas about what parents should transmit to children and children should return to parents. Siblinghood, the subject of Part III, leads us from the analysis of changing relations within families to that of changing relations between them. When the Nisei's concept of siblinghood is examined in relation to their concepts of "family" and "relative," it turns out to be quite different from the Issei's concept of siblinghood seen in relation to Issei concepts of *kazoku* (roughly translated as "family") and *shinrui* (roughly translated as "relatives"). For the Issei locate siblings outside the *kazoku* while the Nisei view them as enduring members of the "family." Siblings, and in particular sisters, are shown to provide the main interfamilial links that constitute the kinship networks of the community, while the relationships among sisters and the emergence of women-centered kin networks are used to illustrate one of the ways the Nisei create "Japanese tradition" in light of the "Japanese American" present.

PART ONE

MARRIAGE

I begin this part with an analysis of the differences as well as the similarities in the marital experiences of two generations, the Issei and the Nisei. Japanese American marriage has been transformed as one generation's cultural reasoning has been succeeded by another's. At the same time, each generation encompasses marriages characterized by different residential and occupational histories, and by variation in the conjugal division of labor and conjugal power relations. Indeed, the cultural reasoning shared by the members of each generation is best revealed by the way in which their diverse conjugal histories are seen by them as variations on a common structure of marriage.

In Chapter 2, my discussion of the kinship context of Issei immigration and marriage focuses on the difference between marriages that were expected to provide the successor to a parental household and marriages that were not. Examination of this difference, which was a product of the Japanese stem-family system, reveals the link between the families formed by the Issei in the United States and the ones they came from in Japan. It also serves to correct previous afamilial accounts of Issei marriages and to display further significant differences among them. Thus while the predominance of petty capitalism in the Seattle Japanese community before World War II allowed variations in the division of labor between Issei husbands and wives, it was the position of an Issei couple vis-à-vis parental households, sometimes on both sides of the Pacific, that shaped their particular conjugal power relation.

Turning to Nisei marriage, Chapter 3 introduces the historical drama of the World War II imprisonment of Japanese Americans, which both differentiated the Nisei as a generation internally and increased their differentiation from the Issei. I discuss both the immediate effects of these events—for instance, on the rate of employment of Nisei wives and on the frequency of different types of postmarital residence—and their more enduring consequences for Nisei in successive marriage cohorts, among which perhaps the most notable is differential social mobility. Over time, however, there is a striking convergence in the employment patterns of Nisei wives from all cohorts, and the conjugal division of labor among today's Nisei couples is similar. As a generation, then, it would appear that the Nisei share much more than their genealogical relation to the Issei.

In Chapter 4 I examine the system of symbols and meanings underlying each generation's norms of marriage. The differences between the two systems form the basis of my conclusions about the transformation of Japanese American marriage. I focus especially on Issei and Nisei conceptions of gender domains, authority, and leadership in marriage because these provide a key to understanding what the two generations do and do not share. Moreover, this symbolic analysis contributes in two ways to our understsanding of Part I: it reveals the Issei cultural logic that underlies the relationship, discussed in Chapter 2, between variations in conjugal power and variations in kinship contexts; and it reveals the Nisei cultural logic behind the convergence, discussed in Chapter 3, of what were initially different patterns of the conjugal division of labor.

Although some of the symbols and meanings the Nisei employ in interpreting their conjugal relationships are unique to them, their model of gender domains is common among other Americans. Later, in Chapter 9, I address the issue of what is and is not shared by the Nisei and other Americans. I introduce the issue here only to avoid any misconstruction of my meaning when I say that Nisei marriages constitute a generation of marriages. For what I mean is that they differ from Issei marriages in a way that lends unity to their diversity.

CHAPTER 2

Issei Marriage

THE NOTION THAT ISSEI MARRIAGE—the event that, in most accounts, creates the Japanese American family—brought family relationships to a population previously without any, is one that has some basis in historical fact. Whether they were married or single, most early Japanese immigrants were men who planned to return home—"birds of passage" as they were often called (Miyamoto 1939, 65). The absence of families and, indeed, of an adequate supply of marriageable women during this period is wholly consistent with such a picture of the "frontier" Japanese American community.

The analytical consequences of this notion have been most unfortunate. Having represented the period preceding Issei marriage as one in which Japanese American families were nonexistent, most authors are inclined to overlook the family relationships, both in Japan and the United States, to which even the youthful Issei bachelor was tied. While they are certain to describe or at least allude to the "traditional Japanese" family values of the Issei, they are just as certain to overlook the families that continued to shape the Issei's behavior long after their arrival in the New World.[1] Marriage, however, is a process as much involved in reproducing existing families as in creating new ones. In this chapter, then, I shall be looking back at Japanese families while at the same time looking forward to Japanese American ones.

IMMIGRANTS AND KIN

It has long been recognized that the Issei came to the United States with the goal of accumulating savings and returning to Japan within

[1] John Modell (1968, 74) is one of the few to emphasize the family context of immigration, and to point out that a substantial percentage of the Issei had siblings who also emigrated to the United States.

four or five years. Where the desire to avoid conscription in the Japanese army also motivated a young man's emigration, a longer period of temporary residence abroad may have been anticipated. At age 20, every male citizen was required by Japanese law to undergo an examination and subsequent conscription in the military service. Emigration was an effective way to escape from this service because residence abroad (except in China) allowed one to postpone the examination indefinitely (Ichihashi 1932, 87). If one remained abroad until reaching the age limit of 32 years (raised to 37 in 1910), moreover, one was entirely exempt. Anti-Japanese sentiment on the West Coast, including discriminatory land laws and the exclusion of the Japanese from American citizenship, reinforced the Issei's disinclination to remain permanently in the United States. Not one of the Issei I interviewed claimed to have left Japan with the idea of settling permanently in the United States.[2]

A less well recognized fact of Issei immigration is that a substantial proportion of the Issei had parents and siblings who also immigrated into the United States. Table 1 shows the kin who preceded, accompanied, or followed the couples in the Issei marriage sample to the Seattle area. Two-thirds of the couples had at least 1 parent or sibling of one of the spouses in the Seattle area for some period of time before World War II. Not all these kin remained in Seattle. Two-thirds of the 21 parents returned to Japan before World War II, as did half of the 26 siblings.

Fewer Issei women than men in the marriage sample had parents or siblings in the area, because women generally came to join husbands rather than the members of their natal households. Yet a third of the women accompanied or joined parents or siblings and later married Issei men. Most of these women came as the young daughters of parents who were immigrants themselves. A few came to live with brothers (and, in addition, one woman came to live with her aunts) before they were married to Issei men in the community.

Whether the Issei were accompanied by parents and siblings on their journey to America or whether they preceded or followed them, the movement of family members was usually part of a coordinated parental strategy for overseas migration. A common pattern was for sons to follow fathers who had been working in the Northwest for several years. Father and son then labored side by side in sawmills, lumber camps, and farms, or they operated a small business together. Where

[2] The Issei's retrospective accounts of expectations held over fifty years ago might be suspect if they were not so consistent with early reports of their intentions (e.g., Ichihashi 1913 and 1932; Miyamoto 1939).

TABLE 1

Immigration into Seattle Area of Parents
and Siblings of Issei in Marriage Sample

Immigrant family members of Issei couple	Number of couples
Both husband's and wife's parents and/or siblings immigrated	5
Only husband's parents and/or siblings immigrated[a]	8
Only wife's parents and/or siblings immigrated	3
No parents or siblings of either husband or wife immigrated	8
TOTAL	24

[a]This includes a couple in which the wife was a Nisei; although her parents and siblings were in the area, they are not counted as immigrating with her.

there was a successful business, fathers appear to have remained longer after the arrival of their son (or sons), and sometimes additional family members were brought to Seattle. The early careers and fortunes of many immigrant brothers also were closely linked by joint business ventures, coresidence, and the exchange of loans and labor. In Chapter 7 I will have more to say about such Issei siblings tied together by immigration, as well as about those who were geographically separated by it.

My Issei marriage sample probably overestimates the percentage of all Issei couples ever residing in Seattle who had kin in the area. As I note in the Appendix, the sample is biased towards younger Issei who came in later immigration periods and who had survived into the 1970's, when I conducted my research. John Modell (1971) reports that a higher percentage of Issei who immigrated after 1907 (the date of the Gentlemen's Agreement) had relatives who also immigrated. That being the case, the Issei in my marriage sample would have been more surrounded by kin in their early years in Seattle than Issei who arrived before them. This bias does not, however, detract from a crucial implication of Modell's and my own findings: the arrival of brides and wives was accompanied by the arrival of siblings, parents, and other kin. In short, at the same time that Japanese American families were formed through Issei marriage, Japanese family relationships were transported to the United States. Far from creating the first Japanese American families in isolation from Japanese ones, Issei marriages were from the beginning embedded in families that crossed national boundaries.

Kinship and Locality Ties of Issei Marriage

It is clear from the arrangements leading to Issei marriages that they were of social consequence to people in Japan as well as in America. Whether an Issei marriage was arranged in Japan or in the United States, family and kin were involved at every stage of the process except in the most unusual cases. It was the rare Issei who married without the approval of parents. Most marriages were initiated by the Issei's parents and many were financed, at least in part, by them.

Case I.21a. The events leading to Katsumi and Tatsuyo Takitani's wedding were typical of Issei marriages arranged in Japan. By the time he was thirty-five years old, Katsumi had been working in America for twelve years. As he was the *chōnan* (first son), his widowed mother in Japan was anxious to see him married. Tatsuyo's father's sister lived next door to Katsumi's married sister in Katsumi's village, and thus was one of the first to hear that his mother was seeking a bride for him. She told Tatsuyo's parents about this and they in turn arranged a *miai* (viewing session) in which Katsumi, who was back visiting his family, and his mother (his father was deceased) met Tatsuyo and her family. Katsumi was satisfied enough with what he saw, and as Tatsuyo's response to her parents' query as to whether she would like to go to America was that she "didn't mind," the parents proceeded with the arrangements. Each family already knew enough about the other's history and bloodline, as they lived in adjoining *mura* (villages) separated by only two miles. Consequently, there was little need for either to invest much time investigating the other's background, and the wedding took place one month after the *miai*.

As Case I.21a illustrates, more kin than parents were often involved. The participation of a range of kin and neighbors was made possible by the close genealogical and geographical distance between affinal households in Japan. There were no prescribed categories of marriageable kin, nor were there prohibitions against marriage between consanguineal kin except for members of the nuclear family and direct descendants. However, marriage alliances were generally limited to households of similar social standing within a restricted geographical area (Nakane 1967, 160-64). As a result, marriage between households already linked by consanguinity or affinity was extremely common, especially (but by no means exclusively) among the upper strata of a community, for whom political alliances were more important and the field of marriageable households more limited. Marriages between cousins (both cross and parallel) and between households already linked by an affinal tie were sometimes preferred because they reinforced existing ties, and incurred less expense than marriages that created new alliances between households (ibid., 165).

Understandably, then, the expectation that the couple was to reside in a foreign country did not remove Issei marriages from the densely connected network of kinship and locality ties in Japan. In my Issei marriage sample, 3 of the 14 marriages in Japan involved *shinrui* households—that is, households already connected by a consanguineal or affinal tie. Moreover, in 12 of the 14 marriages arranged in Japan, the bride's household and the groom's household were located in the same prefecture and separated by no more than six miles. In 5 of these 12 cases, the households were located in the same village or town. In the 7 marriages where the households were in different villages or towns, the distance between them varied from two to six miles, with an average of about four miles. The two cases where the distance between the natal households of the bride and groom were far greater than usual were both rather exceptional, each for different reasons. In the first case, the woman's age (28) and her career (as a normal school teacher) made the search for a suitable spouse more difficult when her father decided she should marry out of the household rather than re-main as the wife of an uxorilocal husband. He subsequently arranged her marriage to the younger brother of a man he had met several years earlier when they worked together as miners. In the second marriage in which the spouses were from different prefectures, the bride had been working as a prostitute in Japan for a year before she heard that a friend's sister, who had a restaurant in Seattle, was trying to find a bride for an Issei bachelor who operated a pool hall in Seattle. In contrast to other Issei marriages, this one was arranged by friends and associates of the bride and groom rather than their relatives. No doubt the bride's occupation had something to do with this.

In all but 1 of the 14 Issei marriages arranged in Japan, the parents of the couple expressed their affinal relationship through visits and the exchange of gifts if not through exchange of labor. Their relationship, moreover, was recognized by their neighbors and kin in the surround-ing community, some of whom had participated in the marriage ar-rangements and the wedding party. Where the bride's and groom's households were connected by previous consanguineal or affinal links, the significance of the marriage for local kinship relationships was even clearer.

Case I.19a. By marrying her father's brother's wife's brother's son, Ayano Ton-omiya strengthened the *shinrui* relationship between her household (number 1 in Figure 1) and that of her husband, Heihachiro Sugita (household 3). These two households already were linked by their sibling relations with a common household (household 2). In her parent's generation, Ayano's father's natal household (household 2) had received a bride from the Sugita household. With

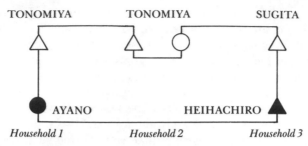

Fig. 1. Kinship ties in Sugita marriage

Ayano's marriage to Heihachiro, the Tonomiyas had in turn sent a bride to the Sugitas. In light of the history of ties between their natal households and kin in Japan, the fact that the couple planned to reside in America for the first years of their marriage did not lessen the concern of all the parties involved for the stability and success of the marriage.

In the case of Issei marriages arranged in Seattle, the resulting affinal relationships depended for their significance on the presence of the spouses' parents. Marriages arranged in Seattle by Issei men whose parents had remained in Japan did not create socially significant *shinrui* relationships between parental households; thus no man in this category from my sample chose a wife from his own prefecture. Still, important affinal relationships were often created between households in Seattle: Haruteru Eto's marriage, for example, added an affinal relationship to what had already been a business association between him and his wife's brothers. Where both the groom's and bride's parents were present in Seattle, the marriage created a *shinrui* relationship similar to that between Issei spouses' parental households in Japan, except that the households were located in Seattle.

Case I.17a. The marriage of Chiyo Morishima and Bunkichi Nakanishi involved geographical proximity of their natal households in Japan, the presence of both sets of parents (in Bunkichi's case these were his adoptive parents) in Seattle, and previous genealogical ties between the two households (see Figure 2). The Morishima and Nakanishi homes were but a few blocks from each other in the same town, and Bunkichi and Chiyo were second cousins. In addition, in the preceding generation, Bunkichi's father's sister (4) had married Chiyo's father's brother (3), and in their own generation Chiyo's eldest sister (5) had married Bunkichi's eldest brother (6). Thus, a series of affinal ties over two generations linked the descendants of the two sisters (1 and 2) who were the grandmothers of Bunkichi and Chiyo. The spatial proximity of these genealogically connected households was replicated in Seattle, for the couple set up

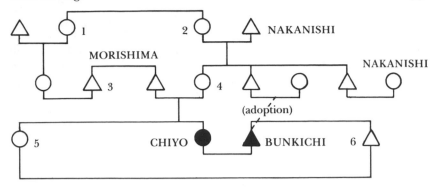

Fig. 2. Kinship ties in Nakanishi marriage

their household next door to her parents, her eldest brother, and his wife, and within a mile of his adoptive parents.

Only 1 of the 24 Issei marriages in the sample was a marriage by proxy, or what is commonly referred to as a "picture-bride marriage." In all the other cases, the wedding either occurred in Seattle or the groom returned to Japan to marry.[3] In some of the latter cases, these grooms, like those in picture-bride marriages, had consented to marry women whose photographs had been sent by parents in Japan. Rather than electing to be married by proxy in Japan, however, these Issei returned for the wedding.[4] My marriage sample would appear, therefore, to underrepresent a category of marriage featured in popular accounts both about the Issei and by the Issei. The extent to which it does is difficult to assess, however, because there are no reliable figures on the numbers of Issei proxy marriages. Yamato Ichihashi (1932, 291-96) notes that estimates of the number of picture-bride marriages among the Issei vary greatly and those made by the advocates of Japanese exclusion were undoubtedly inflated in the interest of arousing sentiment against the immoral, undemocratic customs of the Japanese. The estimates, as he points out, are made more problematic by American confusion over Japanese custom. The label of "picture bride" may have

[3] Weddings in Japan were held very soon after the *miai* so the groom could avoid conscription in the Japanese army. Japanese men residing abroad lost their military deferment if they remained in Japan for more than thirty days (Ichioka 1980, 342).

[4] Proxy marriages of brides in Japan were permitted from 1908 to 1921. After February 1921, the Japanese government refused to issue passports to such brides "on account of due respect to the customs and ideals of Americans concerning marriage" (Ichihashi 1932, 296).

been applied not only to brides who were married by proxy to men they met for the first time upon arrival in the United States (the dramatic scenario), but also to brides who had been selected by photos even though the groom then returned to Japan for the wedding. Estimates from later sources are no more conclusive. In the late 1960's Kazuo Ito, a journalist from Japan, solicited autobiographical essays from a large number of Seattle Issei with the help of the Seattle Japanese Community Association. In his section on women (Ito 1973, 247-88) are a number of accounts of marriage arrangements and weddings. Of 31 such autobiographical accounts, 6 are said to be "photo-marriages," 17 are clearly not, and 8 are ambiguous, as, for example, when a woman writes, "I came to the United States at the request of my husband" (wherein it is not clear whether they were already married at the time of his request). If we assume that the ambiguous cases have the same proportion of proxy and nonproxy marriages as the unambiguous ones, this yields a considerably higher proportion of proxy marriages (6 out of 23) than my marriage sample (1 out of 23).

There is no reason to think that the kinship and locality ties of proxy marriages or the affinal relationships they created were any different from those in which the groom was physically present for the wedding ceremony. A man who lacked the financial resources for a return trip to Japan would still need the kinship resources to procure a bride for his American sojourn; in fact, he might need them all the more.

Divorce is also noticeably lacking in my marriage sample. Here the sample would appear to more accurately reflect the characteristics of the population from which it was drawn. It appears from U.S. census figures that only 1.6 percent of Issei marriages ended in divorce (H. Kitano 1976, 206). Yet both my informants' reports and the Japanese-language newspapers of the 1900's and 1910's (Ichioka 1980, 349-52) present a picture of greater marital instability than this figure suggests. According to the Issei I interviewed, there were many women who left their husbands to live with other Issei men, particularly in the period before 1930. In some of these cases, they said, the woman took with her all, or the youngest, of the children; and both she and her children adopted her new husband's name without obtaining a legal divorce or adoption. Several women who left their husbands were said to have moved to Portland or other West Coast communities. Others were reputed to have become prostitutes. Ito (1973, 288) concludes from Seattle Issei accounts that the highly imbalanced sex ratio made "wife stealing" commonplace. The early Japanese-language press is replete with *kakeochi* (desertion) announcements in which the guilty pair are named and described, as well as *kakeochi* stories which, although embellished to teach moral lessons, are based upon actual incidents (Ichioka 1980, 349-51). Although the rates of separation and divorce are difficult to assess on the basis of these anecdotal accounts, it seems highly likely that many dissolutions were not legally recorded.

While Issei immigration and marriage were linked to the social and economic dynamics of parental households in Japan, not all the Issei were equally committed to supporting those households. Neither did they all plan to return to them. This unevenness of commitment was the product of a family system that entailed two kinds of marriage, each of which in turn generated a different conjugal strategy. An understanding of these differences requires placing Issei marriage within the Japanese stem-family system as it then was.

MARRIAGE, SUCCESSION, AND THE JAPANESE STEM FAMILY

The basic kinship unit of Japanese society at the turn of the century was the *ie*, or household. The term *ie* referred not only to the physical structure of the household and its current membership but also to its past and future members (Nakane 1967). Whether in towns or villages, households were considered discrete units of production, consumption, and property ownership. Each person was a registered member of a household, and village size was figured on the basis of the number of constituent households rather than individuals.

The household was perpetuated through the marriage of the successor, ideally the biological son of the previous head. One son (biological or adopted) of the household head succeeded to the headship of the household, managed its economic activities, inherited the bulk of its property, and worshipped its ancestors. In most areas of Japan, including the regions from which the Issei emigrated, primogeniture was the preferred mode of succession, although in some other areas ultimogeniture was practiced (Nakane 1967, 9). If the eldest son died, was deemed incompetent, or chose to leave the household in favor of some other pursuit, a younger son would replace him. Where there were no sons, the head would adopt a son or son-in-law (*yōshi*) who acquired the head's surname and the same jural status as a biological successor. When the household head had no children of his own, a boy was adopted, raised in the household, and trained for the successor's position; or an adult male was adopted and a bride then brought in for him.

If the head had a daughter but no sons, he would find a husband for her whom he then adopted as his successor.[5]

As only one son succeeded to the headship, all other sons were expected to leave the household and establish their own households. Although these nonsuccessor sons might inherit small portions of the family's land or other property, the successor (*sōzokunin*) inherited the family home and the greater share of the family property. The sisters of the successor also left the household upon marriage and joined their husbands' households. Consequently, married siblings rarely resided in the same household.

The selection of a suitable marriage partner for a son or a daughter was made by the household head and his wife. Parental authority over marriage was legally reinforced in the 1890's by a clause in the Meiji Civil Code requiring parental consent for marriage up to the age of thirty for men and twenty-five for women (Fukutake 1967, 44-45). In some families the son's or daughter's wishes were given partial consideration and a *miai* was held. Daughters, however, generally were merely viewed at these sessions, and had less say than sons in their choice of marriage partners. As households linked by marriage also considered each other the most appropriate to ask for help in the form of labor and even money, it was preferred that the two households involved be of the same or roughly similar social and economic standing (Fukutake 1967, 43; Nakane 1967, 153). The household receiving the bride was concerned not only with her procreative and productive capacities but with the social, symbolic, and economic resources that the affinal ties with her natal household would bring. The receiving household gave a gift (*yuinō*), regardless of whether the new member was a bride or a groom. In a virilocal marriage, the bride brought a trousseau that usually consisted of little more than a few pieces of furniture and personal items such as clothing and cosmetics. Among the peasantry in nineteenth-century Japan, dowry was not a significant form of property. According to Thomas C. Smith, "even if [the bride] took a sum of money or rights to land, these were usually trifling compared to what the groom stood to inherit in the form of a house, furniture, heirlooms, land rights and tools" (1977, 97).

Succession by one son generated two distinct kinds of marriages: those that involved a successor and those that did not. The marriage of

---

[5] In such a case, known as *muko-yōshi* (groom-foster-son), the daughter's husband took his father-in-law's surname and forfeited any inheritance and succession rights to his own natal household. For this reason, adopted sons and adopted sons-in-law were generally later-born sons.

a successor entailed the movement of a woman (or a man if it was a *yōshi* marriage), from one household to another, and the simultaneous transfer of rights over her procreative and productive capacities. The bride in a successor marriage moved into a household consisting of her husband, his parents, and his unmarried siblings. The siblings of the successor would subsequently marry and leave the household. As the parents grew older, the successor and his bride would succeed to the offices of househead and house mistress. Hence, the structurally weak position of the young bride in a virilocal marriage, a position that has been extensively described in the literature on Japanese kinship, was at least transitory (Nakane 1967, 25).

In a nonsuccessor marriage, the bride and groom established their own household. Nonsuccessor marriages, therefore, do not conform as well as successor marriages to the image of Japanese marriage as "primarily a social and economic arrangement between two families" (Embree 1939, 203), nor to such statements as "Marriage under such an *ie* system is a matter not so much for the two marriage partners as for the two *ie* to which they belong" (Fukutake 1967, 43). For the young couple starting their own household, the economic disadvantage of receiving little or no property was somewhat compensated for by their escaping the authority of the husband's parents. This compensation was apparently considerable enough for many young women to prefer marriage to a nonsuccessor son (Nakane 1967, 24).

Yet, while the wife in a nonsuccessor household was her own mistress and did not have to compete with her mother-in-law for the loyalties of her husband and children and for control over the management of female spheres, she still was not the jural equal of her husband. As in the successor household, authority resided in the househead, and children were considered the legal offspring of the household, not of their mother. Furthermore, if a nonsuccessor couple resided on land received from the husband's natal household, they were surrounded by his kin.

If a nonsuccessor household was endowed with sufficient landholdings or other resources to ensure its economic viability in the community, it might evolve into a three-generation household after the marriage of its successor. When these resources were insufficient, nonsuccessor sons were forced to marry uxorilocally as *yōshi*, or emigrate to other rural areas where land might be obtained or to towns and cities where they sought employment or engaged in trade. If their fortunes allowed it, these migrating sons would eventually marry and found new households.

SUCCESSOR AND NONSUCCESSOR MARRIAGES

Not all Issei men were successors. Hence, Issei marriages were of two types: successor marriages and nonsuccessor marriages. Because primogeniture was the preferred mode of inheritance in the regions from which the Issei immigrated, a son's status as successor usually depended on his birth order. As long as he remained registered in the village *koseki* (household register) as the first-born son of the household, a man held the status of successor. The head of the household, however, had the right to remove the first son from the register and so from that status. The head could replace the first son with any individual of his choosing. Generally, the replacement was the next oldest son, the adopted husband of a daughter, or an adopted son. Given the right of the head of the household to choose the successor, it cannot be assumed that every Issei man who was a first-born son was the designated successor of his natal household, nor that every second-born, third-born, or fourth-born son was not.

On the basis of the Issei men's reports or their wives' reports of their positions within parental households at the time of their marriage, I have classified 12 of the 24 marriages in my Issei marriage sample as successor marriages.[6] Seven of these successor marriages involved first-born sons who were reportedly listed as such in their natal households in Japan at the time of marriage. Although when they married two of these men were living in Seattle with their parents, their households remained in the registers of their home community. The remaining 5 successor marriages involved men who were not first-born sons, but who were reportedly registered as successors at the time of their marriage. In one case, the Issei was a second-born son whose older brother had been disinherited by his widowed mother, the de facto head of the household, because he refused to marry the bride of her choosing. Three other Issei men who were not first-born sons had been adopted when they were young men by couples who had no sons and were registered as the only sons of their households. Finally, one Issei man was the *yōshi* husband of an Issei woman who herself was the adopted daughter of her father's brother and wife.

[6] There are no data on the percentage of successors among the immigrants to Seattle or to the continental United States against which to compare my Issei marriage sample. Considering birth order alone, however, the proportion of first-born sons in my Issei sample (7 of 24) is lower than that reported by Modell, who states that within any given family, "the eldest son was half again more likely than his younger brother to emigrate to America" (1968, 74).

I have classified the remaining 12 marriages in the Issei marriage sample as nonsuccessor marriages, again on the basis of their or their wives' reports of their status at the time of marriage. In all these cases, the Issei husband was a second-, third-, fourth- or fifth-born son, and each of them had an older brother who, at the time of the Issei's marriage, was reported to have been registered as the successor of the household. The eldest brothers of most of these Issei men were living with their parents in Japan and were already established as the new household heads. In a few cases, the older brother was also in the United States at the time of the Issei's marriage, but soon returned to the household in Japan.

As parents had the right to alter the household register, thereby changing the designated successor, the mere report by the Issei of their positions in their households in Japan seems rather weak evidence on which to classify their marriages. It would be helpful to have confirming evidence such as records of a public statement made by the head of the household or a copy of the dated, official household register. Unfortunately, I have no such records, Yet there are data that come close to providing the same information, namely, the postmarital residence histories of the Issei. The postmarital residences of successor and nonsuccessor couples in Japan were expected to be distinctly different. Successors and their wives were expected to reside virilocally, in the husband's natal household (except, of course, in the case of *yōshi* marriage, when they resided uxorilocally), while nonsuccessors and their wives were expected to reside neolocally, although they might settle near the husband's natal home. Obviously, no Japanese emigrant couple could live virilocally unless the husband's parents had also emigrated. Recall, however, that when an Issei wedding took place in Japan, either the bride and groom or the bride alone remained in Japan for two months or more before embarking for America. Although Issei husbands left shortly after their weddings, all the wives waited at least two months before they emigrated. Hence, every bride who married in Japan could have lived in her husband's parents' household for the period (ranging from two months to four years) between wedding and emigration.

The detailed residential histories I collected from the Issei reveal clear differences between the immediate postmarital residence patterns of successor and nonsuccessor marriages. Of the 12 marriages I classified as successor marriages, 5 occurred in Japan, and in all 5 the bride alone or the bride and groom together resided in the husband's natal household before emigrating to Seattle. The other 7 took place in Seattle. In 2 of these cases the husband's parents were not present, so virilocal residence was ruled out. But in the other 5, the successor couples lived initially with the appropriate parents in all except one case. In comparison, the 12 marriages I classified as nonsuccessor exhibit a very different pattern. Eight of them took place in Japan and could have entailed virilocal residence, but only one did. In the other 7 cases, the initial postmarital residence of the couple (if the husband did not leave immediately) or the bride (if he did) indicated unequivocally that the bride had *not* been incorporated into her husband's household. Where the groom left immediately for Seattle, the bride remained in her own household until she too departed, in some cases as much as six months after the wedding. Where the couple remained in Japan for a month or more after, each spouse remained in his or her respective parental household, the couple went back and forth between their two parental households, or they lived neolocally. The 4 nonsuccessor marriages that were arranged in Seattle precluded any but a neolocal arrangement. In all but 2 of 24 cases, the initial postmarital residence of couples accords with the reported status of their marriage as successor or nonsuccessor. The two exceptions included one adopted successor who did not live with his adoptive parents after marriage, and one nonsuccessor whose wife lived in his parental household before departing from Japan. The former case (that of Nakanishi) is discussed extensively in Chapter 5; it seems to be explained by the ambiguity of the Issei's status in relation to his adoptive parents. (The latter case is more puzzling.)

Two other indicators further confirm the status of Issei marriages with regard to succession. First, the extended visits that several of the Issei made to Japan after marriage provide an opportunity to again ask with whom they resided. Some visits to Japan were too brief for there to be any significant period of coresidence; in others, however, an Issei couple and their children or a wife and her children returned for two months or more and settled in one household. Four of the 5 successor couples or wives and their children who visited long enough to settle in one household lived virilocally. In contrast, the only two instances where nonsuccessor wives and their children returned for a prolonged stay in Japan involved uxorilocal residence.

The other indicator is the home to which a couple sent their children to live in Japan. Like a good many Issei, seven of the Issei in the marriage sample sent one or more of their children to live in Japan with either the parents or a sibling of the husband or wife. The practice has been attributed to the Issei's desire to have children who were properly trained in Japanese language and culture (see, for example, Kitano

1976, 109, 159-60). After all, if they planned to return to Japan, their children would need the language and social skills appropriate to their "home" community rather than the English language and the European-American customs they would adopt through their exposure to the Seattle public schools. Dorothy Swaine Thomas (1952, 63-64), on the other hand, argues that the economic benefit of freeing the mother to work in the family business was the main reason behind the creation of that subclass of Nisei, the Kibei, who spent part of their childhood and adolescence in Japan. Some of the Issei I interviewed told me that the primary reason they sent children to Japan was they were too busy working to care for their young children. But others said that they did so because their parents in Japan insisted that the children be sent to them. In any case, where a child went to live indicated the household to which a couple retained the strongest ties, and where they would take up residence upon their return to Japan. Five of the 12 successor couples sent children to live in Japan, and all but one of these sent them to live with the husband's parents. In comparison, only 2 of the 12 nonsuccessor couples sent children to live in Japan, and in both cases they lived in their mother's natal home.

That the successor status of any Issei marriage in the parental household in Japan was far from unequivocal and unchanging will be seen in Chapter 5. But in spite of this ambiguity (or, perhaps, partly because of it) these differences in status generated not only different relations between Issei couples and households in Japan, but different relations between Issei spouses themselves. In the final section of this chapter, I show that underlying the variations in conjugal power relations of Issei marriages were the different marital goals and strategies of successor sons and their wives and of nonsuccessor sons and their wives. But first, so that I can describe those variations, the conjugal relations of Issei couples must be located in the context of their occupational histories.

ISSEI MARRIAGE AND PETTY CAPITALISM

Until World War II, the occupational histories of the Issei present, for the most part, a collective tale of small business in early twentieth-century America. The 24 couples in the Issei marriage sample show an increasing incidence of entrepreneurship over the first twenty years of marriage. Table 2 shows the rise in the percentage of husbands who were self-employed during the first, fifth, tenth, fifteenth, and twentieth years of their marriages. Just over half the men began marriage as self-employed entrepreneurs and just under half as wageworkers. By the tenth year of marriage, over two-thirds were self-employed, and

TABLE 2

Occupations of Issei Husbands During First Twenty Years of Marriage

Occupation	Year of marriage				
	1	5	10	15	20
Self-employed					
Number	13	14	16	14	15
Percent	54%	58%	73%	67%	75%
Wage work					
Number	11	10	6	7	5
Percent	46%	42%	27%	33%	25%
TOTAL					
Number	24	24	22	21	20
Percent	100%	100%	100%	100%	100%
In internment camp or deceased	0	0	2	3	4
GRAND TOTAL	24	24	24	24	24

NOTE: Issei who were in a World War II internment camp or deceased are excluded from the percentages for that particular year.

this percentage remained fairly stable through the twentieth year. In all, 17 of the 24 men were occupied in small businesses for a majority of their first twenty years of marriage. Only 7 men were employed largely in wage work.

What is glossed here as "self-employment" and "small business" consisted of a range of enterprises. For a few, the business was a well-capitalized grocery store supplemented by wholesale importing from Japan; more often, however, it was a small workingman's hotel or a vegetable-and-fruit stand. The businesses operated by the Issei in the marriage sample included hotels and apartments, greenhouses, barber shops, laundries, gardening services, vegetable-and-fruit stands, grocery stores, restaurants, wholesale groceries, peddling routes, and an import-export business. In addition, as we shall soon see, some men were engaged in business by themselves, others operated a family business with their wives, and yet others worked in a family business with parents and siblings.

The occupational histories of the 24 women are somewhat more complex than those of their husbands, because Issei women experienced more shifts in their work activities over the first twenty years of marriage. As Table 3 reveals, close to half the women were occupied exclusively as housewives during the first year. The percentage of those who were also employed remained around 60 until the twentieth year,

TABLE 3

Occupations of Issei Wives During First Twenty Years of Marriage

Occupation	Year of marriage				
	1	5	10	15	20
Family business					
Number	5	10	10	10	12
Percent	21%	42%	42%	45%	52%
Wage work					
Number	8	6	4	3	5
Percent	33%	25%	16%	14%	22%
TOTAL					
Number	13	16	14	13	17
Percent	54%	67%	58%	59%	74%
Housewife					
Number	11	8	10	9	6
Percent	46%	33%	42%	41%	26%
In internment camp					
or deceased	0	0	0	2	1
GRAND TOTAL	24	24	24	24	24

NOTE: Issei who were in a World War II internment camp or deceased are excluded from the percentages for that particular year.

when it rose to 74. Subject to this general rise in employment (which, it should be remembered, was in addition to a woman's own housework), work, generally unpaid, in family business and work for wages followed different trends, with the former increasing and the latter declining. The family enterprises in which women worked were as diverse as those of the men. The wage-work occupations of women included domestic servant, seamstress, chambermaid, cook, waitress, and greenhouse worker.

Figure 3 charts the shifts in the combined work activity of each Issei couple during the first twenty years of marriage. Each couple is included in the category of combined work in which they began their marriage. Where a couple moved to another category, a directional line points to it. Category *G* has a different border from the others because it is the only one in which none of the couples began their marriage, but into which several moved. In some cases (Hongo, Isoshima, Arashi, Suwa), there was more than one shift, so the line must be traced beyond its first step. The most complex path, that of the Suwas, entailed four steps—which eventually brought them back to their initial category.

Several conclusions can be drawn from this chart. First, there was considerable change in couples' combined work activities. Of the 24

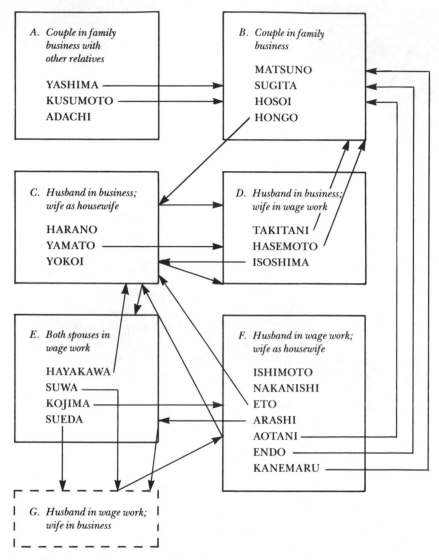

Fig. 3. Shifts in combined work activity of Issei couples over first twenty years of marriage

couples, only 8 experienced no change at all. Second, the direction of change was away from wage work by both or either of the spouses and toward business for one or both spouses. This can be seen by comparing categories *A*, *B*, *C*, and *D*, all of which entailed at least one spouse in business, with categories *E* and *F*, which entailed no business activity by either spouse. The directional lines originating from categories *A*, *B*, *C*, and *D* point exclusively toward one of the other categories within that set. None of the lines originating from *A*, *B*, *C*, or *D* point toward categories *E* and *F*. In contrast, all but one of the nine directional lines that originate from categories *E* and *F* point away from that set and end in categories *B*, *C*, or *G*.

Such an inclination toward self-employment is not difficult to understand when we consider the goals of the Issei and the opportunities available to them before World War II. Anti-Asian sentiment in labor unions as well as among white employers barred Issei men from better-paying blue-collar positions. Language and cultural differences were additional barriers to these and to white-collar positions. The only wage-earning positions available to them were low-paying laboring and service jobs that offered little financial security and few benefits. Men found it difficult to support their wives and growing families with wages, let alone accumulate savings for the return to Japan or for remittances to parents. The jobs available to Issei women were even more limited. Domestic service in the homes of middle-class and wealthier whites or work as dishwashers, chambermaids, seamstresses, and laundresses in either white or Japanese-owned establishments were all an Issei woman could hope to find in the wage market.

No doubt, as Miyamoto suggests, the Issei's entry into petty capitalism was encouraged by their acquaintance with an entrepreneurial tradition that was "well laid in the customs of Japan" (1939, 74). Even though many Issei came from rural farming families, most of them were familiar with small business enterprises. Not only did nearly a third of the Issei in the marriage sample have parents who were engaged in trades and services, but most came from those areas of Japan where the market economy was most developed (see Appendix). The *kenjin-kai* (prefectural association) enhanced this orientation by recruiting Issei into trades that had proven successful for fellow *kenjin* (people from the same prefecture). Issei learned from *kenjin* how to operate hotels, restaurants, and nurseries, and obtained cooperative financing through rotating credit associations known as *tanomoshi* (Miyamoto 1939, 75; Light 1972, 27-29).

The assistance provided by prefectural associations and rotating credit associations, however, is better viewed as an accompaniment to, rather than the determinant of, Issei enterprises. The types of business into which the Issei ventured required a small amount of capital. In the 1920's, for example, a few hundred dollars was all that was needed to lease an old building, make a few repairs, and begin renting rooms to single workingmen. A grocery stand or peddling route required even less capital. Although rotating credit associations were useful to the Issei, in some cases enabling them to expand businesses or see them through a difficult period, none of my Issei informants started their businesses with money from a *tanomoshi*. Loans from relatives, friends, the local Japanese bank, and, above all, their personal savings provided the initial capital for their businesses.

If Japanese entrepreneurial tradition provided the knowledge and the Issei's goals as immigrants the motive for small businesses, the economic history of the Northwest provided the opportunity. At the turn of the century Seattle was an "expanding frontier community wholly willing to accept a new immigrant group that would offer them much-needed small-shop services" (Miyamoto 1939, 76). Economic booms precipitated by the Alaska-Yukon expedition and the outbreak of World War I created a demand for services that the Issei moved quickly to provide. Issei in all urban West Coast communities moved into small businesses, but in Seattle they did so at an even greater rate, which by the mid-1930's gave the Japanese American community an overwhelmingly entrepreneurial character.

Owning a family business meant that a couple could make optimum use of a wife's labor. The predominance of small business enterprise among the Seattle Issei allowed high rates of female participation in economically productive work during the period that Issei women were bearing and raising children. It will be seen from Table 4 that Issei women whose husbands were entrepreneurs worked more continuously in such productive activities than did women whose husbands were wage earners. In fact, 8 of the 17 wives of entrepreneurs worked continuously in the business themselves. In contrast, 5 of the 7 women married to men who were primarily wage earners worked intermittently, except for housework, throughout the first twenty years of marriage, and only 1 worked continuously.

When a couple had a business of their own (or with relatives), the wife could adjust both the type of work she did and her work schedule in order to care for children. As the family often lived behind or above the business (in the case of apartment and hotel owners they lived in

TABLE 4
*Work Activities of Issei Husbands and Wives
over First Twenty Years of Marriage*

Occupation of wife	Primary occupation of husband	
	Business	Wage work
Works continuously in:		
Business	8	0
Wage work	0	0
Both	2	1
TOTAL	10	1
Works intermittently in:		
Business	0	1
Wage work	2	3
Both	2	1
TOTAL	4	5
Always housewife	3	1
GRAND TOTAL	17	7

one of the units in the building), Issei women often worked while attending to children. In some cases, the couple changed their line of business to accommodate child-care needs. The Matsunos, for example, closed their restaurant and opened a store and bakery because Mrs. Matsuno found it too difficult to work in the restaurant and watch her children at the same time.

In contrast, the wife of a man who worked for wages and did not have a business in which she could be flexibly employed, found it difficult to work for wages at the same time she was bearing and caring for young children. Either she had to quit working or start a business which was compatible with child rearing. Three such women married to wageworkers started their own businesses sometime during the first twenty years of marriage; in one case the business was a barber shop, in the other two a rooming house or hotel business. Other women married to wageworkers lacked the resources or the initiative to accomplish this. Instead, they worked for wages during the very early and later years of their marriage, but quit their jobs when child-care duties were most demanding—usually from the second or third to the fifteenth year of marriage.[7] The incompatibility of wage work and child care is

[7] As Issei women had an average of five children, many had preschool children past their fifteenth year of marriage. By that time, however, mothers could be relieved of much of their housework and child-care duties by their eldest daughter(s).

reflected in the fact that none of the five women who worked solely in wage-earning jobs worked continuously throughout her first twenty years of marriage.

VARIATIONS IN ISSEI CONJUGAL RELATIONS

In describing both the division of labor and the power relations of couples, there is the temptation to reduce what are complex configurations to unidimensional features. Yet we know that different activities can be organized in very different ways. Spouses who have highly differentiated tasks in child care, for example, may not manifest the same degree of differentiation in another domain, such as income-producing work.[8] Likewise, the dominance of one spouse over decisions in one sphere may not be mirrored in all spheres. Thus a wife who has little control over the operation of the family business and the family economy may exercise a great deal of control over the care, education, and occupational future of children. As my aim here is to both display diversity and order it in a way that will lead to our understanding of it, I have avoided characterizing relationships according to single summary features such as the extent of "inequality." Instead, I have chosen to organize the Issei's marriages into several categories, each of which entails certain core features but at the same time incorporates marriages that differ in other features. First, I describe four patterns of the division of income-producing tasks between Issei spouses. Second, I describe four configurations of husbands' and wives' comparative control over four spheres of activity.

The Division of Labor

The organization of housework and child care in the Issei marriage sample exhibited little variation. By far the most common division of these tasks was one in which the wife did the bulk of the routine, daily tasks of housekeeping and child care while her husband lent his labor to nonroutine tasks such as carpentry, electrical repair, plumbing, yard work and, in some cases, automobile repair and maintenance. Eighteen of the 24 couples were characterized by this pattern, in which husbands rarely ever did any housekeeping or child-care chores with the exception of occasionally disciplining children and taking them on recreational outings. Two variants of the predominant pattern were for the wife to be relieved of a considerable part of these tasks either by a cores-

[8] For an illuminating study of variation in role differentiation across domains of activity, see Platt 1969.

ident mother or mother-in-law or by sending children to be raised in Japan. Thus 4 women were relieved of caring for one or all of their young children when they were sent to Japan. Otherwise, however, these women fulfilled the remaining housekeeping tasks by themselves. In the case of 2 other women, the bulk of these tasks were taken over by a mother or mother-in-law. Only 2 Issei couples exhibited a categorically different pattern in which the husband contributed significantly to child care and housekeeping tasks. In one case, the husband's help came primarily in the area of child care; in the other, the husband helped with housework as well.

Greater variation existed in the Issei's organization of income-producing tasks than in that of their household tasks. Here, there are four patterns into which an Issei marriage at any point in time can be sorted: one in which only the husband engaged in income-producing work, while his wife's work was restricted to housework and child care; and one in which both spouses worked to produce income, but separately from each other. Included here are couples in which the husband was in business and the wife in wage work, couples in which both spouses were wageworkers, and couples in which (after several years of marriage) the wife was in business and the husband in wage work. These were rather unstable combinations, and many couples moved in and out of this pattern throughout their first twenty years of marriage.

The other two patterns are not at all what one might expect from the prior discussion of occupational histories. This is because lumping together all couples in which both spouses worked in a family business obscures differences in how their work was organized. There are, in fact, two very different patterns. On the one hand, four couples who operated a business together had a clear task division between husband and wife. In three of these four cases, the wives assumed tasks that were more menial, brought them into less contact with customers and tradespeople, and entailed fewer decisions. The tasks that required a sound knowledge of the financial state of the business and of its dealings with the public were handled by their husbands. For example, Mr. Yashima made all the arrangements with wholesalers, local farmers, and importers to stock the couple's grocery store, and he managed its finances. His wife's work was restricted to cleaning the store, stocking shelves, and waiting on customers. Although there was some overlap in their work—they both waited on customers—their tasks were for the most part different, but coordinated. The fourth couple, the Kusumotos, also had a clear task division, although their roles were reversed (the husband drove the laundry truck while the wife kept the accounts).

On the other hand, there were couples who displayed considerable overlap and flexibility in fulfilling their tasks. Five couples who operated a business exhibited this pattern. Here, wives as well as husbands waited on customers, made arrangements with retailers or wholesalers, and handled bank accounts and customer billing. Mr. and Mrs. Hasemoto, for example, were both involved in all aspects of their hotel business, including the procuring of loans and decisions about expansion.

That the Hasemotos overlapped considerably in their work tasks but the Takitanis, who also operated a hotel, did not, demonstrates that the division of labor in any marriage was not determined by the character of the enterprise itself. When we add the fact that other hotel businesses, such as the one run by Mr. Yokoi, did not employ the labor of wives at all, it is even more apparent that a particular type of Issei enterprise could be operated with a variety of patterns of the conjugal division of labor. What determined the pattern in any given case? Comparison of similar Issei businesses that had different patterns suggests the involvement of several factors.

1. *The scale of the business and its margin of profit.* Whether a wife worked in the business alongside her husband or whether a husband joined a business started by his wife depended partly on the demand for additional labor and the feasibility of hiring paid labor. The wealthiest of Issei businessmen could afford to hire paid workers and did not require their wives' labor to make a living. But they were a small minority. At the other end of the financial continuum were the Issei whose businesses were too small to make it worth including a wife's labor. Consequently, these wives worked for wages, and not in the family business. In the middle of the continuum were the majority of businesses, which were large enough to usefully employ wives, but not profitable enough to replace them with paid workers. It was these wives who worked continuously throughout their first twenty years of marriage.

2. *Availability of other sources of unpaid labor (other family members).* As we have seen, several couples lived in stem-family households whose members worked together in the business and shared in housework. In some cases this meant the wife spent more time working in the business while her mother or mother-in-law specialized in housekeeping and child care. Mrs. Kusumoto, for example, worked full-time in the family laundry and did very little in the way of housework or child care because her adoptive mother took over these functions. Mrs. Yashima, on the other hand, because the other members of her household (her father-in-law and brother-in-law) were men, assumed all the housework as well as working in the family store. Thus, while the availability of

other family labor had an impact on the kind of work a wife did, the consequences differed depending upon how that additional labor was employed. Furthermore, additional family labor was not limited to members of the couple's household. Where children were sent to live with relatives in Japan, family labor came in the form of assistance in child care by geographically distant kin.

3. *The knowledge, skills, and ambitions of the spouses.* Thus Mrs. Hasemoto, who came to her marriage with a family background in the hotel business and with an ambitious streak as well, took the lead in the couple's entrepreneurial activities. In contrast Mrs. Takitani, who had no experience in the hotel business and no special skills in the financial arena, was relegated—at least at the beginning of her marriage—to the tasks of cleaning rooms, making beds, and washing sheets.

4. *Task differentiation and control over the business enterprise.* Finally, control over the business enterprise and the marriage as a whole appears to be linked with the form of task differentiation among Issei in business. Where one spouse (almost always the wife) had little knowledge and control of the management of the business and its financial affairs, husband and wife had clearly differentiated tasks in the business. However, this raises the question as to whether control over the business influenced task differentiation or whether task differentiation influenced control over the business. Before this question can be addressed, I must describe the variations in the power relations of Issei couples.

Power Relations: The Control of Spheres of Activity

Whereas the conjugal division of labor refers to the tasks and functions each spouse fulfills, the conjugal power relation refers to who controls these activities and their products. That these are empirically as well as analytically distinct aspects of the conjugal relationship is apparent when we consider marriages in which wives worked continually in the couple's business but had little control of business decisions or income. Because, as I stated earlier, we cannot assume that all tasks and activities in any marriage were subject to the same balance of power between spouses, I have grouped their activities into four spheres.

1. *The family economy.* Included in this sphere are decisions about the kind of work in which each spouse engaged, the operation of the business if there was one, and the use of the family income whether the income was derived from wages or business profits. In assessing the extent to which each spouse controlled the family economy, I examined the participation of each in decisions about whether and when the wife should work and in what kind of job or business, how the business

should be run, how income should be spent, for what purposes savings should be accumulated, and when loans should be obtained or given.

2. *Housekeeping*. I include here decisions about the appearance of the home and its furnishings, the purchase of household goods and supplies, food consumption and meal preparation, the clothing of family members—in other words, what are commonly labeled "domestic" tasks.

3. *Children*. Any decisions about the location, care, supervision, education, and future of children are encompassed in this sphere.

4. *Social activities*. This sphere covers decisions about the social activities of family members, including their church affiliations, membership and participation in community organizations and associations, recreational and leisure pursuits, and visiting patterns, including the entertaining of guests in the couple's home.

When Issei spouses' control over these four spheres of activity in the first decade of marriage is examined, four major configurations of conjugal power relations emerge (Table 5).[9] Configuration 1 includes only two couples, one of whom resided with the husband's parents and the other with the wife's parents during the first decade of marriage. As the junior couple in the household these Issei did not themselves control decisions in any of the spheres of activity, but had their parents to contend with. In the Adachi case, as the first son and designated successor of his father, Mr. Adachi was from the beginning of his marriage included in decision making. Over time his control over the family economy and his and his wife's social activities increased as his father gradually handed over the headship of the household. Mr. Adachi's mother was in charge of housekeeping and so Mrs. Adachi, who had no children, had control over no sphere of activity. The situation was somewhat different for the Kusumotos, because they lived with the wife's adoptive parents. As the in-marrying affine, Mr. Kusumoto was not given control over any sphere of activity. His wife's adoptive parents firmly controlled the family economy and his wife's mother made the housekeeping decisions. The senior couple would have made all important decisions regarding their grandchildren and the social activities of all members of the household as well, if Mr. and Mrs. Kusumoto had not objected.

Configuration 2 also includes only two couples. In this instance, however, what differentiated them from the rest of the Issei was their joint

[9] Two of the 24 Issei couples in the marriage sample are excluded from the table because I did not have sufficient data on one couple, and the other had a unique relationship that appears to have been a consequence of the husband's alcoholism.

TABLE 5

Four Configurations of Issei Conjugal Power
Relations in the First Decade of Marriage

Issei couple	Family economy	Housekeeping	Children	Social activities
Configuration 1:				
Kusumoto	Wi's parents	Wi's mother	Wi's parents	Wi's parents
Adachi	Hu's father & Hu	Hu's mother	—	Hu's father & Hu
Configuration 2:				
Hasemoto	Joint	Wi	Joint	Joint
Yamato	"	"	"	"
Configuration 3:				
Yokoi	Hu: Wi sometimes consulted	Wi	Joint	Hu; Wi has considerable autonomy
Yashima	"	"	"	"
Eto	"	"	"	"
Hongo	"	"	"	"
Hosoi	"	"	"	"
Sugita	"	"	"	"
Nakanishi	"	"	"	"
Sueda	"	"	"	Unknown
Endo	"	"	"	"
Kojima	"	"	"	"
Configuration 4:				
Hayakawa	Hu; Wi not consulted	Hu	Hu	Hu; Wi has no autonomy
Takitani	"	"	"	"
Harano	"	"	"	"
Isoshima	"	"	Hu; Wi consulted	"
Ishimoto	"	"	Hu	"
Suwa	"	"	Hu; Wi consulted	Unknown
Matsuno	"	"	"	Hu; Wi has no autonomy
Aotani	"	"	Hu	"

control over all spheres of activity with the exception of housekeeping, which was controlled by the wife. This does not mean that in both marriages husband and wife had equal influence over any particular decision or set of decisions. It seems to have been Mrs. Hasemoto, for instance, who formulated the couple's economic strategies, while Mrs. Yamato often went along with her husband's suggestions. But in both marriages, husband and wife had full knowledge of their financial and social affairs, deliberated over matters together, and arrived at a mutual decision.

Configuration 3 was the most prevalent one. Here the husband controlled the family economy, although he sometimes consulted with his wife on major decisions. He also controlled the couple's social activities; but here again his wife had some degree of autonomy over her own social activities. Housekeeping, in turn, was the wife's domain and decisions about children were made jointly. Mr. Yokoi, for example, made all the decisions about the couple's financial affairs, including his business affairs with his adoptive father and, later, his own bottling business. He also decided on investment strategies when he had later accumulated savings. But, at the same time that he was firmly in control of the family economy, he often discussed financial matters with his wife and considered her suggestions when she offered them. Mrs. Yokoi, on the other hand, had rather free rein over the running of the home. Likewise, although Mr. Yokoi decided which church and community associations they joined as a couple, Mrs. Yokoi had her own sphere of social activities which her husband did not control. She led, in fact, a rather active social life, visiting her parents and sisters, as well as her female friends in the community, and entertaining them at home; she also participated in female clubs organized around hobbies, such as flower arrangement, and around social service. Although Mrs. Yokoi's control over the running of the home was typical of other women in this category, her social life was not. Most of them led less active social lives, but because of their more limited resources (of both time and money) rather than of their husbands' efforts to control them. In addition, all the couples in this category made major decisions about their children's upbringing, schooling, and future occupation (if they had one in mind) together. Wives had a great deal to say about their children's lives, especially their education and social activities.

Finally, configuration 4 included eight couples with a power relation that is the easiest one to characterize—namely, as husband dominated. In these marriages, husbands made decisions about the family economy without consulting, and often without even informing, their wives. The wives knew very little about family finances and the husband's expenditures, even though in three cases the couple worked together in a family business. Where wives were employed in wage-earning jobs, their husbands controlled their earnings and decided when and where they should work. These wives also had little control over the management of the home; their husbands allocated money and supplies and expected both to last over a given period of time. When a wife had used up her grocery allowance she had to request another allocation. She had no direct access to cash or savings. Thus, in contrast to the women in the preceding category, these wives had little or no domestic autonomy. As one woman put it, "Everything but what we ate was his decision." Some wives did not even have a free hand in this area, because their husbands dictated the contents of family meals.

The dominance of husbands in configuration 4 in most cases extended to decisions about children. Five of the men made important decisions about their children without consulting their wives. In some cases, the decisions concerned children's formal education, work activity, or community associations. In other cases, men arranged to have their children sent to Japan to live with relatives. Their wives often learned of these decisions only as they were being enacted. For example, when Mrs. Hayakawa arrived in Japan with her eldest daughter on what she had thought was a vacation, she discovered that her husband had arranged to give the child to friends in Japan. As the combined forces of his parents and her parents were on hand to enforce his decision, Mrs. Hayakawa had no choice but to obey. Mr. Hayakawa also had arranged with midwives for the delivery of their four children without consulting his wife as to her wishes, and he alone selected the children's names. (The other three husbands in this category, while also making the decisions about their children's futures, at least consulted their wives before enacting their plans.) The wives in this category had no social independence either. Unless their husbands brought home guests or took them, on rare occasions, to a community picnic, these women had little social intercourse outside the home, place of work, or church. Their husbands, however, belonged to community organizations—in some cases they were extensively involved in them and held leadership positions—and had their own recreational pursuits.

SUCCESSOR STATUS AND CONJUGAL POWER RELATIONS

What determined these variations in the Issei's conjugal power relations? The multidimensional character of the relations forbids a simple answer. Two factors, however, were clearly not among the determinants: the couple's work activities, and the presence or absence of the wife's contribution to income-earning activity.

Table 6 displays the relation between work activities and the conjugal power relation in the first ten years of marriage. It will be seen that couples who began marriage in a particular type of combined work pattern

TABLE 6

Work Activities and Conjugal Power Relation of
Issei Spouses in First Ten Years of Marriage

Combined work activities of husband and wife in first year of marriage	Type of power relation in first ten years of marriage				
	1	2	3	4	Total
Family business with other relatives	Adachi Kusumoto		Yashima		3
Couple in business together			Sugita Hongo Hosoi	Matsuno	4
Husband in business; wife a housewife		Yamato	Yokoi	Harano	3
Husband in business; wife in wage work		Hasemoto		Takitani Isoshima	3
Both spouses in wage work			Kojima Sueda	Hayakawa Suwa	4
Husband in wage work; wife a housewife			Endo Eto Nakanishi	Ishimoto Aotani	5
TOTAL	2	2	10	8	22[a]

[a]See note 9 for an explanation of why only 22 of the 24 couples in the Issei marriage sample are included in this table. Note that one category in Figure 3 (husband in wage work, wife in business) is omitted here because none of the couples began marriage in this pattern of combined work activity.

are not concentrated in any single configuration of power relation.[10] For example, the 3 couples who began with both spouses working with other relatives in a family business are distributed between configurations 1 and 3. The distribution is even broader for couples who started out with the husband in business and the wife as a housewife: in this case the 3 couples are distributed among as many configurations of power relations (2, 3, and 4). The 5 couples who began marriage with husbands working for wages while wives remained at home are divided between configurations 3 and 4.

The fact that the couples who started out in any one category of work activities are not distributed over the entire range of configuration of power relations should not be read as an indication of the restrictions placed by the work activities of spouses on the form of the conjugal power relation. For it must be remembered that configuration 1, in

[10] The hypothesis that the type of work activities resulted in a particular configuration of power relations assumes that the former comes before the latter. Therefore, I have sorted couples according to their initial category of combined work activities.

TABLE 7

*Issei Wife's Income-Producing Work and Conjugal Power
Relation in First Ten Years of Marriage*

Labor contribution of wife	Type of power relation				
	1	2	3	4	Total
Both husband and wife engaged in income-producing work (whether in business or wage work)	2	1	6	5	14
Only husband engaged in income-producing work	0	1	4	3	8
TOTAL	2	2	10	8	22

which the Issei couple was either under the control of, or shared control with, a senior couple, could not have characterized the 19 couples who did not live in stem-family households. Moreover, the great majority of couples (18 of 22) were distributed between configurations 3 and 4. When these latter two configurations are examined, we see that couples from a wide range of types of work patterns are included in each of them.

The wife's participation, or lack of it, in income-producing work can also be rejected as a major factor in the balance of power between Issei spouses. Table 7 ignores the kind of work women did and categorizes them simply according to whether or not they engaged in income-earning activities. It is apparent that couples who began their marriages with wives engaged in income-producing work nevertheless exhibited a variety of power relations.

If variations in the conjugal division of labor cannot explain variations in the power relations of Issei couples, what can?[11] Here I return to the differences in the successor status of Issei marriages—in other words, to the different expectations about the relationships between Issei couples and their parental households. For it appears that these two aspects of Issei marriage were closely interlinked. As Table 8 reveals, couples in which the husband was, at the inception of the marriage, the designated successor of his parents' household, whether adoptive or biological, were more likely to be characterized by a husband-dominated

[11] The confidence with which we can reject the conjugal division of labor as a significant determinant of the power relation might be increased if we were to examine the relationship between the shifts in the work activities of spouses and the shifts in their power relations. Unfortunately, I lack sufficiently detailed information on either.

TABLE 8

*Distribution of Successor Sons and Nonsuccessor Sons
Among Four Types of Conjugal Power Relation*

Successor status	Type of power relation				
of husband	1	2	3	4	Total
Successor	1	0	3	6	10
Nonsuccessor	1[a]	2	7	2	12

[a]This couple was involved in a "successor marriage," but as it was an uxori-local marriage in which the husband was a *yōshi* I have included him in the category of nonsuccessor sons.

power relation (configuration 4) than by any other power relation. In contrast, the bulk of the nonsuccessor sons were in marriages in which wives had domestic and social autonomy as well as joint control over the children, and were at least consulted in decisions about the family economy (configuration 3). The remaining nonsuccessor sons were in marriages characterized by configuration 2 (joint control, two couples) and configuration 1 (parental control, one couple in a uxorilocal marriage).

It is not hard to see why an Issei husband's status as successor should have such an impact. Successor husbands had both the authority and the interest to exercise firm control over the family economy; moreover, that authority was considered as legitimate in Seattle as in his home community. A successor was expected to bring with him on his return to Japan sufficient wealth to maintain the household and, in many cases, support his parents and a younger sibling or two. To accomplish this he had to accumulate savings from the income generated by his, his wife's, and—later—his children's work. Although some wives shared their husbands' goal of returning to their family homes in Japan, others did not look forward to entering households where they would be placed in the weak position of in-marrying affines. Since wives preferred to use the income they produced to advance their own conjugal families, and perhaps even to aid their parents and siblings in Japan, successor sons and their wives often had different economic interests in both the short and the long term. These divergent and potentially conflicting interests appear to have led many successor husbands to insist upon exclusive control of the family economy. Wives were treated less as partners in a marriage intended to create a household in Seattle—even if that household might eventually be relocated in Japan—than as workers whose labor was to be controlled and directed toward the maintenance of the husband's natal household.

Such treatment extended beyond the family economy into the sphere of housekeeping and children. By refusing to grant his wife autonomy in the management of the household, a successor husband placed her in the subordinate position of the young bride in a virilocally extended household. In this sense, Issei successor husbands assumed their mothers' prerogative of control over domestic activities. As their mothers were not present to supervise the *yome* (young bride) and teach her respect for the ways of the household into which she had married, these men took on this task themselves. Far from being spared the dominance of a mother-in-law, wives married to successor sons felt the full brunt of their subordination to the interests of their husband's household through the agency of their husbands alone. Successor husbands' exclusive control over children again derived from a view of the marriage and its products as means for the perpetuation of the husband's natal household. If children were sent to live with the husband's parents in Japan, this did not require explanation or the wife's consent, for children were merely the youngest generation of members in their father's natal household.

The successor husband's exclusive control of all spheres of activity appears to have been mitigated by one factor: the kinship resources that the wife brought to the marriage. The three wives of successor sons who enjoyed domestic and social autonomy and joint control over the children (configuration 3), all had parents living in Seattle during their early years of marriage. In contrast, only one of the six women married to a successor son who dominated all spheres of activity had parents—or any close consanguineal kin, for that matter—in the Seattle area. It was not merely the parents' presence that enhanced the position of Issei wives, however, but their relative economic and social standing, and hence the resources they offered the couple. In two of the configuration 3 marriages just mentioned, the wife's parents in Seattle were noticeably wealthier than the husband's parents in Japan and had social and business ties of direct benefit to the husband's entrepreneurial activities. Undoubtedly, both Mr. Yokoi and Mr. Yashima had this in mind when they married the eldest daughters of men who were highly successful in the hotel or grocery business—areas into which each of these Issei men themselves had recently entered. If there were no immediate economic resources coming from the wife's parents, there was the possibility of future transmissions and the benefit of being affinally connected to a family of high social standing. Neither of these wives could be treated as the subservient *yome* by her husband. The resources, both material and symbolic, that they brought with them in marriage placed them in a position quite different from that of the Issei women who, particularly in their husbands' eyes, came to marriage with no more to offer than their labor. The third configuration 3 marriage with a successor husband involved a couple, the Nakanishis, who were already connected by close consanguineal and affinal ties (see Case I.17a). This, with the presence of both sets of parents in Seattle during the early years of the marriage, appears to have placed the marriage in a kinship context that obviated the husband's desire (or ability) to control all spheres of activity. The remaining seven women married to Issei successor sons lacked any such kinship resources and therefore any such power. Six of them experienced their husband's control over all spheres of activity throughout both the first and second decades of marriage. The seventh, Mrs. Adachi, was in a marriage that began with her husband and his parents in control of various spheres and that only much later—in its third decade—shifted to one in which the husband, while in exclusive control of the family economy, granted some domestic autonomy to the wife.

Even though nonsuccessor sons shared in the common Issei intention to return to Japan, their jural status produced a different set of goals, interests, and power relations. Nonsuccessor sons did not view their marriages and their wives as resources to be harnessed for the benefit of their parental households. Marriage for them, as for their wives, was more an end in itself, or at least the first stage in the creation of a conjugal family household. Husbands and wives both shared the desire to return to Japan with the economic resources that would enable them to establish a viable household, in the husband's or the wife's natal community, or it might be in neither's. If there were disagreements as to where they would resettle in Japan, these were not of the same order as the divergent interests between spouses that characterized the marriages of successor sons. For regardless of where they might eventually reside, the common interest of nonsuccessor husbands and wives was to employ their labors and accumulate savings toward the establishment of an independent household. Where a wife in these marriages felt obligations to kin in Japan, these had to be balanced against the interests of her own conjugal family and its social mobility, rather than against her husband's family's competing goals of household perpetuation. The same was true of husbands' obligations to kin in Japan. Wives could have domestic autonomy, participate in decisions about children, and even have a say in the family economy, because their interests did not diverge significantly from those of their husbands. The income earned by husband and wife created a conjugal fund that, although certainly not equally controlled by both parties, was perceived as the property of the couple themselves, not as a resource to be used in the interests of the husband's parental household. Children too were viewed as members of their parents' household and human resources for its own future.

As in the successor-son marriages, the kinship resources brought by the wife of a nonsuccessor son enhanced her sphere of control and created power relations that were even more egalitarian. Thus Mrs. Hasemoto, whose parents were successful hotel and apartment owners in Seattle, enjoyed as much if not more control over all spheres of activity as her husband from the outset of their marriage. The Kusumotos, who in their second decade of marriage were freed from parental control when the wife's parents returned to Japan, were the second of three couples who had joint control over the family economy, children, and social activities. In this marriage, the couple's social and economic position derived from the wife's (adoptive) parents and their laundry business, which the Kusumotos inherited. These benefits of his *yōshi* marriage brought Mr. Kusumoto a decidedly brighter economic future than he had had as a handyman.

Power relations in Issei marriage, therefore, were shaped by the married couple's actual and anticipated relations to kin in Seattle and Japan rather than by their income-earning work.[12] I must emphasize here, however, the incompleteness of my analysis of Issei marriage. I have demonstrated that a linkage exists between Issei conjugal power relations and kinship contexts, and have argued that the reasons for that linkage lie in Issei husbands' and wives' goals and strategies for succession, independence, and social mobility. But my explanation of how these power relations were generated cannot be complete until I have shown how the Issei themselves connect these aspects of marriage. To do so, I must first examine the constructs and system of meanings through which the Issei interpret and conceptually order these aspects

[12] The apparent connection between task differentiation in the family business and inequality in the couple's power relation is best explained by the effect of the power relation on the division of labor rather than vice versa. Men with the means and motive to maintain exclusive control over the family economy would have relegated their wives to tasks that required and brought with them little knowledge of the business, keeping the tasks that entailed decisions and social contacts for themselves. In contrast, wives who had some say in decisions about the family economy would have engaged in some tasks that overlapped with the ones their husbands performed. Unfortunately, there are too few cases of couples in my Issei marriage sample who began their marriage with both spouses working in the business (and without other kin) to demonstrate this relationship statistically.

of marriage. For the connections the Issei draw between the power relations, division of labor, and kinship context of marriage are not
shared by the Nisei. As will be seen in the next chapter, Nisei experience
of the conjugal relation was forged in rather different historical circumstances that brought with them rather different notions about it.

CHAPTER 3

Nisei Marriage

Given their demographic discreteness, Japanese American generations might seem the proper units of comparison in any study of change. Each generation, after all, has been labeled differently by the Japanese American community. Yet the differences within a generation may be as crucial as the differences between generations. In the previous chapter, analysis of variations in conjugal relations among the Issei illuminated the kinship structures that at once created different marital goals and strategies and yet held them together as an immigrant generation. Here, the differences in occupation, education, and social mobility among the Nisei will also be found to display similar patterns.

Were the Nisei to be treated as a kind of grand marriage cohort so as to compare them with the Issei, the striking differences between these two generations would be readily apparent. The shifts in the mean ages at marriage of women and men in and of themselves suggest substantial changes in marriage strategies. Nisei men married at the mean age of 27.8 years in comparison to their Issei fathers, who were on the average 1.4 years older. Nisei brides, on the other hand, were on the average 3 years older than their Issei mothers, who had married at the mean age of 21.4.[1] Family size in the two generations is no less radically different. The mean completed fertility of Nisei married women has declined to close to half that of Issei married women: 2.4 children com-

---

[1] These figures on Nisei mean age at marriage are derived from the JACS fertility sample of 170 Nisei married women, while the figures on Issei mean age at marriage are derived from these women's parents (Seattle Japanese-American Community Study 1978, 10).

pared to 4.3 children.[2] Whereas the Issei had an average of 8 years of formal education in Japan, the Nisei have an average of slightly more than 12 years of American schooling.[3] Finally, whereas the Issei were predominantly self-employed entrepreneurs, the Nisei are predominantly salaried employees.

The contrast between the occupations of Issei and Nisei is heightened when we compare the historical trends in occupations *within* each generation. While the early occupational history of Issei couples is a tale of movement from wage labor to small business and, after the war, back to wage labor, that of the Nisei is one of movement from small business to salaried jobs. The movement from wage labor to petty capitalism characterized not only the aggregate history of the Issei as a marriage generation, but the life histories of individual Issei and the marital histories of Issei couples. As I showed in the preceding chapter, the vast majority of Issei men began working as wage laborers and only later moved into their own businesses; such was the common experience of their generation, and it did not vary much from one individual to another. The Nisei movement from family business to salaried employment, in contrast, was less a generational trend than a historical shift in occupation that brought different Nisei rather different occupational and economic histories. By lumping the Nisei together in a way that emphasizes their unity vis-à-vis the Issei, we leap too hastily to aggregate characteristics and thereby overlook some very significant, temporally ordered differences among Nisei marriages.

FOUR PERIODS OF NISEI MARRIAGE

Most of the Issei married and had children over the same limited period. Accordingly, the period over which those children married was also a limited one. Indirectly, then, the temporal concentration of Nisei births and marriages was a consequence of the immigration policies and strategies affecting their parents' marriages. About half the Seattle Nisei were born in the ten years from 1916 to 1925; nearly 80 percent were born in the twenty-year period between 1916 and 1935. Table 9 shows the age structure of the Seattle Nisei as derived from the 1940 U.S. census and from my Nisei survey sample. Aside from a slight ov-

[2] Figures on mean completed fertility of Issei and Nisei married women are based on the JACS fertility sample of 98 Issei women and 170 Nisei women (Watanabe 1977, 28).

[3] In the Seattle Japanese American Community Study it was found that 57 percent of Nisei men (N = 117) and 51 percent of Nisei women (N = 118) had some post–high school education. Twenty-four percent of the women and 34 percent of the men had college degrees.

TABLE 9
Birth Cohorts of Seattle Nisei

Birth cohort	Nisei survey sample (N = 102)	1940 census data[a] (N = 4,099)
Before 1901	-	1%
1901-5	2%	1
1906-10	2	3
1911-15	14	10
1916-20	24	20
1921-25	32	30
1926-30	13	17
1931-35	5	10
1936-40	8	8
TOTAL	100%	100%

[a]U.S.-born Japanese in Seattle, from *Characteristics of the Non-white Population by Race* (U.S. Bureau of the Census, 1943b), table 33: "Japanese Population by Age, Nativity, and Sex for Selected States, Urban and Rural, and for Selected Cities, 1940."

TABLE 10
Distribution of Seattle Nisei Marriages by Five-Year Periods

Period	Number of marriages	Period	Number of marriages
1926-30	1	1951-55	4
1931-35	3	1956-60	6
1936-40	4	1961-65	3
1941-45	13	1966-70	3
1946-50	11	TOTAL	48

errepresentation of the 1911-15 and 1916-20 cohorts and an underrepresentation of the 1926-30 and 1931-35 cohorts, the age distribution in my survey sample corresponds generally to the age distribution reported by the 1940 census.

It is not surprising, then, that the vast majority—approximately 85 percent—of Seattle Nisei marriages occurred in the thirty-year period between 1930 and 1960.[4] Table 10 shows the year of marriage of the 48 couples in my Nisei marriage sample by five-year periods. In Table 11 these periods have been converted into historically differentiated mar-

[4]A Seattle Nisei marriage is defined here as a marriage in which at least one spouse was a Nisei who had lived in Seattle before World War II.

TABLE 11

Distribution of Seattle Nisei Marriages
by Major Historical Periods

Period	Number of marriages	Percent
Prewar (1926-40)	8	17%
War (1941-45)	13	27
Resettlement (1946-55)	15	31
Post-resettlement (1956-70)	12	25
TOTAL	48	100%

riage cohorts.[5] I have chosen this arrangement because the experience of each cohort was indeed radically different from the others'. For example, the expanded job opportunities available to Nisei after the war had different social consequences for the younger men who married at that time than it did for older married men. Analysis of a national survey of Nisei men by Edna Bonacich and John Modell (1980) has disclosed the extent to which these changing circumstances generated different educational, occupational, and mobility characteristics for successive birth cohorts. In particular, they have shown that educational levels and the proportion of professionals were higher in each successive birth cohort. These results are paralleled in my marriage sample of Seattle Nisei.

In this section I shall describe four historical periods of Nisei marriage and the four marriage cohorts that had their beginnings in them. A cohort is usually defined as "the aggregate of individuals (within some population definition) who experience the same event within the same time interval" (Ryder 1965, 845). Birth as the defining event that yields birth cohorts is only the most common example of this kind of temporally defined aggregate. Although "generation" is often used synonymously with "cohort" in the social science literature, I use each term to refer to a different group in this study. The first generation, Issei, is defined on the basis of birthplace and immigration status. It includes Japanese born in Japan who emigrated to the United States. The second generation, Nisei, is defined on the basis of kinship and territorial criteria; these are the American-born children of the first generation. In a sense, the Issei are a cohort as well as a generation,

[5] A similar distribution, with the peak during the war and immediate postwar years when the largest Nisei birth cohorts reached marriageable age, is documented by Donna L. Leonetti's sample of 166 Nisei women (1976, 38, 108-14).

since they all experienced the event of immigration during the period from 1880 to 1924. But the Issei as a generation can be divided into cohorts on the basis of a number of events, including time of birth, marriage, and immigration. Likewise, the Nisei as a generation can be divided into cohorts. Here, I am concerned with the differences and similarities in the experience of Nisei marriage cohorts.

The four marriage periods and their respective marriage cohorts are not based on the standard five-year intervals employed by demographers. Two reasons lie behind this departure from convention. First, as is obvious from Table 10, the division of my Nisei marriage sample into five-year marriage cohorts reduces the cases in many cohorts to so small a number as to make ridiculous their treatment as an "aggregate" of individuals. The small size of my sample and the nature of my data, of course, rule against any refined statistical analysis of the differences between cohorts. Yet even though I must forgo any such analysis, the treatment of a cohort's marriage histories as "macro-biography" (Ryder 1965, 859) requires some minimal mass of cases. The second reason follows from the first: if I am to expand the time interval within which the defining event occurred, it seems analytically more productive to define the boundaries of the time intervals on the basis of historically specific and, therefore, socially salient events.

Prewar Period: 1926-1940

One fact above all differentiates the circumstances of prewar Nisei marriage from those of marriage at later periods: before the war the economic resources of the Seattle Japanese community were firmly controlled by the Issei. Employment opportunities outside that community were severely restricted by the racial discrimination or lack of interest of white employers, in both the public and the private sectors (Ichihashi 1932, 356-59). Neither the higher-paying (and unionized) blue-collar jobs nor the more prestigious white-collar positions were available to the Nisei who came of age before the war. Professional occupations such as medicine, dentistry, and law were no solution to the employment problems of the Nisei, because the pool of potential clients was limited primarily to the Japanese population.

The barriers to employment in white-controlled business and government sectors and the Issei domination of the trades and services combined to make most Nisei dependent upon the Issei for employment. Although some Nisei were self-employed, the majority were workers in Japanese businesses. Of 165 Seattle Nisei who in 1940 were working in wholesale or retail trade and personal services, 26 percent were at that time self-employed, 58 percent were working for a Japanese employer, and 16 percent were working for a Caucasian employer (Thomas 1952, 605). This dependency was not unique to the Seattle Nisei, but was characteristic of West Coast, urban Japanese communities before World War II. Modell has extensively documented the restrictions on Nisei employment in Los Angeles in 1940, and the consequent dependence of Nisei upon first-generation enterprises. Only about 5 percent of the Nisei in urban Los Angeles at that time were employed by Caucasians, and even then they were very often in "Japanese" occupations such as produce wholesaling and retailing (Modell 1969, 258). The coincidence of the Great Depression with this early period of Nisei marriage exacerbated the problem of Nisei employment. Rising unemployment in Seattle—23 percent by January 1931—was accompanied by a decline in retail sales (Mullins 1973, 123). The Issei's enterprises, which catered largely to Japanese farmers in outlying areas and to lower-income white workers, suffered from decreased trade. In October 1931 the Furuya Bank, the only Japanese bank in Seattle, collapsed. Scores of Issei lost their savings and many businesses were forced into bankruptcy. The interdependence of the economic fates of individuals and families in the community was never more obvious than during this financial crisis.[6] Issei businesses were in no position to expand to accommodate the increasing number of available Nisei workers. During the 1930's, in Seattle as well as in Los Angeles, "the Nisei needed employment by their parents' generation more than their parents needed Nisei employees" (Modell 1969, 260).[7]

The arrangements leading to Nisei marriages in the prewar era ranged from Issei control to Nisei independence. But the former largely predominated. Many of the earliest Nisei marriages involved Nisei daughters and Issei men, a situation that increased parental control of marriage arrangements. Because the preferred age at marriage of Japanese women—around twenty—was six or seven years earlier than the age at which men were deemed ready for marriage, at the time that the earliest birth cohorts of Nisei women were, in the eyes of their parents, ready to marry, most of the eligible bachelors were Issei men. These early Nisei marriages tended to be Issei affairs into which Nisei brides were pulled as the least and last informed participants. Before

---

[6] For Issei recollections of the bank closure and the depression in general, see Ito 1973.

[7] Nisei sometimes suffered wage discrimination from Issei employers (Bonacich and Modell 1980, 86). According to F. E. LaViolette, Caucasian workers in Japanese wholesale produce houses in Seattle received higher wages than Nisei employees who did the same kind of work (1945, 80-81).

the war, many marriages of Nisei men were also arranged by parents, who were particularly interested in finding suitable brides for their first sons. Of the eight prewar marriages in my Nisei marriage sample, six fell into this category. Although I do not have data from a larger sample to confirm this apparent correlation between early marriage cohort and early birth order, it undoubtedly holds for the larger Seattle Nisei population. In Leonetti's sample of 149 women from five Seattle Nisei birth cohorts, each successive birth cohort evinces a higher average birth order (1976, 112). The same relation between birth order and birth cohort should hold for Nisei men, with predictable social consequences. If the Issei were amenable to making concessions to American customs of marriage at this early date, they were not ready to concede so critical a relationship as the one they expected to maintain with their first son. The combination of historical time, social and economic circumstances, and birth order made the first marriages of the Nisei a rather overdetermined test of Issei intentions.

Toward the end of the prewar era Nisei marriage arrangements began to acquire more of an American appearance. Where earlier marriages had been arranged by Issei parents, these later marriages were often the result of Nisei-initiated courtship. The shift toward mutual selection of spouses by Nisei—though with parental approval still of great importance—was facilitated by demographic factors. By the late 1930's, the largest Nisei birth cohorts were beginning to reach young adulthood. The sheer size of these cohorts gave the Nisei the numerical strength to construct their own version of American adolescent social life. As they were generally excluded from the friendship and dating circles of their white classmates, they developed their own parallel social clubs and activities. Just prior to the outbreak of World War II, there was a proliferation of social events sponsored by Nisei clubs, many of which were attached to Japanese churches (both Buddhist and Christian). Within the whirl of these unabashedly courtship-oriented activities—skating parties, "splash" (swimming) parties, dances (to the big-band tunes performed by groups such as the Nisei Melodians), bazaars, and picnics—the Nisei had more than sufficient opportunity to meet and evaluate potential spouses.

Over time, an increasing proportion of Nisei marriages were the result of Nisei choice followed by Issei approval. Some parents, of course, adamantly opposed their child's choice and successfully vetoed it. But others found it as acceptable as one they might have arranged themselves, and graciously conceded to the "American way." At least a few Issei were rather relieved when their children found suitable spouses, as this saved them the worrisome task of arranging a marriage. The Issei, moreover, could be reasonably well assured that even if they did not pick the actual spouse, there were clearly understood restrictions on the kind of individual a child of theirs would dare to entertain as a potential one.

Before the war, the pool of marriageable spouses was limited by both racial and community endogamy. Interracial dating and marriage were as unacceptable to the Issei as they were to the Nisei's white classmates and their parents, and the two groups had sharply segregated friendship networks. Even other Asians, such as Chinese, Koreans, and Filipinos, were excluded from Nisei social activities, and close friendship with blacks was unthinkable. Less than one percent of Japanese marriages in Seattle between 1930 and 1942 involved a non-Japanese.[8] A second limitation was the Nisei's low geographical mobility. Before the war, few Seattle Nisei left to seek employment or education outside the community. Consequently, their pool of potential spouses was limited to Nisei who lived in Seattle or one of its outlying rural communities. Over 85 percent of Seattle Japanese who married between 1935 and 1942, the great majority of whom were Nisei, married another Japanese resident of Seattle (Leonetti and Newell-Morris 1982).

Even with the rise in Nisei courtship activities, before the war parental approval was, for the great majority of Nisei, a prerequisite of marriage. The Nisei, as we have seen, were too economically dependent upon their parents and their parents' associates in the community to risk proceeding with a prohibited marriage. Parents were therefore almost always involved in the marriage arrangements before the engagement was announced. The usual sequence of events was for the couple to decide to marry and then for each to seek approval from their respective parents. As often as not, the Issei parents had already made inquiries about the individual (and his or her family background) their child had been seeing. If they had not already announced their disapproval, they were likely to accept their child's choice. Once they had approved of their son's decision, the groom's parents would enlist a *baishakunin* (go-between) to approach either the bride's parents or a friend of the bride's parents. Eventually this would lead to a formal meeting attended by both sets of parents and the *baishakunin*.

Prewar Nisei weddings appeared rather uniform in ceremonial form. Their size and lavishness varied, however, according to the par-

---

[8] This figure is derived from an analysis of marriage license applications in Seattle–King County between 1930 and 1942 (Leonetti and Newell-Morris 1982). These were predominantly Nisei marriages, although a few involved Issei.

ents' wealth and social standing in the community and the birth order of the Nisei involved. The wedding of a first son or daughter was as elaborate as the parents could afford, whereas that of a second son or daughter was less grand. An Issei man who held leadership positions in community organizations or whose business depended heavily on a community clientele had to be more generous with his children's weddings than did a wage earner. Following the wedding ceremony at the Buddhist temple or one of the Japanese Christian churches, a formal dinner was served in the banquet hall of a restaurant or at a rented community hall. The guests gave wedding gifts of money calculated precisely to defray the cost of their dinner, and the formal program was a modified version of a Japanese wedding feast. An Issei master of ceremonies introduced a routine sequence of events which included a toast to the couple, a congratulatory song, introductions of all relatives and important guests, and speeches by representatives of community organizations. The second half of the program generally included musical entertainment provided by community musicians and guests.

The wedding expenses were not always paid fully by the groom's parents, although this practice predominated before the war. Where it was clear that the Nisei bride was to be incorporated into her husband's parents' household, the wedding costs were paid by the receiving household. But in marriages arranged by the Nisei themselves, the lack of clarity—and, in some cases, the lack of agreement between parents and children—as to the Nisei couple's future relationship to the groom's or (less often) the bride's parents made the payment of wedding costs problematic. It was no longer obvious that the groom's parents should pay for the wedding costs if the couple stated their intent to reside separately from them. On the other hand, it was not clear that the couple should follow what they perceived to be standard American custom, and ask the bride's parents to pay for the wedding, or whether they should simply pay for it themselves. In these instances, a variety of arrangements were negotiated among the couple and their parents. In some cases the two sets of parents shared the costs of the wedding, each side paying for the guests they invited and dividing the other costs; in others, the costs were shared by the groom and the bride's parents. Yet even where it seemed likely that the Nisei couple would set up a separate household, the groom's parents—whether out of sheer cultural habit or concern for their social standing in the community, or as a strategy for establishing future claims on the couple—often paid the wedding expenses anyway.

The occupational histories of the 8 men in the Nisei marriage sample who married during the prewar period display clear continuities with Issei occupational histories. All 3 men who started their marriages in a business (newspaper publisher, greenhouse operator) or in a profession (pharmacist) continued at these careers throughout their entire working lives. But the 5 men who were engaged in wage work in their first year of marriage, with one exception, shifted jobs before settling into their final occupation. The wage-earning jobs they started in were all laboring or semiskilled occupations such as sawmill worker, grocery clerk, or factory worker. Three of these wage-earning men shifted to businesses of the type operated by the Issei, and all but one remained in these enterprises. By their twentieth year of marriage, then, half of the 8 Nisei husbands in the prewar cohort were operating small businesses. In contrast, the wives' employment histories reveal a shift away from business operated by couples. The women in this marriage cohort devoted their labor primarily to child rearing and housework during the first fifteen years of marriage. When they did work later, it was either as employees in other businesses (store clerks, cashiers, greenhouse workers) or as domestic servants. Only 1 woman worked continuously throughout the first twenty years of marriage in a family business with her husband, although 5 husbands had businesses.

War Period: 1941-1945

By the outbreak of World War II, the ascendance of greater numbers of Nisei to adulthood had already modified Nisei patterns of marriage arrangement. Given Issei economic dominance, however, the power of the Nisei to define the social meaning of the relationships created by marriage was limited. This was particularly true of first sons, who were still expected by most Issei to fulfill the role of successor. By the late 1930's, more second sons were reaching marriageable age and new questions about their marriages were being raised. But the aftermath of the Japanese attack on Pearl Harbor in December 1941 rendered moot the issue of how second-son marriages were to be treated in the context of an Issei-controlled community. The decision by the U.S. government to "relocate" the West Coast Japanese American population—both Japanese citizens (Issei) and American citizens (Nisei and a few young Sansei children)—in detention camps destroyed the Seattle Japanese community's prewar economic and social organization.

Even before the announcement that all such Japanese would be "evacuated" to internment camps in militarily "safe" zones, the impact of the war was felt by Japanese families in Seattle.[9] A quick sweep of the

[9] The "zones" were in eastern California, Idaho, Arizona, Wyoming, Colorado, Utah, and Arkansas.

Issei suspected by the FBI as harboring the most pro-Japanese sentiments (and therefore deemed to be the most subversive elements in the
community) resulted in the removal of the community's leaders—Buddhist priests, heads of voluntary associations, businessmen with ties to
Japan, and even veterans of the Russo-Japanese War. The imprisonment of these Issei men left many Issei wives and their children to operate family businesses by themselves or to seek outside employment—
neither of which, given the growing anti-Japanese sentiment, was a
particularly easy task. Some families regrouped to weather the crisis,
with Nisei children hurriedly returning from college or jobs in other
areas of the country. Relatives left without economic support when Issei husbands and fathers had been imprisoned were incorporated temporarily into other households. As rumors spread of the impending
imprisonment of all Japanese, Nisei who were planning to get married
moved the wedding date forward to ensure their joint removal. Trau-
matic as they were, these immediate responses to the war were of minor
consequence for the long-term future of families. It was the imprisonment of the population that altered irrevocably the community and its
familial structure. By autumn of 1942, 6,801 Japanese from Seattle
were in prison camps, 89 percent of them in Camp Minidoka in
Idaho.[10]

Through imprisonment the Issei lost their businesses and earnings,
and therefore the economic basis of their control over their children.
The administrative policies of the War Relocation Authority (WRA),
which governed the internment camps, did equal damage to the Issei's
political leadership. As much by its general attitude as by specific administrative rules, it encouraged the Nisei to lead the camp population
and to subvert Issei attempts at leadership. It went so far as to segregate
the "loyal" from the "disloyal" internees by means of a questionnaire
that demanded a declaration of each individual's national loyalties and
willingness to serve in the U.S. Armed Forces. The questionnaire precipitated intense conflict within families. Many Nisei found themselves
in bitter disagreement with fathers and mothers; brothers and sisters
chose opposing sides. The WRA policy of encouraging Nisei to "relocate" in the Midwest and East Coast regions generated similar conflicts.
For many Nisei, the WRA relocation program offered the first opportunity to act independently of their parents, and many chose to go—
often against their parents' wishes. As it was the older Nisei sons and

[10] Of the 6,801 Japanese from Seattle interned in 1942, 6,040 went to Camp Minidoka
(where they constituted 61.3 percent of the camp population), 712 went to Camp Tule
Lake, in northeastern California, and the remaining 49 were distributed among other
camps (Leonetti 1976, 22).

daughters who jumped at the chance to leave the stifling atmosphere of the camps, many Issei were left behind with only their younger children. In some families all the Nisei children left camp for college, employment, or military service.[11]

In the midst of these unsettled years, more Nisei married than had married during the entire prewar period. This was not so much an outcome of the imprisonment as a continuation of the increase in marriages as the large birth cohorts of Nisei reached marriageable age. Although some Nisei had married a few months earlier than they might have otherwise, their haste did not significantly alter the age at marriage. The thirteen couples in my Nisei marriage sample who married during the war years hardly differed in their mean age at marriage (24.5 years for the men and 21.8 years for the women) from the prewar cohort's (25.8 years for the men and 21.6 years for the women). On the other hand, imprisonment did not deter the Nisei from marrying. Indeed, camp life brought even greater opportunities for the Nisei to meet potential spouses than they had enjoyed in the prewar community. Nisei social life boomed along the same lines that had marked its development before the war, and the dreary surroundings in which the Nisei found themselves did not dampen their appetite for dances, sports, and courtship-oriented recreation. In the confinement of the camps, ironically, many Nisei experienced increased liberty from parental control in their courtship activities. The WRA policy of providing separate (albeit barely private) rooms for married couples offered added incentive to marry.

Their authority undermined in the camps, the Issei had less control over their children's marriage decisions. Instead of seeking their parents' approval, Nisei sons and daughters were more likely to simply inform their parents of their decision to marry. Moreover, they were now marrying Nisei from a wider range of communities. Whereas between 1935 and 1942 only 14 percent of Seattle Japanese married someone other than a Seattle Japanese resident, during the war the figure increased to 39 percent (Leonetti and Newell-Morris 1982). Although most of the Seattle Japanese were concentrated in Minidoka, they lived alongside Japanese from other communities in Washington, Oregon, and California. After the WRA implemented its policy of segregating the "loyal" from the "disloyal," the Issei and Nisei who had been branded as disloyal were removed to the Tule Lake camp, where they

[11] Seven out of ten of the Japanese American internees who relocated before the evacuation order was rescinded were men and women between the ages of fifteen and thirty-five (Thomas 1952, 115).

joined internees from all areas of the West Coast. The thinning of the dense social networks of prewar communities and the resulting lack of acquaintance with other families' social biographies made it all the more difficult for the Issei to control their children's choice of marriage partner. The parents of Nisei who married while on extended leave from the camps were even further removed from the marriage arrangements.

The employment histories for the first ten years of marriage of the 13 Nisei men in the wartime marriage cohort reflect the instability of the times. None of the husbands in this cohort started their marriages in the occupations in which they would eventually settle. For most, these first ten years were spent in a series of temporary jobs ranging from foundry worker and mechanic to warehouse manager. By the tenth year, 9 of the 13 had settled into the occupations they would keep for the rest of their working years; the remainder entered such occupations sometime during the next eight years. Those who became settled earliest were the ones who entered into businesses, either by themselves or with parents. The other men, who settled into semiskilled or skilled blue-collar jobs or into managerial or professional occupations, spent longer periods in interim jobs.

Like the women in the prewar marriage cohort, the wives in the war cohort remained primarily housewives for the first fifteen years of marriage. When, around the fifteenth year of marriage, they began to work, the jobs they obtained spanned a broader and slightly higher range than those held by wives in the prewar marriage cohort. They were not only waitresses and factory workers; some had their own businesses, while others became secretaries.

Resettlement Period: 1946-1955

While the incarceration, in its later period, was characterized by the dispersal of families, the years following the closing of the camps in 1945 were a period of both reunion and separation. Not all the Issei returned immediately to Seattle; for many, the reunion with children took place in cities such as Chicago and Minneapolis. Parents whose single or married children had found jobs or were enrolled in colleges and schools in these cities joined them there. Sometimes the temporary stay lengthened into several years; in other cases it became permanent. More often, however, at least some of the family members returned to Seattle, leaving one or more Nisei children (and their spouses) who had decided that the Midwest or East Coast offered better opportunities than the West. Many of the families reunited in Seattle after the war were therefore incomplete. By 1946, 60 to 70 percent of the prewar Seattle Japanese American population had returned to resettle in the area (Miyamoto and O'Brien 1947). The reconstituted population exhibited an age and sex structure remarkably similar to that of the prewar period (Leonetti 1976, 61).[12]

The Nisei continued to control the selection of their spouses as they had during the war. Right after the war, marriages to non-Japanese climbed to just above 10 percent. Parents regained some of their former involvement in marriage arrangements, although for the most part this was merely a symbolic concession by the Nisei. If the Issei tried to go beyond the boundaries of the social formalities permitted by their children they were likely to be rebuked. The Issei, moreover, now had less reason to initiate marriage arrangements for their children. If a daughter was passing what they saw as the prime of her marriageable years, parents could see new advantages in having her remain single. Nisei women were finding respectable and well-paying jobs as secretaries and clerks. Those whose older brothers had not returned to live with parents found that they did not experience the parental pressure to marry that they would have before the war. The same was true of second sons whose older married brothers were not living with their parents. When Issei parents realized that first sons might never return to fulfill their obligations as successors, they became less interested in marrying off their remaining single children.

With the rebirth of community social organization—the reconstitution of prewar churches, civic groups, and voluntary associations, and the creation of new ones—weddings once again became events for affirming the relationships created by marriage and reaffirming kinship and community ties. But the financial constraints of the times kept most weddings from matching the prewar period in elaborateness and size. Moreover, as second, third, and later sons and daughters married, parents grew less concerned with the social implications of weddings for their prestige in the community; more often than not, it was the couple themselves who paid for the bulk of the wedding expenses. The Nisei were less concerned with displaying their present wealth than with planning for future social mobility; as a result, most reception par-

---

[12] Interestingly, the Chicago Japanese population, which was established during the war as people left the internment camps, in 1950 exhibited an age structure similar to that of Seattle and other West Coast Japanese populations. Leonetti (1976) concludes from this that, despite the extensive migration of Nisei from the internment camps to the Midwest, the reconstituted Seattle community did not have a significantly smaller proportion of Nisei.

ties were small, including only kin and close friends, or else the formal sit-down dinner was foregone and replaced by what the Nisei conceived of as an American-style buffet.

The Nisei who married between 1946 and 1955 faced their first years of marriage during a period characterized by both the greatest economic insecurity and the most promising economic future. Plagued by a severe housing shortage, their own lack of savings, high rates of unemployment, and the social and psychological difficulties of readjusting to urban American life, the Nisei who married in this period at the same time began to achieve the occupational mobility that had been denied the older members of their generation. Returning war veterans who had fought in all-Nisei battalions in Europe flocked to universities and colleges with the aid of the G.I. Bill. Other Nisei enlisted (many were to use their Japanese-language skills in the occupation and reconstruction of Japan) with the educational and social benefits of veteran status in mind. Despite the absence of assurance that their educational achievements would lead to comparably high-level jobs in a society in which anti-Japanese sentiment still lingered, many Nisei pinned their hopes on college degrees. They had few other prospects to pursue. What small part of the community's former entrepreneurial base had been resurrected was far too meager to employ more than a small number of Nisei. There was even less reason to think that, in the near future, whites would be likely to patronize Nisei businesses than there was to hope that they might hire Nisei as employees. Already in the first years of the resettlement young Nisei women were finding secretarial jobs in white firms and government offices, and Nisei men with college degrees and technical skills were for the first time being hired in jobs that matched their educations.

Case N.41a. The early married years of William and Kimie Nishikawa illustrate the dynamic and unstable, yet hopeful, character of the resettlement period. The couple first met while they were on work leave from Minidoka harvesting sugar beets in Montana. They had not known each other in Seattle, as Kimie's family were farmers in the Puyallup Valley about thirty miles south of the city. Soon after they met, William took advantage of the relocation program to take a job as gardener in Spokane (in eastern Washington, and thus outside the prohibited zone). In the meantime Kimie also left Minidoka for Chicago to join her older married sister, whose husband had offered her a job as a waitress in his restaurant. Both Kimie's and William's parents remained in camp. William soon moved to Chicago, where he was drafted. Following a tour of duty in Europe, he was discharged in 1946 and returned to marry Kimie. In the intervening years, Kimie's widowed mother had joined her two daughters in Chicago. William's parents, however, had returned to Seattle. In the year following their wedding in Seattle William and Kimie lived first with his parents and then in their own apartment while he worked as a full-time gardener and she worked as a waitress. In late summer of 1947 they moved back to Chicago, where William enrolled in college with the help of the G.I. Bill. Their first child was born just about the time William started his first semester, but Kimie was able to work full-time in her brother-in-law's restaurant because her mother cared for their child. At the end of a year of school, William decided that a West Coast university offered a better program in architecture and he transferred to that school leaving Kimie to live with her mother until he got settled. Within a year Kimie and their daughter joined him. Over the next three years while William worked toward his bachelor's degree in architecture both he and Kimie worked part-time. Just before he graduated, their second child was born, and Kimie stopped working. A few months later they returned to Seattle, where, after working for another business for two years, William opened his own architectural office. Two years after he started his business, their third and last child was born and the couple purchased their first home in the Beacon Hill neighborhood, a middle-income area with a high proportion of Japanese residents.

The Nishikawas' early years of marriage were not untypical. Of the 15 couples in the Nisei marriage sample who married between 1946 and 1955, 9 had similar configurations of school attendance and employment in interim jobs by husbands. All but 1 of the wives of these 9 men worked full-time during these years. However, not every couple who married during the resettlement period was engaged in a strategy of occupational mobility that rested upon a husband's college degree. Six of the 15 husbands, in fact, had already settled into their career occupations by their first year of marriage. Significantly, none of these men had a college degree.

Although their initial period of postmarital employment was prolonged, the women in this marriage cohort, like their counterparts in the two previous ones, made child rearing and housework their primary activity for the first fifteen years of marriage. Fourteen of the 15 women in the cohort were working at full-time jobs during the first year of marriage, but by the tenth year, when most of the husbands had attained their career positions and the couples' families were well under way, only a third were employed. That their strategies for upward mobility were concentrated almost exclusively on male educational achievement is reflected in the fact that only 1 of the women returned to school after marriage. The other women, while they started their marriages in jobs considered more desirable than those held by women in the earlier cohorts, did not experience any occupational mobility after marriage. Most were in secretarial and clerical positions, but 2 had semiprofessional jobs, 1 as a nurse and 1 as a librarian. A couple were workers in family businesses, but only 1 was a wage-earning blue-collar worker.

Post-resettlement Period: 1956-1970

By the middle of the 1950's, the era of economic insecurity, housing shortages, and interim employment had been replaced by a period of economic stability and relative abundance for families and community. Couples who married during the resettlement had settled by now into the homes their higher income levels afforded them and—along with the older members of their generation—were preoccupied with raising their children. The late 1950's and the 1960's were the Nisei counterpart to the Issei period of family building in the 1930's. Once again community social organizations were oriented toward providing services to complement and buttress family functions. With the Nisei now in leadership positions, community social life took on the familistic tenor that pervaded American society in general during this period. Churches in the community once again promoted the sports leagues and youth organizations designed for the children of members—now the third generation (Sansei). If the community seemed to be continually losing its physical integrity, as families moved into areas of the city, and even the suburbs, where few Japanese had been found before the war, for most families it continued to be where most of their kin and friends were to be found.

In this context of a relatively stable, familistic community that had just recovered from the upheaval of internment and resettlement, the last Nisei marriages took place. As a marriage cohort, the Nisei who married between 1956 and 1970 were at the same time more homogeneous and more heterogeneous than any of the other marriage cohorts. Their heterogeneity lay in the wide span of ages at which they married. The 12 husbands in my sample of post-resettlement marriages were as young as 23 and as old as 45 at the time they married; their brides ranged from 21 to 39 years old. These Nisei were a mix of younger Nisei from the latest birth cohorts (dating from the 1930's) and late-marrying Nisei from middle birth cohorts (dating from the 1920's). Because of the high proportion of Nisei in this cohort who married late (that is, after 30), the mean ages at marriage of men and women were considerably higher than in previous cohorts: 32.7 for men and 27.3 for women.

However dissimilar in age, the couples in this cohort had remarkably

similar occupational histories in their early married years. In contrast
to the high percentage of husbands in the resettlement cohort who
were employed in interim jobs during their first years of marriage, all
but one of the 12 husbands in this cohort were settled into their careers
when they married. It was not just the late-marrying men who had already attained their career levels, but also the men who married in
their mid- to late twenties. Very few of these couples changed residence
during their first five years of marriage—a sign of their comparative
affluence. Indeed, a majority of them were able to purchase homes at
the time of marriage. Like the husbands in the resettlement cohort,
these men had high occupational levels. Aside from 2 men who were in
business, all were concentrated in professional and managerial jobs.
Their wives attained similarly high occupation levels; not a single one
was a worker in a family business or a factory or service worker. When
they worked it was either in such acceptable female professions as
teaching and librarianship, or as office workers.

Marriages in this period continued to be predominantly the outcome
of Nisei dating and decisions, although there was a noticeable resur-
gence in parental involvement in wedding plans and even in the selection of spouses. With community social life once again centering on the
family, the comparatively small number of Nisei who were eligible for
marriage in this period conducted their courtships in the absence of a
flourishing peer culture. The circumstances leading to their marriages—and their accounts of these circumstances—display a greater
sense of continuity in their relationships with parents than the independent, and sometimes rebellious, spirit conveyed by the Nisei who
married during the war. Many of the older Nisei who married in the
post-resettlement period had continued to live with their parents or a
widowed mother throughout their single adult lives, and, as a result,
had developed close parental ties. Although the late-marrying men in
my marriage sample were both first and second sons (there were even a
few third sons), the late-marrying women were all first or only daughters. The siblings of these Nisei had come to expect them, by virtue of
their continued residence in the parental home, to take primary responsibility for the parents. In Chapter 6 I will discuss the ways in
which the Nisei's ideas about the filial obligations of different members
of the sibling group developed and changed over time. For the present,
suffice it to say that unmarried Nisei children whose siblings had already married commonly found themselves left with more filial responsibilities than they might have initially expected. A good proportion of the Nisei who had not married by their early thirties were to

remain unmarried.[13] Those who eventually married often did so in ways that spoke strongly of filial obligations.

Case N.35a. When Joan Kimatsu married for the first time at the age of thirty-eight, it was to a forty-seven-year-old Nisei, Torao Nagaoka, whose deceased parents had been members of her parents' church and who owned the apartment building in which she and her parents lived. Joan was the only child of her parents and had never left home, though her postgraduate degree and career as a nurse certainly gave her the financial option to do so. Torao, on the other hand, as the first son in a sibship of seven, had always lived and worked with his parents in their apartment business. After their death he continued to operate the apartment business by himself. Although Peggy and Torao dated before their marriage, her parents were from the beginning closely involved in encouraging the relationship, and it was they who planned the wedding with the groom. Torao, of course, knew full well that by marrying Joan he was accepting responsibility for the financial security of her parents. After they married, Joan moved into Torao's apartment and her parents remained in their apartment on the upper floor. Although they continued to pay rent, there was little question but that if, in the future, they could not afford it, their son-in-law would be obliged to absorb the financial loss.

Even some of the marriages of the younger Nisei during this period display the influence of parents. Thus when Dan Fukumoto and Betty Yokoi met at the University of Washington and began dating, her father entered quickly into their plans by informing Dan that they could not marry until he had graduated. After he did, Mr. Yokoi arranged a formal meeting, attended by the couple and both sets of parents, in which they all agreed to the marriage. Mr. Yokoi had even wanted to engage the services of a *baishakunin*, but the couple drew the line here and refused. They did not, however, reject his request for a large wedding. This, too, was a sign of the times. The Fukumoto-Yokoi wedding, like many others in this period, closely resembled the prewar ones, with their emphasis on kinship and affinal relationships and on the community associations of parents. But if the dramatic form of the wedding reception party—its full complement of formal speeches, introductions of relatives, and Japanese musical entertainment—was almost indistinguishable from its prewar predecessors, the financial arrangements behind it spoke of a rather different set of filial and affinal relationships. The bride, who had been an elementary school teacher for five years, paid for all but a few of the costs of the wedding ceremony with her own savings—a sizable amount as she had lived rent-free with

[13] Nuptiality rates of Seattle Nisei women are high, but later birth cohorts have higher rates of nonmarriage than earlier ones (Leonetti 1976, 112).

her parents. The groom paid for the flowers and the liquor served at the reception. The expense of the formal dinner party for 250 guests was paid by the bride's father, who saw the wedding as his final chance (she was the last of his three daughters to marry) to repay obligations to his business associates and friends in the community. The groom's parents gave the couple a small gift of money. They, of all the principal actors who participated in the Buddhist wedding ceremony and the dinner reception, were by far the least involved in planning them. Like the bride's parents, they submitted to the bride a list of the relatives and friends they thought should be invited to the wedding. It was, however, the bride herself who, in close consultation with her mother, sisters, and friends, coordinated and staged the wedding at which her parents-in-law were only the most interested of the spectators.

PERIOD EFFECTS AND SOCIAL CHANGE

Like the elaborateness of their weddings, several features of the Nisei's marriages exhibit the immediate effects of the circumstances in which they were initiated. A comparison of husbands' employment patterns, for instance, reveals striking differences between the first year of marriage in each historical period. Table 12 shows the small numbers of husbands in the war cohort and the resettlement cohort who were employed in their career jobs during the first year of marriage. The relatively large numbers of husbands who were in camp, the army, or an interim job resulted directly from the incarceration and its aftermath, which delayed attainment of the career jobs into which these men would eventually settle.

The fact that half the men in the prewar cohort also began married life in interim jobs reflects their very limited opportunities at that time. As I explained in my discussion of this cohort, it was the men who started out in laboring or semiskilled wage-earning jobs who later changed careers in an attempt to move into business. Members of the same cohort who began marriage as entrepreneurs or professionals did not change careers. In contrast, the very small number of men in the post-resettlement cohort who began married life in interim jobs reflects the vastly improved occupational opportunities open to the Nisei by the latter half of the 1950's. These occupational shifts among the Nisei men in my marriage sample parallel those of the Nisei men in the national survey reported by Edna Bonacich and John Modell, with one exception. From the prewar period until the mid-1960's, only the professionals in their national sample remained in their prewar occupations. All other occupational categories, including proprietors and

TABLE 12

*Occupation of Nisei Husbands in Four Marriage Cohorts
During First Year of Marriage*

Cohort	In interim job	In camp	In army or school	Total not in career job	Total in career job
Prewar (*N* = 8)	4	0	0	4	4
War (*N* = 13)	4	9	0	13	0
Resettlement (*N* = 15)	4	0	5	9	6
Post-resettlement (*N* = 12)	1	0	0	1	11

TABLE 13

*Nisei Wives in Four Marriage Cohorts
Employed in First Year of Marriage*

Cohort	Number employed	Percent employed
Prewar (*N* = 8)	3	38%
War (*N* = 13)	1	8
Resettlement (*N* = 15)	14	93
Post-resettlement (*N* = 12)	7	58
TOTAL (*N* = 48)	25	48%

managers, lost more than half the Nisei men who had been in them before the war (1980, 158). The entrepreneurs in my Seattle prewar marriage cohort, in contrast, returned to their line of work after the war.

The impact of the period on the first year of Nisei marriage is even more starkly displayed by the employment status of Nisei wives (see Table 13). The very low employment rates for war cohort wives were due to the imprisonment, while the very high ones for wives in the resettlement cohort accompanied the high percentages of husbands in the army or school. Given the involvement of husbands in military service, college, or interim jobs, wives in this cohort worked in the initial years of marriage, most of them until their husbands' attainment of a secure career job, or the birth of a child, or both, temporarily retired them from paid employment.

The postmarital residence patterns of the four marriage cohorts differ markedly for the same reasons. In my analysis of filial relationships in Chapter 5, I will examine closely the effects of the wartime incarceration and subsequent resettlement on those patterns. For the present, however, it can be noted that no fewer than 92 percent of the couples in

TABLE 14

Postmarital Residence of Nisei Couples
During First Ten Years of Marriage, by Marriage Cohort

Cohort	One year or more in stem-family household		Only neolocal	
	Number	Percent	Number	Percent
Prewar (*N* = 8)	5	62%	3	38%
War (*N* = 13)	12	92	1	8
Resettlement (*N* = 15)	5	33	10	67
Post-resettlement (*N* = 12)	6	50	6	50
TOTAL (*N* = 48)	28	58%	20	42%

TABLE 15

College Graduates Among Seattle Nisei,
by Marriage Cohort

Cohort	Percent college graduates	
	Men	Women
Prewar (*N* = 8)	25%	0%
War (*N* = 13)	31	15
Resettlement (*N* = 15)	53	40
Post-resettlement (*N* = 12)	50	33

the war cohort but only 33 percent of those in the resettlement cohort spent one or more of their first ten years of married life in a stem-family household (see Table 14). It was neither the Nisei who married during the resettlement period, nor those who had married before the war who contributed most to the very high rates of coresidence during that period, but those who married during the war.

Because social change has varying consequences for people at different stages of life, and because these consequences may extend far into people's later lives, it may differentiate cohorts in historically significant ways (Ryder 1965, 844). Among the Nisei, this interweaving of demographic and social process manifests itself most significantly in the cohorts' differential social mobility. Tables 15 and 16 exhibit the higher educational and occupational levels of later marriage cohorts. The altered opportunities of the postwar era quite obviously had different, and differentiating, consequences for successive cohorts. Nisei birth cohorts similarly exhibit different educational and occupational characters. Later birth cohorts of Seattle Nisei, like later Nisei birth cohorts

TABLE 16

Occupations of Nisei Men, by Marriage Cohort

Occupation	Prewar	War	Resettlement	Post-resettlement	Total
Unskilled and semiskilled	2	2	0	0	4
Craftsmen and technicians	0	3	3	2	8
Sales and clerical	1	2	1	2	6
Managerial and administrative	0	1	3	2	6
Professional	1	1	5	4	11
Self-employed businessmen	4	4	3	2	13
TOTAL	8	13	15	12	48

nationally, display greater proportions of college graduates and professionals (Leonetti 1976).[14] The changing educational and occupational character of successive Nisei marriage cohorts should accordingly be viewed as the combined outcome of two sets of characteristics: those of Nisei from later birth cohorts who have been marrying in step with their respective cohorts; and those of late-marrying members of earlier birth cohorts. These latter Nisei tend to have more education and are more likely to be professionals than their cohort peers. The steady rise in age at marriage in the four cohorts should be viewed in the same way. The age at marriage of husbands rises from a marriage cohort mean of 25.8 for the prewar period to one of 32.7 for the post-resettlement period. The corresponding increase for brides is from 21.6 to 27.3. Again this trend is a consequence of the rise in age at marriage of successive birth cohorts (Leonetti 1976, 108-14) combined with the late marriages of Nisei from earlier birth cohorts.

To compare birth cohorts and marriage cohorts, then, is to illuminate Nisei social mobility and to recognize it as a process that was far from equally generous to all members of that generation. When popular accounts of Japanese Americans portray the Nisei as a successful generation, they overlook the fact that some Nisei were more successful than others. It is not that these accounts have no relation to social and demographic fact. The Nisei who married after the war, and who at-

[14] The national sample of Nisei in the UCLA Japanese American Research Project also shows a rise in educational and occupational levels among successive male birth cohorts; unfortunately, female birth cohorts are not analyzed (Bonacich and Modell 1980).

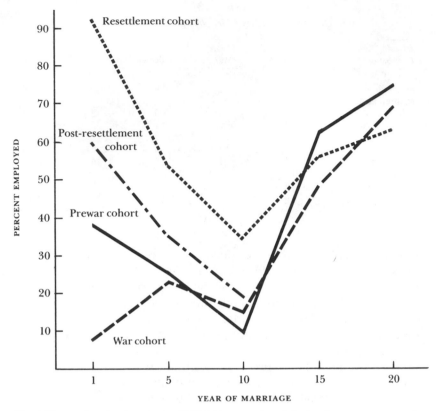

Fig. 4. Fluctuations in percentage of Nisei wives employed during first twenty years of marriage, by marriage cohorts. The post-resettlement cohort is followed only until the tenth year of marriage because its members had not attained later marriage years at the time of the study.

tained higher educational and occupational levels, do in fact comprise more than half their generation (see Tables 10 and 11). Those who married in the five years after the war, after all, are members of the second-largest five-year marriage cohort. The war cohort immediately preceding them is larger. But, less favored as it was by the timing of events, it would not become the model of the generation. Instead, the cohort of Nisei who came of age in the camps, left to seek their educations and futures in the East Coast and Midwest, married with little benefit of or hindrance from parental involvement, and returned to their home communities to ascend the social ladder made available by postwar America, became the symbol of their generation for both those inside and outside the Japanese American community. In short, they emerged as the key cohort of that generation.

As telling as the enduring differences that today give each cohort a distinctive character is the disappearance of certain differences over time. The eventual convergence of cohorts into common patterns despite initial differences generated by period effects mirrors the shared experience holding the Nisei together as a generation. Furthermore, such convergences hint at shared normative and cultural systems that, along with unshared and variable social circumstances, have shaped Nisei marriages. One such telling convergence can be found in the employment histories of wives. In spite of the great difference in the percentage of wives employed during the first year of marriage (see Table 13), over time the four cohorts come to display the same pattern. Figure 4 shows the fluctuations in the employment rate of wives during the first twenty years of marriage for each of the four marriage cohorts. It is immediately apparent that all cohorts manifest the same pattern of change over time. With the exception of the war cohort, where the low rate is due to the incarceration, the common pattern is a steady decline in the wives' employment rate until the tenth year of marriage, followed by a steady rise to the twentieth year of marriage. Although the graph ends at the twentieth year—the historical limit of this study—the prewar and war cohorts exhibit a pattern in which rates remain at this high level until the thirtieth year of marriage, when they begin to fall due to retirement. Not only do the patterns of change in the four cohorts coincide but, in the tenth and (even more so) the twentieth years of marriage, they converge.

POWER RELATIONS IN NISEI MARRIAGE

During the years of childbearing, which for most Nisei women were confined to the second to ninth years of marriage, and the years when their children were of preschool age, most Nisei wives became full-time housewives. After these child-bearing and child-rearing years, wives reentered the labor force in increasing numbers.[15] Clearly, then, the similar trends in wives' employment among the four Nisei marriage cohorts reflect the priority the Nisei place on women's child-bearing and child-rearing activities as opposed to their work outside the home.

Today, the Nisei marriage cohorts that started out with very different employment patterns exhibit similar patterns of the conjugal division

[15] The interval between marriage and first birth for Seattle Nisei women is a mean of 1.89 years and the interval between first birth and last birth is a mean of 6.7 years (Leonetti 1976, 116).

of labor. In the latter respect, couples from different marriage cohorts do not differ as much as they do in their occupational and educational characteristics. It is not that the Nisei are entirely unvarying in their conjugal division of labor and in their power relations. Nisei couples differ with regard to the way in which they divide tasks in a number of spheres, including child care and income-producing work, and thus cannot be described as sharing the same overall pattern of the conjugal division of labor. As regards the conjugal power relation, that is, the relative control of the spouses over activities and their products, Nisei couples differ as to particular spheres such as the family economy and their children's future. But the differences are small in comparison to the differences in conjugal relations among the Issei. Overall, Nisei conjugal relations exhibit a fundamentally common structure.

The Conjugal Division of Labor

Because most Nisei husbands and wives spend most of their time in work separated by time and space, their conjugal division of labor is easier to summarize than that of Issei spouses in small business. Nisei spouses tend to work apart from each other even when one or both are self-employed. Not only self-employed professionals, but men engaged in business enterprises similar to those in which the Issei were concentrated before the war generally work apart from their wives. Of the 14 Nisei wives married to self-employed businessmen, only 5 (36 percent) ever worked in the business compared to 11 of the 17 (65 percent) Issei wives married to self-employed businessmen. Thus not only was there a dramatic decline in the rate of entrepreneurship from one generation to the next, but even where the Nisei operated businesses, wives were almost half as likely to work alongside their husbands as they were among the Issei.

The two primary types of conjugal work patterns among the Nisei, therefore, are separate income-earning work (either self-employed professional or salaried) by the two spouses, and income-earning work solely by the husband. Nisei couples, moreover, tend toward a common timing in their alternation between these two patterns. Furthermore, with the exception of the first few years of marriage when some husbands were in the army, in school, or working part-time, and the later years between the husband's retirement and the wife's retirement, Nisei husbands, even when their wives work full-time, generally earn 60 percent or more of the couple's income. In the first few years of marriage, a working wife may bring home almost as much income as her husband, particularly if he is working only part-time at an interim job.

When a woman returns to employed work after a period as a housewife, however, she usually earns from 25 to 40 percent of the couple's
total income.

As regards the division of tasks around the home, what husbands do
is easier to describe than what wives do because it is much more limited.
Every Nisei husband does at least a small amount of maintenance work
on the house, yard, and automobile. Husbands differ in the extent to
which they help their wives with the rest of the housework. But men in
general have very little to do with meal preparation; they rarely plan,
shop for, or cook meals. A few men occasionally make their own break-
fasts or specialize in cooking a particular kind of food or meal such as
Sunday breakfast. A few also help their wives on an occasional basis in
such tasks as dishwashing, housecleaning, and laundering. The variation is greater in the area of child care. During their children's infancy,
when demands for child care were greatest, some husbands did no
more than change an infrequent diaper and watch the child on the rare
occasions when their wives had to leave the home. Others went so far as
to take over a considerable part of the housework during the weeks immediately following the birth of a child. Some routinely changed dia-
pers, fixed formulas, and got up during the night to tend a wailing infant. Only one husband, however, took any time off from his job to help
his wife after the birth.

Nisei wives with rare exceptions handle all the routine housework
and child care. For most couples the wives' assumption of routine tasks
around the home extends to financial affairs. Daily, predictable expenditures required for the operation of the home are handled by the wife.
A typical arrangement is for a husband to hand his paycheck over to his
wife or to deposit it in a joint checking account from which she draws
funds to pay household bills and make routine purchases. In a few
cases the wife also gives her husband what is commonly known as a
"spending allowance," but in most cases husbands simply write checks
for purchases and withdraw cash for their personal expenses. A few
couples vary this by having the wife make daily, routine purchases while
the husband pays the monthly bills and balances the checking account.
But it is much commoner for one spouse—almost always the wife—to
assume responsibility for both daily purchases and monthly bills.

Not all the Nisei couples began their marriages with the wife in
charge of routine finances. During their first married years, prewar
brides often did not have access to a checking account and had to ask
their husbands for money for even the smallest of extraordinary purchases. Over time almost all these couples have moved closer to the pat-

tern I described as the typical financial arrangement. If a wife has not become the family accountant she at least has access to a joint checking account and better knowledge of the couple's financial affairs. Likewise, most couples who began marriage with property and savings in the husband's name now have joint legal ownership of property and joint savings accounts. The exceptions are business property—an apartment or hotel, for instance—a car, savings bonds, and stocks, all of which remain registered solely in the husband's name. Only one of the wives has property or savings solely in her own name.

The fact that Nisei wives manage routine financial transactions, of course, does not mean that women control or even have parity with their husbands in making important decisions concerning the family economy. Indeed, the fact that wives manage family finances reinforces the point made in the previous chapter about the necessity of analytically differentiating a task from a domain of control. For although women are charged with managing the routine financial transactions, men have greater control of the family economy. This control is apparent in, for instance, the lead men take in making large nonroutine purchases. Men have the final say in whether and when a couple purchases a house, car, and other large items even though wives are usually consulted and are often the originators of the idea to purchase an item at a certain time. As a general rule, moreover, wives do not spend over fifty dollars on an item without first obtaining permission from their husbands. Men are not similarly constrained. Nisei husbands buy such items as stereo equipment, golf clubs, and skis, as well as gifts for their wives, without a prior discussion. Many Nisei wives have gained greater power, and most feel freer, in later married years to buy personal items and gifts, but a good part of this is a consequence of their greater affluence in later married life.

Nisei husbands also control the family economy by managing its long-term financial strategies. Several Nisei husbands I interviewed were at the time members of investment clubs through which they learned of investment alternatives and plotted investment plans. Wives were not members of these clubs, nor did they attend meetings at which such information was transmitted. How much a wife knew of her husband's financial strategies varied. Some wives had been consulted at each step and had detailed knowledge of the couple's fiscal affairs; others were unclear of the extent of their holdings in stocks and bonds or even if these were registered in their husbands' name or both their names. Not surprisingly, wives in the latter position confronted serious problems when they became widows. When wives return to work and provide a substantial portion of the couple's income, they may feel less constrained in their spending habits, but they do not become equal partners in managing the family economy. Nor does the fact that a wife earns more than her husband result in a reversal of conjugal power relations. In all but one of the four cases where Nisei wives earned more than half the couple's income—either at the time of the study or in earlier years—their husbands retained greater control of the family economy. The one exception was a couple in which the husband's physical handicap had come to limit his contacts with people and organizations outside the home. This couple was also exceptional in that the husband did most of the housework and child care while his wife was very active in community affairs and in her career work.

Finally, men were found to exert greater control over the family economy through their influence on their wives' employment patterns. In many Nisei marriages, husbands either decided whether and when their wives should work or at the least had a large part in that decision. Before the birth of the first child, whether a wife worked depended primarily on whether she and her husband thought it a good financial strategy for accumulating savings or seeing them through a lean period. Most wives appear to have been quite willing to either work or not during this initial period; consequently, it is difficult to differentiate cases of mutual agreement from cases in which either a husband's or wife's desires prevailed. After the birth of the first child the mutual agreement of husbands and wives was again at a high level: in all but a few exceptional cases both spouses wanted the wife to devote her full efforts to child care and homemaking. By the time a second or third child had been born and, even more so, by the time the last child had reached school age, the desires of husbands and wives appear to have diverged. Several wives said they wanted to return to work or at least found it an appealing possibility, but were discouraged by husbands who wanted them to remain full-time homemakers. In a few instances, husbands simply forbade their wives to work. More often, however, they made clear that they would not be pleased if the children were neglected or dinners late in being served. Husbands' complaints that their wives were too tired in the evenings, too tense and frustrated by the demands of work, or "trying to do too much" led some women to abandon their jobs.

Recreational and Social Activities

The activities and social relations of married couples outside their so-called work pursuits are generally placed in the category of "leisure" or "recreation," and hence are discussed apart from the conjugal division of labor. But there is no reason why they should not be treated as part of it, especially when one is dealing with the kinship-related activities of Nisei husbands and wives. For it becomes obvious, when one examines this area, that wives take a much more active role in it than husbands. Moreover, a good part of these women's leisure (which can be defined as time not spent at a job or on housework and child care) is spent with relatives. If we add the fact that Nisei wives uniformly arrange and make preparations for family gatherings that bring relatives together, take charge of sending wedding, birthday, and graduation presents (to friends as well as relatives), handle most of the correspondence with geographically distant relatives, and (without exception) send Christmas cards, it becomes even more difficult to ignore the overlap between social activities and domestic tasks.

Corresponding to the kinship-related social activities of Nisei wives are the career-related social activities and recreational pursuits of Nisei husbands. Men's participation in sports clubs, community political associations, and investment clubs brings them into contact with other men who are at the same time both friends and co-workers, colleagues, or potential (if not actual) clients. Many husbands golf every weekend with friends and work associates. Others get together regularly once or twice a month with an informal male friendship circle to play poker. Attending spectator sports, fishing, and drinking at bars (usually bars that have a regular Nisei clientele) are other activities that Nisei husbands do with friends. Most men have a hobby they pursue by themselves such as fishing, skiing, photography, or bonsai. In addition, almost all belong to some voluntary association. Businessmen and professionals are usually members of career-based associations such as the Asian Technical Engineers Association, the Boeing Management Club, the National Society of Packaging and Material Handling Engineers, and the Seattle Japanese Hotel and Apartment Owners Association. Some actively participate in one of the Japanese American churches (Buddhist or Christian), where they are members of standing committees, church social clubs, or boards. A few take an active part in community associations such as the local chapter of the Japanese American Citizens League, the Nisei Veterans Association, and the Asian Employment Office. Men who are members of several associations may attend meetings and other functions as often as twice a week, but most have only one or two evenings a month taken up by them.

Nisei wives are much less often members of voluntary associations— whether professional or community associations or sports groups—

and fewer of them have a hobby that they regularly pursue. The one exception to the former is their participation in church events. Although some of these activities (Sunday service, bazaars, picnics) are ones they attend with husbands, most women who are active church members also participate in other church events by themselves. Thus they may be members of the women's association (*fujin-kai*) or a service committee. But aside from their attendance at Sunday services, only a few women spend more than one evening or afternoon a month at a church meeting. At the time of this study, less than a fourth of the Nisei wives in my sample were members of a community service organization such as a school parent-teacher association, a hospital auxiliary club, or other volunteer service group. Unpaid volunteer work was not something Nisei wives as a group had taken up, and less than a third of the Nisei wives interviewed said they had a hobby.

There is great variation in the frequency with which spouses participate in leisure-time activities together, without their children. A few Nisei lead an active, couple-oriented social life that includes attending plays, concerts, and movies, playing regularly in a bridge club, and having dinner with other couples. Most couples, however, participate in these shared activities less frequently than in their separate recreational pursuits. Moreover, in a great many of the social events that husbands and wives attend together, one of the spouses has the primary tie to the group sponsoring the event. As a general rule, husbands bring their wives into contact with business associates and friends, and wives pull their husbands into family and kinship-based groups. There are, of course, exceptions to this general pattern. A few wives have close ties with women friends, and thus pull their husbands into this friendship circle. Likewise, there are some men who have strong ties with their parents and siblings. But they are by far the exception, not the rule. The implications of this conjugal division of labor—for that is what it is—will be explored in Chapter 8.

We have seen how the drama in which Japanese Americans were swept up during World War II was accompanied by a dramatic change in the circumstances of marriage. From Issei to Nisei, and through the succession of Nisei marriage cohorts, much more changed than the way in which spouses were selected. That Nisei husbands and wives no longer worked together in family businesses, but worked separately for individual salaries and wages—this, in social import if not emotional drama, equaled the shift from arranged marriage to romantic marriage. The employment patterns of wives over time, the conjugal division of labor (including its leisure-time activities), and the power relations of husbands and wives all differentiate the Nisei from their parents. Neither are Nisei conjugal relations shaped by the successor status of the husbands, or by the marital strategies that motivated the Issei before the war. Even where the Nisei have remained in the kinds of businesses in which the Issei were concentrated before the war, wives manifest similar patterns of employment as those whose husbands are in professions or salaried occupations.

What forces are responsible for this transformation? The question requires more than a comparison of the social histories of marriage cohorts, for such a comparison cannot tell us, for example, how changes in the conjugal division of labor are linked with changes in the power relations of spouses. We need to explicate the system of symbols and meanings through which people interpret and act upon marriage before we can arrive at an understanding of its historical transformation.

CHAPTER 4

The Transformation of Marriage

M ARRIAGE AS A SOCIAL INSTITUTION entails much more than the residential and economic histories or even the power relations of married couples. It also involves a cultural system of meanings through which people create different marital histories and interpret them as variants of a common structure of marriage. An analysis of the transformation of marriage must illuminate the changes in the connections people make between various aspects of their marital histories so as to make sense of them. It should tell us how, for example, people make sense of and, in so doing, forge the links between particular employment histories and particular conjugal power relations. In this chapter I present a comparative analysis of the system of symbols and meanings through which the Issei and Nisei interpret and act upon their marriages. In addition to examining the ways in which the two generations locate marriage in a social universe of relationships, I explore the constructs through which each generation conceptually orders the actions and interactions of spouses.

THE ISSEI INTERPRETATION OF MARRIAGE

Marriage as Giri

Issei men and women locate their marriages in that phase of their lives in which they have had to bear the greatest burdens and responsibilities. Marriage, bound up as it is with continuing obligations to parents and newly created responsibilities to children, is thought of as inseparable from adulthood: just as one has to meet the demands of being an adult, so one has to meet the demands of marriage. One does not choose to marry. Rather, marriage is a natural stage in the course of one's life.

Issei men associate their marriages with the attainment of full adult status. Whether marriage entailed their headship of a new household or brought them a step closer to succeeding to the headship of an old one, it redefined their relations with parents, siblings, and other kin. This redefinition brought them a sense of being more active agents in the shaping of their lives and futures. For Issei women, on the other hand, marriage also coincided with adulthood, but it brought them little sense of greater personal control or activity. Instead, marriage is portrayed by these women as having entailed the transference of obedience from one's parents to one's husband. Indeed, marriage often brought them greater subordination than they had experienced in their natal families—a subordination that was doubly oppressive if untempered by compassion. In spite of this difference in men's and women's experience, marriage for both sexes is depicted by the Issei as enmeshed within a web of obligations and responsibilities to kin and community. It is a relationship rooted in *giri*, that is, in specific binding obligations.

The success of a marriage, then, is seen as having depended on the fulfillment of these obligations by both spouses. What people did—the correctness of their behavior toward each other and toward parents and other family members involved in the marriage—determined the form of their marriage, its integrity, and its emotional content. This emphasis on correct action and behavior does not preclude a concern for emotional commitment and affection. For example, the husbands of whom Issei wives are most critical are the ones they accused of lacking compassion or feeling. A woman whose husband sent their children to Japan without consulting her expressed bitter resentment toward him even after his death. Similar resentment was still felt by a woman whose husband had engaged in a prolonged extramarital affair with another woman in the community. In both cases, however, the impropriety and incorrectness of the spouses' actions were emphasized rather than the absence of emotional commitment they exhibited. Neither of these women, moreover, felt they had been bad or improper wives for having resented and disliked their husbands most of their married lives. Indeed, both claimed they had fulfilled their conjugal obligations. As long as their behavior was correct, they could not be faulted for harboring ill will or feeling little, if any, affection for their husbands.

Issei who express greater satisfaction with their marriages describe the character of their conjugal relationships in terms of "compassion," "respect," and "consideration." Husbands praise wives for the respect they have shown and the emotional support they have provided. Wives speak of the compassion and consideration exhibited by esteemed husbands and of the confidences they have shared. A few say that they became "good friends" to each other. On the rare occasions when "love" is mentioned, it is portrayed as an affection that evolved over years of married life. Love, however, is a relatively minor theme in Issei discussions of their conjugal relationships; the key features of a happy and satisfying marriage are compassion, respect, and consideration.

For most Issei women, the end of marriage is associated with release from life's greatest burdens. Issei widows, except for those widowed before their children reached adulthood, describe their present life as one of relative ease and freedom. Whether they are relieved to be free of a domineering husband or miss the companionship of an esteemed one, these widows say they can now rest peacefully knowing they have fulfilled their obligations and duties as wives. Sending or personally delivering a husband's ashes to his home in Japan was mentioned by several widows as fulfillment of their final conjugal obligation. As for the widowers, given the age differential between Issei spouses that I mentioned in Chapter 2, life after the death of a spouse is something few Issei men experience. All but two of the Issei men I interviewed had surviving wives. The two widowers, however, did not view the end of married life as an emancipation from burdens and obligations but rather as an incompleteness. One described his present life as unhappy, because there is "no mental support," and the other complained of his loneliness.

Male and Female Domains: "Inside" and "Outside"

Marriage for the Issei is a relationship between a man and woman that necessarily brings together two different but complementary sets of activities, interests, and characters. The primary conceptual structure for Issei norms about this relationship is derived from their view of women's and men's gender domains, the core symbols of which are "inside" and "outside."

By far the commonest way in which the Issei described the responsibilities, activities, and concerns of spouses was to say that wives took care of things "inside" the house, home, or family, and husbands took care of things "outside" it. When English words were used, most Issei used at least one term from each of two sets: they said "inside the house," "inside the family," or "inside the home" in referring to the wife's domain; and "outside the house," "outside the home," or "outside the family" in referring to the husband's domain. When Japanese was spoken, Issei commonly used the phrase *uchi no koto* (things inside, things indoors, or things of the household) to describe a wife's domain, while the husband's domain was sometimes described as *soto no koto* (things outdoors or outside). A few Issei, however, only clearly specified the wife's domain as including matters "inside" the house, home, or family. They described the husband's domain as including "everything else."

My purpose here, as I said in Chapter 1, is to explicate what such terms, whether English or Japanese, may mean to the people who use them. It is the sum of the usages, not the sum of the dictionary definitions, that is of primary relevance. Indeed, the dictionary alone is rarely helpful. For instance, the phrase *uchi no koto* can be interpreted in several ways. *Uchi* can be translated as "the inside," "the interior," or as "one's house," "one's home," or as "one's household." The addition of the possessive marker *no* and *koto* (things) makes it possible to interpret *uchi no koto* as referring to things physically inside the physical structure of the house, things indoors in general, or things *of* the home or household (and not necessarily physically inside them). Similarly, *ie no naka no koto* can be interpreted in a number of ways depending on whether *ie* is taken to refer to the physical structure of the house, a home, a household, or a family. As it can mean any of these things or all at the same time, it would be a mistake to pin our interpretation on any one literal translation. Much the same is true of the meaning of the English phrases "inside the house," "inside the home," and "inside the family," which the Issei used to define the domain of wives. Here as well there is some ambiguity as to whether that domain is a physically circumscribed one (the interior of the physical structure of the house or the property on which the home sits) or a more socially circumscribed one (the relations within the family). For the above reasons, I have not emphasized the literal definitions of such terms as *kanai*, the Japanese term of reference for one's wife, which means literally "inside the house," or *okusan*, the term of reference for another man's wife, which means "the person of the interior" or "of the depths" (*oku*, with the honorific *san*).

Aspects of differentiation. In its narrowest sense, the opposition between the female, inside domain and the male, outside domain refers to the contrast between indoor and outdoor tasks. Everything inside the walls of the house is said to be the responsibility of women and everything outside them the responsibility of men. Women wash dishes, cook meals, iron, sew, and clean everything in the house. Men do the yard work, maintain the external appearance of the house and its structural soundness, and wash and repair the automobile. The division of indoor and outdoor tasks extends to work in the family business. When a couple operated a hotel, for example, the wife was said to take care of cleaning everything inside the building, while her husband took care of the exterior. When a couple operated a laundry, she worked in the back and he made the deliveries.

The boundary between inside and outside also divides familial space from nonfamilial. Both the home and family business are considered "inside," first, because they are sociospatial areas controlled by the family. Although people outside the family may enter this space, they do so only with its permission. Thus, while a woman's work in the family business brings her into contact with people outside the family, it does so in a space that is controlled by the family and thereby separated from the nonfamilial world. Second, in interactional terms, a woman remains "inside" to the extent that she interacts primarily with family members or people with whom the family is familiar, even if she does so outside the home. A major disadvantage of working outside the family in wage-earning jobs is that it requires women to interact with nonkin and strangers—employees, clients, and fellow workers. In a family business, however, women can be assigned the tasks that entail little interaction with such people. Issei women who worked in family businesses often said they were fortunate to have worked "inside" the family, whereas those who held wage-earning jobs complained of having been sent "outside" the home to work.

The outside domain of men includes both the sphere of extrafamilial activities and the interstitial sphere that links the household to individuals, groups, and institutions outside it. Politics, community organizations, and the construction of a social world outside the household are the proper concern of men, who bear the ultimate responsibility for the security and reputation of the household in that world. Men represent the household in the community, and their relationships outside the household make up the larger community in which households exist. Wives need no such extrafamilial relationships because their social identity is derived from their place within the family and through the public statuses of their family members.

At another level of contrast, however, within the household itself there is an "inside" sphere and an "outside" sphere. The inside one encompasses specific tasks such as child care, housecleaning, and any of the routine, day-to-day chores necessary for the operation of the household. Because these tasks are considered of little consequence for the family's relations with the outside, "inside" in this sense also connotes "small" things, including small purchases, decisions of little consequence, and even small children. As one Issei woman put it, "Everything small, I took care of." Large purchases, decisions of great importance, and older children belong to the male domain. The same is true of decisions in the family business. Even the use of men's and women's earnings can be differentiated by gender domain. Several Issei women explained that when they earned wages, they used them to purchase groceries and other routinely needed supplies, leaving their husbands to pay for the house, car (usually bought cash down), and other exceptional items. Likewise, the care and supervision of small children, whose actions have little impact on relations outside the household, are viewed as almost entirely the responsibility of mothers, but when a child begins to interact with the world outside the home his behavior becomes a concern for his father. Fathers, therefore, should make decisions about the formal education and careers of children and their participation in churches, social clubs, and other community organizations.

Finally, "inside" and "outside" symbolize the different motives and intentions of women and men. Women's proper motives are above all to provide for the well-being of their family members. Indeed, motive appears to be the ultimate criterion for evaluating the gender correctness of female behavior. A woman who goes outside the home to work or to engage in any social activity is judged according to whether she is motivated by a concern for the family or by other interests. As one Issei man stated, "If she [a wife] wants to work because her family needs the money that's fine, but if she wants to work just to kill time or get out of the house, that's her problem." Accordingly, if an Issei woman happens to have been a successful entrepreneur, she explains her actions as motivated solely by her desire to provide for her family. Mrs. Hasemoto, for one, took great delight in recounting the details of the financial transactions and strategies she had employed to build her apartment business. But she always punctuated these narratives with reminders that she had been compelled to be aggressive and shrewd to support her children after her husband died, thereby glossing over the fact that she had begun her business long before his death. She further explained that she had bravely gone "out" to work at two wage-earning jobs so she could earn money to enable her parents to enter the apartment business. She downplayed the fact that a good proportion of her earnings, along with loans from her parents, had been used to capitalize her own business ventures.[1]

Men's actions, of course, are also subject to evaluation on the basis of intention. But because men are expected to have a broader range of concerns than women, they can engage in a wider range of activities with a wider range of people without having to justify their actions. No Issei man I interviewed felt the need to explain his strivings for wealth or social advancement as motivated by sheer concern for his family. Although men are expected to have these concerns, they are also expected to have other (potentially competing) concerns arising from their wider sphere of relationships outside the family. Thus it is acceptable for a man's motives for financial gain to derive not only from his commitment to his family but from his desire for public acclaim and power in the community. Furthermore, the boundaries of the male domain are comparatively vague and more difficult to locate, because "the outside" is somewhat of a residual category that can be defined only in contrast to "the inside." As I mentioned earlier, several Issei said that wives took care of everything "inside" the house, home, or family, and men took care of "everything else." The image conveyed by these statements is that of a bounded female sphere, clearly delimited by a male sphere that is unbounded, except by the exclusion of female elements, and expansive.

The symbolic opposition of inside and outside is flexible enough to encompass a range of diverse patterns in the division of tasks and activities. It not only allows people to explain and make common sense of different patterns of action, but it enables them to criticize the same patterns in other contexts. An Issei wife who worked in a wage-earning job may, in one instance, explain that it was necessary to help support the family and, in another, express bitterness that her husband sent her "outside" the home to work. Conversely, an action that appears incongruent with gender categories according to one dimension of meaning can appear congruent with them when assessed on the basis of another dimension. Mrs. Arashi's management of her own restaurant, for example, brought her into close contact with a variety of strangers, mostly single working men, which in interactional terms placed her squarely in a male domain. But, she emphasized, this was a "family" business

---

[1] Mrs. Hasemoto is an excellent illustration of how seemingly inappropriate behavior can be interpreted as deriving from the most legitimate of motives. That others beside Mrs. Hasemoto interpreted her actions in this light is evidenced by her having been awarded the title of "Mother of the Year" by a Nisei organization.

which she operated with her children and so these interactions occurred within a familial ("inside") context.

Coordination and control. Ideally, in an Issei marriage, these different but complementary gender domains are harmoniously coordinated. Each spouse fulfills his or her proper responsibilities without interfering with the other's. Men should not engage in housekeeping and child care, nor should women represent the household in its relations with the community. If a woman steps beyond her sphere it is because something is amiss: either her husband has not properly met his responsibilities, or unusual circumstances compel her to assume them. Mrs. Arashi explained that she was forced to take a job as a waitress and later opened her own restaurant because her husband, who was an alcoholic, was "in a constant state of irresponsibility." As she put it, "I considered myself dead, so I might as well get a job." Mrs. Hasemoto recounted how, after her husband died, she became an aggressive and shrewd businesswoman to support her children. Both of these women felt that in order to assume their husbands' roles effectively they would have to change their interpersonal styles and adopt what they saw as "male" characteristics—being "tough" and "stern" with the children, for instance. Neither men nor women ever discussed the situation in which a man had to assume his wife's tasks and responsibilities. In speaking of cases where widowed men were left with young children, the Issei said it was necessary for a new wife or other female relative to be brought into the household—either that, or for the children to be sent to live with relatives. Thus whereas women can, albeit with some uneasiness, take over their husbands' domains, it is not conceivable for men to take over their wives' and certainly not to adopt roles and styles of interaction perceived as female.

Although they view the two domains as complementary, the Issei do not view them as equal. From Issei men's point of view the female, inside sphere is encompassed within the male, outside sphere, and is therefore governed by male authority. The wife may be mistress of her own sphere, but he is master of the whole and she must follow in the direction in which he leads the entire family. His knowledge of the world outside the family as well as within it gives him a broader base upon which to make decisions and shape strategies. In the best of all possible marriages, a man does not have to intervene in his wife's sphere, because she constantly adjusts her actions to fit his. If she does not, he should correct her. He may be compassionate and understanding but, more importantly, he must exercise firm leadership as head of the household.

Women's notions about the control over the two domains and the relations between them are similar to men's, if a bit more ambivalent. On the one hand, they emphasize the necessity of male leadership. A good Japanese wife, they affirm, is quiet, reserved, nonaggressive, and somewhat subservient. Above all, she is constantly loyal and obedient to her husband, who ideally is a responsible and wise leader. But, they emphasize, a good husband also gives his wife the freedom to manage her sphere without interfering in or closely overseeing her affairs. In addition, he keeps her informed of important matters affecting the family and confides in her, so that they have a mutual understanding of their affairs. Although ultimately he makes the decisions, he is considerate of her concerns and wishes and does not bully her into submission. He does not, as Mrs. Hayakawa contended her husband did, treat her merely as "a servant serving his guests." Thus, while they accept the legitimacy of male authority and men's right to make decisions that women may not like, Issei women often complain about the inconsiderate manner in which a particular husband exercised that authority. One woman even described her husband as a "tyrant" and her marriage as "utter subjugation."

Issei women also give more expression to the disjunction between men's and women's concerns and interests. A common theme that runs through the women's accounts of their conjugal relationships is resentment of their husbands' interests outside the family. In these complaints, they portray the family and the outside social world as competing for limited resources; expenditures of energy and money in affairs outside the family draw resources away from it. When a husband becomes overly involved in social pursuits outside the family, it is his wife and children who are seen to suffer. In some marriages, it was the husband's drinking or sexual exploits that incurred his wife's resentment. But even socially respectable interests outside the family were sometimes resented. One woman explained that her husband was too compassionate toward outsiders at the expense of the family. He gave money freely to the Buddhist church and other community organizations, but was miserly with his wife and children. He loaned money to families whose children wore better clothing than his own children. And, when they were interned in Camp Minidoka, he helped so many other people with their vegetable gardens that he often neglected his family's garden. These altruistic actions may have enhanced his reputation in the community, but in his wife's opinion he should have, literally, tended his own garden first. For other Issei women, the outside sphere on which the couple's limited resources were being wasted included the husband's parents and siblings. Fulfilling obligations to parents was acceptable, but husbands were sometimes criticized for going beyond the call of duty.

Given their joint commitment to male authority, it is not surprising that Issei husbands and wives have different ways of describing their participation in the construction of marital histories. Men tend to portray themselves as active agents in shaping their own and their wives' activities, as well as their conjugal relationship in general. They do not hesitate to complain of political and economic forces and historical events beyond their control, but they take a stance of self-determination when it comes to interpreting developments in their marriage. They are correspondingly less willing than women to express dissatisfaction with their marriages. Mr. Kojima, who was obviously unhappy about his wife's return to Japan years ago, represented it as his decision, although there was strong indication that it was his wife's family's decision. Similarly, Mr. Kusumoto—after he had forgotten that he had told me he was required, as a *yōshi* husband, to take his wife's parents' name—claimed in a later interview that he had chosen to change his name to Kusumoto because he was tired of getting mail addressed to other men with his original surname. None of the men characterized any decisions or developments in the course of their occupational, marital, or personal histories as shaped by their wives' wishes, decisions, or actions. In contrast, Issei women generally portray their conjugal activities and histories as determined by other people's decisions and actions. If they worked outside the home, it was because of their husbands' orders; if they were housewives, it was because their husbands would not allow them to work. If they had little knowledge and influence over financial matters, it was because authoritarian husbands denied it to them; if they had knowledge and influence, it was because they were married to generous and kindly husbands. Whether they express satisfaction or bitterness over the outcome of events, Issei women are inclined to deny their role as actors in the shaping of those events. Several wives expressed considerable unhappiness over their married lives and displayed a resentful detachment from the role they were "forced to play." Mrs. Takitani, for one, would have liked to have had more control over her early married life but, as she put it, "I had no choice but to play the role" of obedient wife.

As the Issei were unwilling to talk about sexual relationships, I obtained very little information on sexual attitudes and practices. The only informants who spoke of such matters were three widows, all of whom represented intercourse and pregnancy as something beyond the control of women. Men were portrayed as lustful, "dirty" (*kitanai*) people, akin to animals or more specifically dogs, who could not be controlled; a woman was "subject to the whims" of her husband and, regardless of her own mood, she had to submit to him. It was never claimed that women did not enjoy sexual relations, but rather that, like other aspects of the conjugal relation, it was something they did not control.

"Japanese" and "American" Marriage

"American" marriage, in which they include the marriages of the Nisei, is for the Issei the symbolic opposite of "Japanese" marriage, which is how they categorize their own. Japanese marriage, in their view, is rooted in *giri* (duty), while American marriage is based on romantic love. Japanese marriage is enmeshed in a structure of obligations to parents and family; American marriage is free from these burdens. The freedom to choose one's own spouse is the key symbol of the freedom—the lack of constraint and restraint—which characterizes American marriage and renders it for them the antithesis of Japanese marriage.[2] The main differences in the conjugal relationship of a Japanese marriage and an American one, aside from the emotional content of the relationship, are the extent of male dominance, the degree of task differentiation, and the extent of communication. Japanese marriage entails male dominance and female subservience; in American marriage women have a much greater role in decision making. Whether they describe the greater influence of wives in negative terms (wives as "too bossy" and husbands as "henpecked") or positive ones (men show women greater "respect"), the Issei agree that American marriages are more egalitarian, and that their own marriages were fundamentally Japanese. So, according to Mrs. Harano, their marriage was "the same as in Japan—all decisions were made by the patriarch." A few Issei, both men and women, however, said that their marriages were somewhat "American" because the wife's opinion in family matters was taken into consideration by the husband.

A rigid division of labor into separate male and female tasks is also considered a characteristic of Japanese but not of American marriage. One woman cited the fact that her husband cooked and did the laundry when she needed his help as evidence of the "American" aspects of their marriage. In Japan, she claimed, it was unheard-of for a man to do these things, even if his wife were gravely ill. An Issei husband at-

---

[2] "American" was the adjective the Issei used most frequently to refer to this category of marriages. The term *hakujin* (white people) was also used occasionally.

tributed his and his wife's joint tasks and shared responsibility for the
rearing of children to his liking for the "American" style of marriage. It
is not that the Issei view white Americans as lacking gender-differen-
tiated tasks, but rather that they view white American men as more willing to "help" their wives with "women's work" and white American
women as more demanding of such help. Finally, the spouses in an
American marriage are said to communicate more with each other.
American couples talk over family matters in order to reach decisions
together, and generally share their experiences and feelings. A Japanese husband tells his wife very little about his business or financial decisions, and even less about his social affairs. As Mrs. Isoshima put it,
her husband was "Japanese style": he told her to shut up and stay out
of his way, so she knew very little about his business dealings. If it had
been the "American way," she claimed, she would have known more.

The opposing categories of Japanese and American marriage crosscut the types of conjugal division of labor and power relations discussed in Chapter 2. Although the Issei's constructs of Japanese and
American marriage also speak to the same subjects, they do not do so in
the same way as my types. What one Issei labels a "Japanese-style" marriage may be what another labels an "American-style" marriage. Thus
a marriage in which husband and wife have different spheres of activity
and control may be called "Japanese" by one Issei who points to the differentiation of tasks, and "American" by another who emphasizes the
relative degree of autonomy enjoyed by the wife. Moreover, the constructs are flexible enough for most people to label their marriage as
either type or as a blend of both types, depending on the elements they
highlight in a specific context. In one interview, for example, Mrs. Hasemoto said her marriage was "American" style, because she and her
husband made joint decisions about important matters; but in another
interview, she cited the fact that she always served her husband first at
meals as evidence of their "Japanese" marriage. In other words,
whereas Japanese marriage and American marriage are spoken of at
times as if they signified two distinct categories of marriage, they actually refer to various dimensions of contrast that exist in all conjugal
relations. Furthermore, "Japanese" and "American" in this context are
evaluative constructs, that is, they are often employed by the Issei to
express approval or disapproval of people's marriages. This does not
mean there is a simple and constant equation in which one or the other
type of marriage is considered good and the other bad. In some contexts, to classify one's marriage as Japanese implies one's dissatisfaction
with the marriage, as when an Issei woman says about her knowledge

of the couple's financial affairs that her husband was a "Japanese" husband. In another context, the same woman may claim they had a "Japanese" marriage because she treated her husband with deference, implying that she properly fulfilled the role of a good Japanese wife. One must know the specific context, then, in order to determine the evaluative meaning of the labels "Japanese" and "American."

THE NISEI INTERPRETATION OF MARRIAGE

American, Japanese, and Japanese American Marriage

Opposition between the categories of American and Japanese marriage is even more central to Nisei discourse on the subject than it is to the Issei's. Indeed, the Nisei's notions about marriage and the terms in which they evaluate their own marriages can be understood only within the framework of this opposition. When they describe their own marriages, on the one hand, the Nisei invariably contrast them with "Japanese" marriage, a model of marriage that they perceive to have been both the rule and the practice in Japan, and of which they see Issei marriages as representative. "American" marriage, on the other hand, is constituted of what they, through direct observation as well as through the images presented by the mass media, perceive to be characteristic of the marriages of their middle-class, white American contemporaries.[3] Sansei (third-generation) marriages are also adduced as examples of "American" marriage, particularly by older Nisei who have married children. The Nisei view their own marriages as falling into neither of these categories but rather as a synthesis, a well-balanced compromise, between the opposing types and, therefore, as definitively "Japanese American."

Within this symbolic system of cultural oppositions, which we shall see underlies all Nisei notions of family and kinship, American marriage and Japanese marriage represent contrastive institutions shaped by different hierarchies of values. The Nisei agree with the Issei on how these institutions differ. American marriage is more egalitarian, entails greater intimacy and communication, and has a more flexible division of labor. It is, moreover, an institution based on romantic love, that is, on the mutual emotional and sexual attraction of two unique individuals. Its core consists of intense emotion and sexual passion, which are

[3] Here again I use the term "American marriage" to label the construct of marriage that the Nisei oppose to "Japanese marriage" because it is the term most frequently employed by the Nisei themselves. However, the Nisei also use the terms *hakujin* (white people) and "Caucasian" to label this category of marriages.

expressed through the intimate contact and mutual identification of husband and wife. Because it is a relationship that "runs on love," it is greatly affected by fluctuations in people's emotions. If the content of either or both spouses' emotions wanes, the quality of an American marriage suffers, and what results is separation, divorce, or at the least, mutual alienation and misery.

Japanese marriage in contrast is seen as rooted in duty and in one's social and ethical commitment to a contractual relationship. Whether one loves the person to whom one is married is irrelevant to the fulfillment of the specific duties of that contractual relationship. This does not preclude affection or even love from a Japanese marriage. One can have intense feelings for one's spouse, and the Nisei recognize that some Issei husbands and wives developed a strong emotional bond. But love in the romantic sense is neither a necessary component nor a sufficient basis of Japanese marriage. It is quite secondary to one's lifetime duty to the fulfillment of the marital contract. Thus, regardless of whether one spouse's love for the other waxes or wanes, he or she is committed to the marriage. A wife is loyal to her husband not because she is emotionally attached to him as an individual but because he stands in the social relationship of husband to her. All this the Nisei see as confirmed in their parents' marriages, many of which they describe as "lacking in affection" and "loveless."

In the Nisei's view their own marriages are a compromise between the all-too-whimsical and dangerously unstable American marriage and the emotionally ungratifying and often burdensome Japanese marriage. Love and affection have been brought into the conjugal relationship, but not at the expense of duty and commitment. The Nisei marriage, unless it is a marriage gone wrong, is said to blend the best elements of the opposing Japanese and American types. The capriciousness of romantic love and its inherent instability are balanced in Nisei marriage by the stabilizing force of ethical duty. One chooses one's spouse on the basis of romantic and sexual attraction—albeit tempered by sound judgment. But once love has brought a couple together and they marry, it becomes more than just an emotional state. It is transformed into an emotional commitment. After marriage, love is not merely the physical and romantic attraction between two unique individuals but the mutual commitment of husband and wife to fulfill each other's needs and desires for intimacy and affection, to care for each other materially and physically, and to embrace happily all their other conjugal obligations.

That such conjugal love is more than the attraction one feels for one's spouse was nicely illustrated in Mr. Arashi's account to me in his wife's presence of an interchange the two of them had had several months earlier. The Arashis had been discussing their views on love and marriage with me, and Mr. Arashi recounted the incident to demonstrate, he said, "how silly women can be about these matters." His wife one day asked him whether he would love her even if she were not his wife. Mr. Arashi's adamant reply had been "Of course not, I would love my wife." Mrs. Arashi explained that she had wanted to know if he loved her for who she was, that is, if he would be attracted to her even if she was not his wife. One would expect that a strong commitment to romantic love as the core of marriage would require the answer yes. Mr. Arashi's answer, however, brought duty and commitment into the picture without dispensing with love: by definition the woman he loves is his wife, for his duty is to love his wife and not some other woman. Mrs. Arashi appeared satisfied with his answer (and with his account of the interchange) because, although it was not what she expected, it conveyed his emotional commitment to her.

Primacy of the conjugal bond. Because the Nisei notion of a proper Japanese American marriage is at once both a synthesis of, and yet another oppositional construct to, both American and Japanese marriage, any particular statement by a Nisei, if interpreted in isolation from the entire range of statements an informant makes about marriage, may give an incomplete or distorted impression of what is meant by it. Sometimes Nisei informants made statements about their marriages that seemed to reflect an overriding concern with its emotional content. But at other times they stressed "duty" and "commitment," and decried the "Americanization" of the Sansei that had made them the victims of self-indulgent emotionality and led to higher rates of divorce. In each instance, the aspects of marriage stressed by the informant were called forth by the explicit or implicit contrast conjured up in his or her mind at the time. If the contrast was between one's own marriage and that of one's children, then Nisei marriage was depicted as rightly rooted in principles of duty and self-discipline. But the same Nisei in another context would highlight the affectionate and romantic nature of his or her conjugal relationship in contrast to the "unfeeling" marriages of the Issei.

What the Nisei say about the priority of the conjugal relationship over the parent-child relationship, however, appears to place them squarely in their category of "American marriage." To the Nisei, their parents' type of marriage, with its "Japanese" hierarchy of relationships, placed an unhealthy priority on the parent-child relationship. Issei parents are described as having "lived for their children" and in turn of having expected too much from them. Their social reliance and emotional dependence on their children in later life is attributed partly to the lack of emotional satisfaction in their conjugal relationship. Having observed and experienced what they consider to be the burdens and dissatisfactions of such a relationship, the Nisei declare their preference for an "American" style of marriage in which the conjugal relationship is the most intimate, solidary, and enduring bond in a person's life. The conjugal relationship should be the "closest" relationship in the family. As strongly as one may feel about one's parents or children, one should confide in one's spouse first, place one's highest trust in him or her, and commit one's loyalty to him or her before any other person.

For the Nisei, then, the married couple is the proper core of the family and the love and unity manifested in their relationship are what shape the other relationships in the family. It is indeed the determining relationship, the one that "makes the family." If this relationship suffers, if it breaks down, then the whole family suffers. For this reason, if a husband and wife find themselves to be irrevocably alienated from each other they should get divorced. The Issei belief that it is better to remain married for the sake of the children is thought to be ill-conceived, for in the end the children will suffer from the absence of love and from the tensions that must inevitably pervade such a family. Indeed, in the eyes of the Nisei, a family without conjugal love and solidarity is no family at all, but merely an empty facsimile of one. Moreover, the priority that the Issei are said to have placed on their relationships with their children can lead only to disappointment and unhappiness, for one's children will one day marry and leave. All my Nisei informants seemed to agree with the Nisei woman who said: "You have to have more than the kids, because the kids are going to leave; you have to think not only of now, but later. You need marriage not only for now but later for the companionship."

This primacy of the conjugal bond, and the integrity that sets it apart from all other relationships in the Nisei family, emerge clearly when the Nisei discuss the issue of coresidence of married children and their parents. Although many Nisei have lived with their own parents, their spouses', or both for some period after marriage, they uniformly contend that it is far better for a couple to live in their own home. Living with parents is a "burden" not only because there may be disagreements over how to run the household and raise children, but because it stifles the spontaneous interaction between husband and wife and constrains the full development of an intimate, solidary conjugal bond. Yet the Nisei's attitudes are more complex and ambivalent than these responses might seem to indicate. When they comment on the marriages of their children and their white American contemporaries, they are often critical of what they perceive to be an inordinate emphasis on the conjugal bond to the detriment of the parent-child relationship. "American" marriage, they say, goes too far in the other direction. American-style parents are too eager to leave their children at home while they seek entertainment and pleasure for themselves. Their egoistic, selfish concern for their own interests and recreational pursuits may lead to the neglect of children—a neglect that they pay for in problem children, juvenile delinquency, rebellion, and ultimately rejection. And while the Nisei may declare their intention never to burden married children by living with them, at other times they confess that they hope their children will be "Japanese" enough to take them in if some unexpected turn of events renders them needy.

Male and Female Domains: Work and Family

The Nisei notion of the unity of husband and wife—a unity that is so deeply felt by some Nisei that they said a spouse was "just like a part of me" or "an extension of myself"—does not entail constant interaction, shared activities, or expressions of affection. It is good for a husband and wife to spend time together, to "learn to play together," to "go out together," to demonstrate their affection, and to provide each other with companionship. A spouse is in a sense one's "best friend." But this does not mean that a couple should spend all or even a majority of their evenings together, nor that they should always share the same activities. Indeed, to the Nisei it is important that each spouse maintain a sense of his or her individuality and separate identity.

The Nisei model of conjugal unity is best described as one of organic solidarity constructed out of a functional division of labor. The terms the Nisei use repeatedly to talk about the different, but complementary, domains of husbands and wives are "work," on the one hand, and "family" or "home," on the other. Men's concerns and responsibilities are said to lie in the area of "work." The foremost duty of a husband is to work to support his wife and children. A husband may be praised for helping his wife with the housework and with the care of young children, or for considering his wife's opinions in decision making. But these are all secondary considerations. What a Nisei man sees as the primary standard by which his success as a husband will be judged is how well he provides for his family's financial needs and security. When I asked Nisei men what a husband should do to help his wife after the birth of a child, several replied that working hard to earn money was the most important contribution a man could make. As one man put it, "My attitude was that I was going to work harder and do better for her; that's how I could best help my wife when she gave birth." Women's domain, in contrast, is that of the "family" or "home." By this the Nisei mean more than that a woman should cook, clean, and provide for the physical well-being of her husband and children. Being a "homemaker" literally entails transforming a "house" into a "home." As the central node in the family's communicative network she should be aware of her husband's and children's needs, activities, and feelings. Because the most important part of her "job" as wife and mother is to "take care of the children," she is responsible for monitoring their behavior as well as making routine decisions about their activities. Men, too, should be concerned with and interested in their children, and should try to "be in touch with them," but their concern with "work" exempts them from having detailed and up-to-date knowledge of their children's lives. Fathers therefore feel free to admit a certain ignorance of and detachment from their children without the fear of criticism or the guilt that might be experienced by mothers. Women, of course, can also work outside the home, but this is considered both secondary to their "job" as homemaker and mother and, at least ideally, a matter of "choice" rather than "duty." Everyone agrees that it is acceptable and, in some instances, desirable for a woman to work after her children have "grown up" and are "independent." Although there are differing opinions as to when this critical point is reached, all Nisei agree a woman should not work as long as any of her children are of preschool age.

Nisei women place great value on the experience of mothering. For them the greatest drawback of an income-earning job is that it takes them away from constant interaction with young children. Several women explained that if you have a job, even if your child is well cared for, "you miss so much." Returning home tired from work reduces your capacity to "enjoy your children" and the "experience of being a mother." For this reason, the women say that if you must work, the best job is one that allows you to be at home when the children return from school, even if this means taking only a part-time job with little security and reduced earnings. Furthermore, when a woman returns home at the end of the day, she wants to leave behind all concern for "work" so that she can devote her full attention to her family. If she has been away for the entire day, it is all the more necessary that when she returns home she is "there for her family"—that is, fully available to minister to their needs. A Nisei woman who is an elementary school teacher and the mother of a preschool child explained that she no longer brought her "work" home as she used to before her child was born, because when she is at home now her "job is to be a mother." Mothering, then, is all-consuming.

The notion that there is an inherent conflict between the demands of a job and the demands of being a wife and mother emerges constantly in Nisei women's accounts of their employment histories. The fact that a man engages in income-earning work outside the home never requires an explanation because "a man's job is to support the family." A married woman's employment—common as it is—invites explanation from the Nisei. So when I collected their employment histories, Nisei wives often volunteered statements about the specific reasons that had led to their employment. If a wife had continued to work after marriage and well into her first pregnancy, she might explain that she knew her husband was not earning much money and there were some "basic things" they needed. If a woman had worked while her children were young, the reason she offered was usually that she wanted to buy things the children needed (such as clothes) or the home lacked (furniture or appliances). As children grew older the reasons women gave for returning to work centered on the financial demands of their children's college educations and on the imminence of their husbands' retirement. After her children had left home, however, a woman's employment could be justified by a wider range of reasons. She might simply be bored or in need of "mental stimulation."

The norm underlying these explanations of employment is that a married woman's job must fulfill specific family needs to justify her absence from her children. A few of the younger Nisei women and men said it was "not healthy" for a wife to have her entire life revolve around the family, as they perceive to have been the case with Issei women, and, therefore, that it was inherently good for married women to work. Yet as long as a woman has children at home, working solely to "get out of the house" and for "mental therapy" is considered frivolous and bordering on irresponsibility. Even for women whose children are grown it has nowhere near the same stamp of legitimacy as working to earn money for family needs. Furthermore, whereas women at times speak of the isolation, boredom, and even depression they experienced during the periods when they were full-time housewives and mothers, these are not the reasons they offer to explain their reentry into the paid work force.

The Nisei often speak of men's income-earning work and women's housework and child care in terms that portray them as functionally different but structurally equivalent. For example, when the Nisei say it is a wife's "job" to take care of the family and the home, they convey a sense of symmetry in the domains of men and women. A marriage functions smoothly if each spouse does his or her "job." Hence, although it is husbands who should "work" at income-earning "jobs" while their wives should take care of the "family" and "home," in another sense both husbands and wives have "jobs." As a couple of women put it when they discussed the conjugal division of labor, "He [the husband] has his job and I have mine." The same notion is conveyed in the Nisei's comments about men's assistance with housework and child care. Neither men nor women feel it desirable for a husband to share equally in the housework or even to do a significant portion of it. A couple of women reported they felt strangely uncomfortable on the few occasions when their husbands had cooked or washed the dishes. According to one Nisei wife, "to Caucasian women it [a husband doing housework] is normal, but to me it doesn't feel normal to see him doing these things." Other women said that although they were aware their attitudes were now considered "old-fashioned" they did not like to see men do housework. When asked why they felt uncomfortable at the sight of their husbands preparing meals or cleaning the house, these women explained that it was not right for a husband to do "two jobs." After all, they added, a man goes to work and does "his job," so he should not have to come home and do "his wife's job." For a husband to do more than infrequently help his wife with the housework, therefore, upsets the balance of what the Nisei view as an equitable division of labor. What a husband must do to earn enough for himself and his family is equivalent to what a wife must do to maintain the upkeep of the home and children. The logic of this equation would seem to break down when a wife takes on a full-time job, for then it would appear that she is doing twice her husband's work. One response, on the few occasions when I confronted Nisei informants with this problem, was to admit the inequality, often in a half-joking manner—as when Mr. Arashi said, "Well, I guess that's just women's lot." Another response was to explain that if a woman "chooses to go to work" then she must be ready to shoulder the burden of both her "real job" or her "first job," namely, housework and child care, and her "other job." It is precisely because being employed in an income-earning job is not part of a wife's normatively prescribed role that the Nisei treat it as something women "choose" to do. They are well aware that in many instances a wife "chose to go to work" because without her income the family would not be able to afford to live in a manner they consider comfortable and respectable or the children could not attend college. Yet employment is considered "optional" for wives and so their burden of choice.

The sense of equivalence and symmetry imparted by the Nisei's discussion of husbands' "work" domain and wives' "family/home" domain extends to their usage of the terms "inside" and "outside." In comparison to the Issei, the Nisei employ these terms in fewer contexts and in ways that convey a narrower range of meaning. For the Nisei, "inside" and "outside" are just aspects of physical space, and they are used primarily to talk about the sexual division of tasks around the home. Men are considered responsible for the upkeep of objects and areas that are physically "outside" the house, including the garbage, yard, automobile, garage, and the exterior walls and roof of the house. Everything "inside" the physical plant of the house is the responsibility of women. No hierarchical structure is implied by the Nisei use of these terms. "Inside" and "outside" are spoken of as two adjacent spatial domains, and neither men nor women convey the sense that one is subsumed by the other. The only other context in which "inside" and "outside" surface in Nisei discussions of the conjugal relation is when people say that men "go out to work" (at income-earning jobs) while women "stay at home." Yet here again it is the work/home contrast that appears more salient to the Nisei conception of male and female domains than the outside/inside contrast.

The Practical and the Natural

For every Nisei, there is a set of tasks that is considered neither male nor female, neither men's nor women's province. Who does these tasks, therefore, is not a matter of normative rules, but is subject to practical considerations, personal interest, or some combination of the two. Practical considerations include knowledge, skill, and time. If a wife takes charge of paying bills and balancing the couple's joint checking account, the reasons given are often that "she has the time to do it" or "she is better at keeping track of such things." If the husband handles such matters, it may be explained that "he is better at managing money" or that because he operates a business and has to write checks for his business purchases it is "easier" for him to pay the home bills at the same time. Such considerations may also be used to explain why husbands usually do certain tasks and wives usually do others. Thus the reason husbands decide what kind of car to buy is that most men are interested in cars and know more about them than women. Conversely, wives select furniture because they care more about the appearance of the house and are more knowledgeable about style and design. Again because of their interest, knowledge, and skill men do more carpentry and repair work on plumbing and electrical appliances. And if wives consistently send Christmas cards and birthday presents and write more letters to relatives, it is because women are said to be "better at remembering those things" and "like to do them." People also adduce practical exigencies to explain why they deviate from normative patterns of task assignment. A husband explains that the reason his wife mows the lawn, even though it is "his job," is that it is too dark to do it by the time he comes home from work, and so his wife cannot get him to do it soon enough for her satisfaction. The same husband makes coffee for his wife in the morning, even though he considers it a "female task," because he has an easier time getting up. Another husband says the reason he does all the grocery shopping is that his wife does not drive and so it is "more convenient" for him to get food on the way home.

The Nisei do not all agree on which tasks are free from normative gender assignments. For example, one Nisei woman said the reason she is the one who makes decisions about where her children may go after school or how much spending money they should be given is that it is her "job" to take care of the children. However, another Nisei woman said her husband has the final say in these decisions because he is the "head of the family." Yet another said she handles these matters because she is "around during the day" and so it is simply more "practical" for her children to ask her for permission. There is a consistent difference in the way people talk about tasks that fall inside the husband's or wife's domain and tasks that are allotted on the basis of practical considerations or interest. The husband's domain of work and the wife's domain of family and home are discussed in ways that convey a firm commitment to their normative character. Men "should support the family" and women "should do the housework" and "take care of the children," and it is not good for these roles to be reversed. Whether they say this is how things should be "just because that is what is right" or because to have it otherwise would be "threatening to the male ego," the Nisei view the assignment of men to "work" and women to the "family" and "home" as a socially constructed and sanctioned practice. At the same time, however, the Nisei view these gender prescriptions as social reinforcements of men's and women's "natural roles." Indeed, that women bear children and are better equipped—both physiologically and temperamentally—to raise them is cited as proof of the correctness of their assignment to the domain of the home. Yet neither do the Nisei conceive of these gender domains as the direct outcome of biology unmediated by social rules. So much is clear from their comments that "men could stay at home" and "women could be the breadwinners," and from their recognition that some people's inclinations run in these directions. The Nisei are ethnographically sophisticated enough to be at least vaguely aware that their own construction of male and female roles is culturally specific. They recognize that in some other societies women "work as hard as the men" and contribute as much or more to production and income earning. They cite their own mothers and "Japanese" women in general as examples of women who worked all the time and who sometimes had little time to spend on their children. Conversely, they cite "women's libbers" as examples of women who would rather work than be homemakers. They do not assume, then, that all men and women would fall naturally into the same pattern of the sexual division of labor if left unconstrained by social rules. Nevertheless, they tend to see their own pattern as more natural and more desirable than the alternatives. It is because it is "better" for families and especially for children if people conform to their more "natural roles," and because their "values" tell them it is right, that the Nisei say they subscribe to these rules for the sexual division of labor. Thus, the gender domains of "work" and "home" are interpreted by the Nisei as social constructions derived from certain "values" that protect a biologically based sexual division of labor. At the same time, these values have adapted the gender domains to the circumstances of contemporary American society.

In contrast, patterns of task ascription that are seen to derive from practical contingencies and from personal interest are presented as falling outside the normative sphere. So people say that if a woman wanted to do carpentry work and acquired the necessary skills, that would be fine and acceptable, if a little unusual. Likewise, if a man is interested in sending Christmas cards, there is nothing wrong with that. Anyone can do these things if they are interested in them and if it is practical for them to do so. Because they place these matters outside the sphere of norms, the Nisei tend to deny that they are socially constructed. This is particularly the case with gender regularities that are said to derive from people's "interests," for these are spoken of as if they were generated by men's and women's inherent characteristics. When I asked people why, if there were no rules about who should send Christmas cards, in all Nisei marriages wives performed this task, they answered that women are "naturally" just more interested in such things—women care more about relatives and friends, and they are more concerned about not hurting people's feelings. Women are por-

trayed as inherently more sentimental as well as more concerned about
social propriety than men, who are seen as more aloof and less emotionally demonstrative. Likewise, when I inquired why men are more
knowledgeable about cars, and are said for that reason to decide what
model to purchase and to take responsibility for its upkeep (whether
they work on the car themselves or farm the work out to a professional
mechanic), the response was generally that men are more mechanically
inclined and intrigued by cars. Women could learn about auto mechan-
ics, people said, but they just are not interested in it.

Male Leadership

If males and females have inherent, biologically determined attributes and interests that render them better suited for certain tasks and
roles, this does not mean that, in Nisei eyes, one sex is superior to the
other or inherently more valuable. Indeed the Nisei are quick to make
known their rejection of the "Japanese" devaluation of females: husbands and wives, men and women, they claim, are equally valuable human beings. All Nisei agree, however, that the husband should "lead"
in the marriage. He should act as the "head of the family" and "be
strong." In particular, he should represent the couple and the family in
community affairs. This does not mean men have the sole right to make
decisions affecting the couple or the family or even that they should
have a greater say in such decisions. A few women said they liked to be
"subordinate" and wanted their husbands to handle all the important
affairs, although they were defensively apologetic about being members of "the old school of thought." Other women said they found it
difficult to be submissive to their husbands and could not accept "Japanese" ideas about female subordination. They were especially critical
of their Issei fathers' attitudes toward women, which they portrayed as
"feudal." But while they rejected the devaluation of women and the
male dominance they associated with Issei marriage, even these women
said that a husband should "lead" in a marriage. Nisei men too drew a
distinction between what they perceived to be the ill-treatment of
women by Issei men and male leadership, which they considered desirable. What was right, they declared, was for a man to be a strong leader,
not a bully.

Issei husbands, then, are concerned about being strong, and fulfilling their leadership role without hesitation. Conversely, wives are concerned not to usurp men's leadership role. Wives, to judge from their
comments, believe that they play an important part in the construction
of male leadership; that if they lean on their husbands, their husbands

will be strong, but if they take the lead too often their husbands will become weak and dependent. One woman commented: "In the papers I read about men getting less and less able to make decisions and relying on their wives. I think this is the consequence. The more you [a wife] boss the more the man will back up into the corner. Someone has to be the primary one to make decisions." The conviction that "only one person can be the boss" is where the Nisei inevitably end up when they discuss authority and power in marriage. In fact, they offer little else than this to explain or legitimate male leadership. No one ever told me that men are inherently stronger or natural leaders, or that women are naturally submissive. To the contrary, the idea that male leadership and strength is a contingent social phenomenon, elicited by women and depending on their consent, is a clear thread running through the comments of the Nisei.

There are also limits to male leadership in Nisei marriage. The rights of wives, the most important of which are knowledge, participation, and autonomy, define those limits. Knowledge entails a wife's right to know about the couple's current financial situation, their prospects for the future, and any strategies or plans a husband may have that could affect the couple and their children. Participation refers to a wife's right to express her opinion, and to have it seriously considered before any "family decision" is made. A husband should involve his wife in the decision-making process by "talking it over with her" before he takes any action. Finally, a wife has a right to a degree of autonomy in her life. Not only should she be allowed a free rein in "running the house," but she should have freedom of movement and the freedom to purchase items she wants, either for herself or others, so long as the cost is commensurate with the couple's income. It was these latter two freedoms that Nisei wives mentioned most often when they described how their marriage had changed for the better over time. Freedom of movement means that a wife should not have to be accountable to her husband for what she does during the day while he is at work; if she fulfills her housekeeping and child-rearing duties, she should be able to spend her remaining time as she sees fit. As one woman said, "As long as the house is clean and dinner is ready when he gets home, what I do during the day is my business." As far as the freedom to purchase is concerned, men and women agree that a wife should not have to justify to her husband every penny she spends. She should have some leeway to buy personal items and gifts and to go out with her friends—always considering the family budget, of course. Martha Kagawa's account was representative of many Nisei wives' reports of their increased freedom in the later years of their marriage. "When we were first married, my husband controlled the finances tightly. He only gave me a grocery allowance. So, if I wanted anything I had to hint around and hope he would notice. Now I decide I need it and I go and get it. I've had an account at Frederick's [a department store] for a while and now I have three charge accounts. So I think that shows I have more freedom."

The freedom of wives to spend money, however, must be considered in relation to their husbands' freedom to spend it. The issue opens up a rather murky area of Nisei marriage, namely, the ownership and control of conjugal income. On the one hand, Nisei express a strong commitment to joint ownership and control over any income earned by husband or wife. What a husband earns, plus what a wife earns if she works, is automatically part of their conjugal fund. Marriage, the Nisei claim, is after all a relationship based on complete sharing and unity. One does not think of one's earnings as belonging to oneself; they "belong to the couple." A married man does not work for himself; he "works for his family," and what he earns goes into their common fund. The same is true of his wife's earnings. This, the Nisei point out, is why they have joint checking accounts, joint savings accounts, or both. Common ownership applies not only to current earnings but to past earnings and to inherited wealth, which may be in the form of savings, investments, or property. As one husband summarized it, "What's mine is hers and what's hers is mine."

Yet there are other things the Nisei say that belie this notion of equal ownership. As I mentioned in Chapter 3, husbands may on occasion make large purchases without consulting their wives beforehand, or they may simply announce that they intend to make them. Wives do not feel free to make such purchases whether or not they are themselves bringing in earnings. Those who were not employed said they did not feel free to spend "his money." Those who were explained they still felt they were "using his money" because their husband earned so much more than they. As we saw in Chapter 3, the reluctance of wives to spend more than fifty dollars or so extends to buying gifts for their husbands. Men think it generous to buy lavish presents for their wives; women feel uneasy at being generous with "his money," even if he is the recipient of their generosity.[4]

The idea that husbands own or at least have a greater right to the

[4] See also Chapter 6. One of the reasons the Nisei give for justifying the norm that sons should take financial responsibility for their elderly parents is that daughters should not have to ask their husbands for money. Again the notion is that men own, as well as have the right to control, the conjugal funds.

conjugal funds emerged from discussions like the one I had with Betty and Dan Fukumoto. The Fukumotos were one of two Nisei couples in the study in which the wife was currently earning more than her husband, who had just left paid employment (as a professional) to open his own business. Betty Fukumoto's income from her teaching job was to be their means of support until his business began turning a profit. I had asked them how they decided to buy different items. Betty said they decided together on the purchase of their bedroom furniture set, the color television, and appliances.

> *Betty:* But the stereo was something he got by himself. [*Laughs*] I had no say in that. [*Turning to me*] He really gets his way.
> *Dan:* I usually buy you what you want.

The implication in Dan's statement was that he buys things for her, not that she has just as much right to buy herself what she wants. Similarly, other Nisei husbands and wives evaluated how "generous" a husband was according to how much money he "gave" his wife to spend. No one ever spoke of a wife's generosity in allowing her husband the freedom to purchase, or to use either his or his wife's earnings. Men are not only accorded leadership in financial decisions, but in a sense they are seen as owning all the couple's money because they usually earn all or more of the joint income. Masaru Arashi perhaps best summarized this view when he said playfully to his wife during an interview: "What's mine is mine and what's yours is mine."

ISSEI AND NISEI MODELS OF MARRIAGE

One area in which Issei and Nisei interpretations of marriage converge is the contrast between American and Japanese marriage. Both generations agree on the features that render the two institutions different, and in many respects opposed, ideal types. By ideal types, I do not mean that either of these is considered the correct, desirable form of marriage. I mean that these are models against which people compare and assess real marriages and observable conjugal relationships, including their own. "American" and "Japanese" marriage are ideal types on the order of constructs such as "folk society" and "urban society." In this case, however, they have been constructed by the natives rather than by the social scientist. They are summarized in Table 17.

How the Issei and Nisei categorize their own and other people's marriages is a more complex matter. Certainly, both generations agree that Issei marriages are more Japanese and Nisei marriages are more American. But, as we have seen, the Issei tend to portray Nisei mar-

TABLE 17

Two Types of Marriage as Viewed by Japanese Americans

Japanese marriage	American marriage
Absence of choice in selection of spouse, to marry or not	Choice in selection of spouse (and, secondarily, to marry or not)
Based on and maintained by *giri* (duty)	Based on and maintained by romantic love
Enmeshed in other family relationships	Free from and, in some ways, opposed to other family relationships
Priority of filial bond over conjugal bond	Priority of conjugal bond over filial bond
Male dominance	Greater equality of the sexes
Rigid division of labor by sex	Flexible division of labor by sex
Emotional restraint, with emphasis on compassion, respect, consideration	Emotional intensity/indulgence, with emphasis on sexual, romantic attraction
Stable	Unstable
Less verbal communication between spouses	Greater verbal communication between spouses

riage as fundamentally American, whereas the Nisei construe their marriages as a Japanese American synthesis. Likewise, the Nisei view Issei marriages as entirely Japanese whereas the Issei sometimes point to the "American" elements in their marriages. Yet both Issei and Nisei acknowledge that marriages in both generations can be arranged along a continuum from "most Japanese" to "most American." Indeed, both generations engage in this conceptual ordering, as when they say that a particular couple has a "more American" or "more Japanese" marriage than they do. All the Nisei, for example, agree that marriages involving Kibei (Nisei educated in Japan) are "more Japanese" than the marriages of American-educated Nisei. Similarly, the Issei comment that older Nisei who married before the war tend to be "less American" in their ways and their marriages than their younger siblings.

The two generations, however, do not agree on the comparative value and desirability of the two types of marriage. It is not that the Issei are rigidly committed to a purely Japanese marriage and the Nisei to a purely American one. For although the Issei decry the instability and selfish emotionality of American marriage, they approve of other aspects of it, some of which they claim to have incorporated or would have liked to incorporate in their own marriages. Issei women more than Issei men look favorably upon the American-style conjugal relationship, in particular its greater equality and the "respect" shown to women. But men too point to the benefits of the closer communication between spouses in such a marriage. What the Issei disapprove of in American marriage is not so much the relationship between the couple themselves, but the place of that relationship in the larger system of family relationships. The Issei's attribution of emotional indulgence, selfishness, and consequent instability to this style of marriage, while it appears to characterize the relationship between spouses, is a thinly veiled criticism of the couple's relationships with other people—in other words, of the relationships that marriage should serve rather than rob. As we shall see in Chapter 6, what the Issei say about marriage is inextricably linked with what they say about the filial relationship. In particular, what they say about marriage and the marriages of their children is as much about relations between parents and their grownup children as it is about relations between spouses.

The Nisei seem more committed to a synthesis of Japanese and American marriage. But again, this synthesis is not an even one. In other words, although they claim to have integrated Japanese and American elements in their marriages, they are not committed to an evenly balanced compromise. When they speak of the need to bring "love" and "affection" into marriage without sacrificing "duty" and "commitment," they balance what they consider to be the best elements of each cultural type. But, like the Issei, the Nisei do not place themselves in the middle of the continuum between the two ideal types when they talk of marriage and the larger system of family relationships. Although they caution against the dangers of too great an emphasis on the conjugal bond, the Nisei view it as the core of the family. When they reject their parents' lack of emotional satisfaction in marriage, they are also tacitly rejecting their parents' expectations of other family relationships. Thus the divergence between Issei and Nisei assessments of American and Japanese marriage arises from different conceptions of these relationships rather than of the conjugal relationship by itself. Likewise, the discrepancy between the ways in which the Issei and Nisei categorize Nisei marriage (the Issei calling it "American" and the Nisei "Japanese American") can only be understood in relation to the different ways in which they categorize filial relationships. There is, however, no disagreement between them as to the contrastive features of "American" and "Japanese" marriage. Thus the opposition between the two ideal types provides a common vocabulary in which Issei and Nisei can speak about marriage.

Male leadership would seem to be another area in which Issei and Nisei notions of marriage converge. Both generations assert that a husband must "lead" in marriage. Both agree there should be constraints on male leadership. Although they have different views as to what constitutes the proper constraints, the "rights" of wives articulated by the Nisei might be viewed as a stronger version of the Issei's ideals of "consideration" and "compassion" in the exercise of male authority. These are not, however, merely variations of the same construct of leadership. The Issei and Nisei share some ideas about men and women and, consequently, some norms and ways of interpreting the actions and relations of husbands and wives. But the pairs of opposing symbols that underpin their norms and interpretations are different. This in turn makes for rather different conceptions of male leadership.

Sociospatial and Functional Metaphors of Gender Domains

Both the Issei "inside/outside" opposition and the Nisei "family/work" opposition conceptually order complex and varying patterns of activities and relations of husbands and wives. Both might appear to fall under the rubric of what Michelle Z. Rosaldo (1974) has called the "domestic" versus "public" and Rayna R. Reiter (1975) the "private" versus "public" opposition.[5] To classify these Issei and Nisei conceptions as forms of a universal domestic/public opposition, however, would obscure the differences that render them the core symbols in distinctly different cultural systems of gender. "Inside" and "outside" express a sociospatial metaphor in which is embedded an inherent structure of authority. "Work" and "family" express a metaphor of the functional division of labor, a metaphor that says nothing about authority.

The sociospatial character of the Issei's gender domains can be seen in the various referents of "inside" and "outside." From their narrowest and most concrete references to physical space ("indoors/outdoors," "inside one's house / outside one's house") to their interactional, consequential, and motivational referents, they chiefly concern the location of men and women, their activities and interactions, and their orientations in a hierarchy of social space. Men are located physically, socially, and motivationally between women and the world outside the home. Women constitute the interior of domestic units that men both shield from and link with an encompassing social order.

The Nisei opposition of "work" and "family/home," in contrast, constitutes a labor specialization model of gender. The central concern

---

[5] More recently these dichotomies have been rejected as analytically unproductive and empirically unfounded (Rapp 1978; Rosaldo 1980). For a critique of the opposition between "domestic" and "politico-jural" more commonly used in kinship studies, see Yanagisako 1979.

here, and the critical difference between male and female domains, lies in the kinds of work people do, that is, in their respective "jobs" or the functions they perform. The core feature of the male domain is income earning, while that of the female domain is homemaking and mothering. Because the kinds of work people do constitute the distinctive features of male and female domains in marriage, the engagement of either spouse in the other's function is problematic for the Nisei. A husband washing dishes does not seem "fair" or "normal" and a woman's income-earning job threatens her performance of her homemaking and mothering functions. On the other hand, the Nisei are not particularly concerned with the relative location of men and women in social space. It is not because income-earning work takes women outside the home that it poses a problem for the Nisei. When the Nisei say "women should stay at home" they invariably add "with the children" or "when the children are young." As we saw, the Nisei reject as "feudal" the restrictions that the Issei placed on the physical mobility and social activities of women. Accordingly, they claim the right of a wife to "get out of the house" and do what she pleases as long as she has done "her job."

This is not to say that the Nisei make no distinctions among the different kinds of social space through which people move. For the Nisei, as well as for the Issei, family space and the relationships carried on within it have different meaning and character from social space and relationships outside the family. But the Nisei do not construe the social world as divided neatly into a female sphere "inside" the family and a male sphere "outside" it. On the one hand, there is a sense in which men are associated with nonfamilial spheres and women with the familial sphere. Men's "job" of income earning requires them to go outside the home, while women's "job" does not. Nisei norms of male leadership, moreover, assign men the responsibility of representing the couple and their children to the world outside the family. On the other hand, not all social activities and relations outside the family are male spheres. Religious, educational, recreational, charitable, and other activities are considered equally open to female participation, if not female leadership. Women's right to participate in social activities outside the home and family renders "inside" and "outside" inappropriate as the core symbols of gender domains. Neither am I claiming that housekeeping and child care are not defined by the Issei as female functions and part of a wife's duties in marriage. They are most certainly considered female tasks that males should not perform. But these functions are not what serve to define the Issei inside domain, any more than income earning serves to define the outside domain. Rather, it is by the *location* of men's and women's activities in social space that the Issei gender domains are set off from each other.

That the Issei gender domains are not based on a functional division between income-producing work and unpaid housework and child care is apparent in the Issei's discussions of work. Thus the labor of wives in family businesses is construed as work "inside" the family, and is not conceptually opposed to housekeeping and child-care tasks. The division of labor in family-operated enterprises, as we have seen, falls into "inside" female tasks and "outside" male tasks. As long as Issei women engaged in such inside work and did not enter into outside spheres, income-producing work was not experienced as problematic. What was problematic, and what Issei women resented most of all, was having to work outside the family and so being placed in inappropriate social space. Wives resented this just as much when they had no children at home as when they did. Issei women, moreover, placed less emphasis on mothering in their accounts of early married life than did Nisei women. We have seen that Nisei mothers considered mothering to be a "full-time job" that required their being constantly available to young children. The "job" of mothering entailed not only physical nurturance but fostering the child's emotional and intellectual development. No such functional conception of motherhood was articulated by Issei women, whether or not they engaged in other work while their children were young. The Issei women whose children were sent to Japan, some as infants and others as young children, did not report any regret or concern at not being able to raise them. They missed their children, but none of them said they missed nurturing them or fostering their development. Indeed, a couple of these women said it was because they wanted to spend more time working in the family business that they had chosen to send their young children back to Japan. Another Issei woman, whose adoptive mother took care of her two sons while she worked in the family business, said it made no difference to her whether she worked in the laundry or "watched the boys." At the risk of oversimplification, it may be said that for the Issei the emphasis is on motherhood (a social identity and relation) rather than on mothering (performing child-rearing functions).

For the same reasons, the Issei and Nisei have different conceptions of authority and leadership in marriage. The Issei construct of "inside/outside" implies a hierarchical structure. The symbolic expansiveness of the male domain, and its association with the larger social order in which families are located, give it precedence over a female domain that is limited to the narrow confines of familial experience. Male authority in marriage, as in society in general, is based upon the priority of the expansive over the restricted, the encompassing over the encompassed, the knowledgeable over the ignorant, the experienced over the inexperienced, and the extrafamilial (that is, the communal and societal) over familial interests and concerns. Hence, in addition to describing the content of two sociospatial domains, "inside" and "outside" define the hierarchical relationship between those domains and the people who occupy them. In the Issei's sociospatial model of gender domains all functions have an "inside" and "outside," and so men's authority and leadership crosscut functional categories. A wife may be assigned the task of caring for children, but her husband oversees her child-care activities and manages their upbringing. Because he has authority over their relations with the world outside the family, he must also have it over their upbringing inside the family. In all areas of activity—including child care and homemaking—husbands have legitimate authority over wives. "Inside" and "outside" represent well the pervasiveness of male authority because they are inherently relational terms. They speak by analogy of the relationship between men and women by portraying it as a relationship that is fundamentally asymmetrical.

In contrast, "work" and "family/home" are not relational terms; in themselves, they say nothing of a hierarchy of functions. The ways in which the Nisei talk about these domains and about male leadership, moreover, reflect considerable ambiguity about authority in the conjugal relationship. On the one hand, the Nisei grant each spouse authority over his or her functionally differentiated domain. "His job," and thus the activity over which a husband has authority as well as responsibility, is to earn money to support the family. "Her job," and thus the activities over which she has authority, is to take care of the home and children. Husbands and wives are therefore cast as having autonomous control over two equally important spheres of functions. Unlike that of Issei men, Nisei men's authority does not penetrate into homemaking and childcare activities. On the other hand, when the Nisei assert that husbands are the heads of families and should provide strong leadership, they appear to grant men authority over the whole of marriage and the family. Closer examination, however, reveals that the Nisei and Issei conceptions of male authority are quite different. Having rejected any sociospatial definition of gender domains, the Nisei do not interpret male leadership as deriving from the inherent asymmetry between inside and outside. Instead, male leadership is attributed to two different and somewhat contradictory sources. The first is the consent of women. Consent is a theme that pervades both Nisei men's and wom-

en's accounts of leadership in marriage and of marriage in general.
When husbands describe themsevles as "leading" by taking a more active role in decision making, they explain that their wives want them to
make decisions. Wives describe themselves as either participating in
decision making or encouraging—or at least consenting to—their husbands' more active role. They "encourage him to take the lead" or "let
him run the show." Whether it is because they think that men would be
unhappy if they did not lead, or that women would not do as good a
job, or that women do not care to lead, the Nisei view male leadership
as they view the institution of marriage, that is, as a relationship that
two individuals enter and construct by their own volition. The second
source is men's greater earnings. We have seen that the Nisei translate
men's greater earnings into men's greater claim to the conjugal fund.
This claim subverts the Nisei notion of equal ownership and the Nisei
construct of marriage as complete sharing by a man and a woman.
Moreover, the Nisei interpret the claim as providing the husband with
a basis of power that applies not only to decisions about spending and
finances, but to other areas too, including whether or not a wife should
hold a job. In Nisei marriage, then, the husband's position of leadership is not conferred on him by his gender domain. Rather, it is a product of conflicting notions about gender, economics, consent, and
power. If in one sense wives let their husbands have their way, in another sense they are in a weak position to do otherwise. If men and
women are, as the Nisei believe, equal, then their inequality in marriage must result from unequal "jobs." In this way the Nisei simultaneously explain male leadership and subvert it. For, by identifying men's
greater earnings as the source of their power, they rob that leadership
of its former legitimacy—a legitimacy that was based not on power but
on authority.

To conclude, it is in the comparative value of a husband's and a wife's
labor that the difference between the Issei and Nisei systems of gender
domains is most clearly revealed. In the Issei system, which is sociospatial, an intrinsic hierarchy entails a parallel hierarchy of value as regards male and female labor. Just as men link women to the world outside the family and so provide the family with a social identity, so male
labor, or rather male management, links female labor to the outside
and renders it socially meaningful. The Issei do not deny women's labor contribution, but cast it as labor in need of direction and management. Women who do not know the world outside the family can only
be workers who lack the knowledge and social relationships to transform their labor into a livelihood. Men have the knowledge and social

ties to transform both their own labor and female labor into such a livelihood. Likewise, it is men's knowledge, social ties, and management that transform female child care—another form of female labor—into the creation of complete persons with social identities. Whether it is labor directed toward production or reproduction, female labor is incomplete and, therefore, less valuable than male labor.

In contrast, Nisei statements about men's "job" of income earning and women's "job" of housework and childbearing portray male and female labor as equally valuable and necessary. At the same time, however, they grant men's labor greater value because it produces the income that supports the family. This contradiction surfaces nowhere more clearly than in their discussions about the division of household chores in marriages where both spouses are employed full-time. Although a Nisei husband contributes little to housework or child care, because it would be wrong for him to do both his wife's "job" and his own, Nisei wives who are employed full-time enjoy no such exemption. Instead, the Nisei either admit the inequity with observable discomfort, or emphasize that the wife has chosen to assume two jobs and so must accept the burden. The first is an admission of contradiction, the second a reminder of, and appeal to, first premises—namely, that marriage is a relationship into which individuals enter by choice with a commitment to fulfilling their assigned functions.

THE TRANSFORMATION OF MARRIAGE

The Issei, as we have seen, construe the relations between spouses as structured by their placement in their respective sociospatial domains, which are hierarchically ordered. Conjugal power relations are therefore shaped by the comparative social resources that each spouse brings to the marriage. A successor husband, as we saw in Chapter 2, had an interest in controlling his wife's labor and directing it toward the maintenance of his parental household; indeed, his very claim to a household in Japan was a social resource that enhanced his power in relation to hers. The Issei did not think that the more labor a wife contributed to income production the more power she acquired in a marriage. Rather—because for them power is derived from relations among people—the source of her power was the kinship relations she brought to the marriage. A wife with parents in Seattle was not entirely dependent upon her husband for a place in a social world—whether in Japan or the United States.

The Nisei, on the other hand, view marriage as the union of men and women fulfilling complementary functions. In spite of the differences in the educational, occupational, and residential experiences of Nisei marriage cohorts, described in Chapter 3, the Nisei share the same gender constructs and norms, and therefore basically the same conceptions of the division of labor and control between spouses. Although different cohorts began with different female employment rates, these rates tended to converge over time as the common constructs of "work" and "family" made themselves felt. For the same reason, Nisei wives of self-employed businessmen were no more likely to work during their childbearing and child-rearing years than Nisei wives of salaried husbands.

PART TWO

FILIAL RELATIONS

In the next two chapters I trace the filial relations and meanings already involved in the formation of Japanese American marriage. For this purpose I focus on the bonds of shared residence, occupation, and property between parents and children in the two generations. For it is the changing meanings of these bonds—what they can tell us about what is transmitted between parents and children—that have transformed Japanese American filial relations. Just as the family is a system of relationships rather than a mere collection of them, so the symbols and meanings by which people enact those relationships form a system. Although no cultural system is entirely consistent and coherent, analysis of how one of its relationships has been transformed remains incomplete until it is integrated with similar analyses of other relationships and other symbols.

In Chapter 5, I follow up the filial histories of Issei successor and nonsuccessor sons whose differing statuses in their parental households were shown in Chapter 2 to be connected to different marriage strategies and conjugal power relations. Whether it was by dint of being a firstborn son, an adopted son, a yōshi (adopted son-in-law) husband of a daughter, or a younger brother of a disinherited son, half the Issei men in my marriage sample were the incumbent successors to households at the time they married. Their filial claims and marital strategies led to more imbalanced conjugal power relations and, where there was a family business, to a more differentiated conjugal division of labor.

In tracing the filial histories of these Issei in their later years of marriage, however, I uncover various uncertainties about their successor status and ambiguities as to the claims entitled by that status. In only a minority of cases, it turns out, did the Issei in my marriage sample who were designated as successors at the time of marriage come to occupy the headship of a parental household and inherit its property. In the second half of the chapter, I show that unstable residential, occupational, and economic ties with parents are just as characteristic of Nisei sons, in spite of the Issei's apparent commitment to perpetuating their households through the successor-son relationship. But that is less surprising, given both the turbulence of the war years, which came at a critical stage in the development of these filial relations, and the Nisei's commitment to freeing their marriages from parental control. Considered together, however, the indeterminacy of succession outcomes and the dynamic negotiation of claims between parents and children in both generations belie any tidy tale of the shift from a Japanese stem-family system with successorship to an American conjugal family system without.

That neither generation's filial histories adhere to "traditional Japanese rules" of succession says nothing of whether Japanese American filial relations have or have not been shaped by such rules. In Chapter 6, I rehabilitate the "Japanese" past in which eldest sons adhered to the aforementioned rules by succeeding to the headship of parental households, inheriting parental property, and fulfilling their filial duties. For, like other aspects of what they think of as Japanese tradition, this filial past is a core concept for both Issei and Nisei. As such it provides a shared vocabulary through which the two generations debate the meaning of the filial bond at the same time that they negotiate its changing social form.

CHAPTER 5

Two Generations of Filial Relations

DIFFERENTIATED FILIAL RELATIONS are central to the reproduction of a stem-family system. If parents are to perpetuate a stem-family household, their relationship with one child, the successor, must differ from their relationships with all other children. A conjugal family system, in contrast, requires all offspring to form independent households upon marriage. Its reproduction rests on the equivalence of filial relations. In the shift from a stem-family system to a conjugal family system, therefore, a system of differentiated filial relations must be transformed into a system of undifferentiated filial relations. In this chapter and the next, I trace that transformation among Japanese Americans. Here again I move from social history to an analysis of the questions generated by it. In order to explicate the symbols and meanings that structure the filial relations of Issei and Nisei today, it is necessary to understand the filial histories that raised particular issues of meaning. The converse is also true; for those filial histories are the products of interactions between individuals whose goals and strategies are formulated through cultural systems of meaning.

The filial histories of the two generations presented in this chapter manifest similarities as well as differences. This is not surprising. Continuity, after all, has been as much a theme as change in discussions of filial relations among Japanese Americans. Indeed, the standard introduction to a discussion of the relations between Issei parents and Nisei children has been a summary of the core values and prescriptions of "traditional Japanese" family relations (see, for example, Miyamoto 1939; Kitano 1976). The continuities and parallels displayed in this chapter, however, consist not in rule-bound filial "traditions," but rather in the ambiguity, indeterminacy, and negotiability of the Issei's and Nisei's filial histories.

ISSEI FILIAL RELATIONS:
SUCCESSORS AND NONSUCCESSORS

In Chapter 2 I demonstrated that the successor status of Issei marriages was of social consequence for their conjugal relations—at least in their early married years. Yet, as I also noted, the question of whether *over time* successor and nonsuccessor couples among the Issei continued to have distinctly different relationships with parents remains unanswered. To answer the question here we must explore the evolution of the Issei's relations with their parents after marriage and at the death of their parents.

Postmarital Filial Relationships of Successors

Successor couples, as I have said, more often resided virilocally during the period immediately after marriage and during prolonged visits to Japan, and more often sent Kibei children to reside in the parental household. There were additional ways in which successor couples affirmed their status in their parental household. Where the relevant parents had also emigrated to Seattle, in all but one case out of five the Issei couple lived with them, for as long as they remained there, in a stem-family household that was a single production-and-consumption unit.

Where the couple's relevant parents (in all the cases involving geographical separation they were the husband's) had remained in Japan, the continuing economic ties between them were usually still evident. All but two of the seven successor couples whose parents were in Japan contributed regularly (usually monthly) to the support of their household. A couple of the most economically successful Issei men provided enough funds to expand the households' landholdings, capitalize new family businesses, and set up younger brothers in branch households. Such remittances, however, did not differentiate successors unequivocally from nonsuccessors, since nonsuccessor sons also sent them when they could afford to do so. Although the latter's remittances tended to be more occasional and smaller, in a couple of cases they were substantial enough to support members of the household in Japan during critical periods. Whether money was also sent to an Issei wife's parents, siblings, and other kin in Japan usually depended upon the extent of the Issei wife's control over the couple's finances, as well as on the comparative wealth of the couple and their kin.

There is a second reason why the men I have categorized as incumbent successors did not all continue to have relationships with parents that were distinctly different from those of nonsuccessors. The reason is that in most cases there was a significant degree of ambiguity surrounding the Issei's status as successor. In other words, as the five cases I am about to summarize will illustrate, the reciprocal rights and duties linking the successor and his parents were not as unequivocal as the succession rules attributed to Japanese kinship would appear to suggest.

Senichi Harano. Senichi Harano (Case I.6a) was the first son of Isao Harano, who was originally a Kashima but had been adopted as a young man by the Harano household. When Senichi was seventeen years old, Isao sold the Harano family farm to his biological brother (a Kashima) and moved to the city of Kure. Senichi remained with his (adopted) grandparents on the farm for a year and then joined his parents in Kure. Shortly thereafter he left for the United States; without the farm there was little work for him at home, even in the pharmaceutical business his father had started. Although it was Senichi's own idea to emigrate to America, his father approved and gave him pharmaceutical supplies worth 200 yen to sell there. When Senichi left Japan in 1902 his parents were living with his six younger siblings—four brothers and two sisters. For the next twelve years, he worked as a laborer and cook in several northwestern states and eventually opened a restaurant in Utah with his own savings. It is unclear whether he had been sending remittances to his family in Japan during this initial sojourn in the United States.

In 1914, Senichi received conscription papers from Japan ordering him to report for a physical examination. About the same time, Isao wrote that he was arranging the marriage of one of Senichi's younger brothers. Senichi wrote back that his father should take care of his marriage first, as he was the eldest son. When he returned to Japan, Senichi brought considerable savings with him and used much of the money to expand the family drugstore and to buy houses and property for several of his brothers and sisters. His parents in turn arranged his marriage to a woman from a family that lived on the outskirts of the city. After their wedding, which was paid for by Isao, Senichi and his wife, whose name was Masami, moved into his parents' home, where they lived for four years. In their fourth year of marriage, Senichi returned to Utah to sell the restaurant he had left in the care of a cousin and then invested his capital in another restaurant in Seattle. Shortly after he bought the Seattle restaurant, Masami joined him.

After his second departure from Japan, Senichi's parents were left with only their youngest unmarried son Kakuzo in the household. In

1930, sixteen years after their marriage, Senichi, Masami, and their children returned to Japan for a visit and stayed at his parents' home. Sometime between 1918, when he left Japan for the second time, and 1930 (and before his father died), Senichi gave his younger brother Kakuzo the family home and business. His reason for doing this, he says, was that he had enough wealth to be generous to his brother and that he wanted to remain in Seattle. Masami remarked that "it was like giving it to him [Kakuzo] on a silver platter."

Jisaburo Hayakawa. By birth Jisaburo Hayakawa (Case I.8a) was the *jinan* (second son) in his family, but his older brother Saburo had been removed from the household register by their widowed mother because he had refused to marry her niece and had arranged his own marriage in the United States. Hence, when he returned to Japan to marry in 1920, Jisaburo expected to succeed to the headship of the household. This expectation did not deter him from also refusing to marry his mother's niece; he chose instead to marry Minako Goto from a nearby village. The marriage was arranged with the help of Jisaburo's younger brother, Yoshio. Because his mother was angered by his choice of bride, the wedding was held at Minako's home and her parents paid for the inexpensive wedding party, which was attended by her close relatives and Jisaburo's brother Yoshio. After the wedding Minako and Jisaburo traveled to Yokohama, where they stayed with a friend for four days before Jisaburo sailed for Seattle. By this time, Jisaburo's mother had become reconciled to the marriage at least enough to accept the bride into her household for the six months before she in turn left for America. Her mother-in-law's treatment of her seemed to affirm Minako's incorporation into the household.

After Minako joined Jisaburo in Seattle, the couple worked first as farm laborers and domestics and then were able to open a hotel with money loaned to them by a wealthy man from their native prefecture. Jisaburo proved a skillful entrepreneur. Soon there was enough money to send to his mother and also to Minako's parents. Meanwhile, Jisaburo's younger brother Yoshio married in Japan, but his wife was sent back to her natal home by his mother, with whom the couple had been living. The only child of this marriage, a son named Shigeo, remained with Yoshio and his mother. When Yoshio became seriously ill with tuberculosis, Jisaburo sent money to finance Yoshio's treatment and to support him, his mother, and Shigeo. Jisaburo fully expected to inherit the family home despite his long absence. He considered his financial aid to his mother and younger brother proof of his fulfillment of his responsibilities as head of the household. Thus, when Yoshio and his mother sold all the family's holdings and moved to Tokyo, Jisaburo was furious and broke off all correspondence with them. In 1930, when he decided that his daughters should be educated in Japan, he sent them to live with his wife's parents with strict orders that their paternal grandmother was not to be allowed to visit them. It was not until after World War II that Jisaburo resumed contact with his elderly mother and his younger brother.

By then Yoshio had remarried, this time to the maternal cousin his mother had long desired as a daughter-in-law. Upon Yoshio's remarriage, Shigeo had been adopted out to his father's cousin, whose daughter he eventually married. Two sons were then born to Yoshio and his second wife, but the first was adopted out to become the successor of a neighboring household. The second son proved to be retarded. After the deaths of Yoshio and Jisaburo's mother there was nothing to inherit but the house in Tokyo in which she had lived with Yoshio, his wife, and their remaining son. At the time Jisaburo himself died, the issue as to who would succeed to the headship of Yoshio's household was still unresolved, the choice being between a retarded son and an alienated son, Shigeo, who had been adopted out.

Bunkichi Nakanishi. In 1912, when Bunkichi Nakanishi (Case I.17b) was thirteen years old and living in Japan, he was adopted by his father's younger brother Ryoichi and his wife, who had emigrated to Seattle and were childless after many years of marriage. Bunkichi was a second son and had already considered going to America to work (his father had previously worked in Seattle for several years). The adoption seemed particularly convenient as it would allow Bunkichi to enter as Ryoichi's son. By 1917, when Bunkichi emigrated, the Gentlemen's Agreement had, for the past ten years, been restricting immigration from Japan to relatives of Japanese in the United States, students, and nonlaborers. A year before he arrived, Ryoichi's wife gave birth to a daughter. Thus, at the time of his arrival in Seattle, Bunkichi's status as Ryoichi's successor was somewhat clouded by this unexpected birth. Still, Bunkichi remained registered as Ryoichi's son, and affirmed this relationship by living with Ryoichi and consulting him before he made any major decisions. On the other hand, Bunkichi remained in close communication with his biological parents and sent them money every month.

When Bunkichi was asked by a friend of his future mother-in-law whether he was interested in marrying Chiyo Morishima (his second cousin), he obtained Ryoichi's consent before agreeing to the match. Since he had his own income as a railroad worker, Bunkichi paid for the wedding expenses himself, and he and Chiyo set up a household next door to her parents and ten blocks from Ryoichi. Six years after Chiyo and Bunkichi were married, Ryoichi, his wife, and daughter returned to their hometown and built a branch house (*bunke*) next to the main household (*honke*), then headed by Bunkichi's (biological) older brother. Bunkichi continued to send money to his (biological) father, but he also sent money regularly to Ryoichi. Several years (just how many is not recalled) after he returned to Japan, however, Ryoichi officially removed Bunkichi from his household, and later arranged a *yōshi* marriage for his daughter. The daughter and her *yōshi* husband lived with Ryoichi and his wife and eventually inherited the home. Bunkichi claimed it was because he was grateful enough for having been invited to the United States that he did not try to hold on to his position as Ryoichi's heir. But he also admitted that he had been forced to "take a step back" when his adoptive parents had a daughter, and he clearly resented their actions.

Shoji Yokoi. Kisuke, the father of Shoji Yokoi (Case I.24a), was a fifth son who lived in a small *bunke* house next door to his eldest brother's larger house, site of the *honke* household. Because the small parcel of property he had inherited was inadequate to support a family, Kisuke emigrated to the United States to work, leaving his wife and children in Japan. Kisuke had in all six children, the first three (all sons) by his first wife, and the second three by his second wife. His eldest son Ichiro died only a year after he had married, leaving a widow and a newborn son. Because Ichiro's marriage had not been registered in the village office (a common practice during the first year of marriage), his son Hiromu had no legal claim to being his heir or, in turn, Kisuke's. Ichiro's widow was sent back to her family and Hiromu was adopted out to another unrelated household. This made Jiro, the second son, the successor to Kisuke. Jiro also emigrated to the United States, where he eventually entered the hotel business in Seattle.

By the time Shoji, the fifth and youngest son, was a teenager, his older brother Jiro (who was eighteen years older than he) had been married several years. However, Jiro and his wife Matsumi never had any children. Kisuke arranged to have Shoji registered as Jiro's first son and told Shoji he should address Jiro as father. In 1919 Shoji emigrated to Seattle, where he attended school and lived with his adopted father Jiro and his wife Matsumi. When he married in 1931, Shoji and his wife moved into an apartment next to Jiro and Matsumi in a building owned by Jiro, and for the next four years Shoji worked in Jiro's hotel business.

In 1935, after he had a stroke, Jiro and his wife returned to Japan and the family home that had been left to them upon Kisuke's death. Jiro sold his hotel business and left Shoji with enough capital to open a business of his own. Shortly after he returned to Japan, Jiro died leaving his wife Matsumi as de facto head of household. Shoji then announced that he had decided to remain in Seattle rather than return to Japan, and Matsumi replaced him with his younger sister Hanako and her husband, who already had two sons, and who now returned to live with Matsumi in the family home (they had been living in Seattle).

During World War II the eldest of Hanako's sons was killed in the Hiroshima holocaust. After the war the younger son decided to return to Seattle where he had spent most of his youth. As the Yokoi household was again left without a successor, Shoji urged Matsumi to adopt Hiromu, Ichiro's son, who, it will be recalled, had been adopted out upon his father's death. Although Hiromu was legally a member of the Kikuchi household, he had lived for periods of time in the Yokoi home. Matsumi, not surprisingly, did not want as the successor a nephew upon whom she had no personal claims. Eventually, Matsumi and Hanako decided to adopt a young woman who was a relative of Matsumi. They then arranged a *yōshi* marriage for her and several sons and daughters were produced. After Matsumi died, this *yōshi* couple succeeded to the headship of the household. Finally, upon her husband's death, Hanako returned to Seattle to join her surviving son.

Denkichi Adachi. The parents of Denkichi Adachi (Case I.1a) owned a successful grocery store in Seattle. Denkichi was the eldest of two sons who emigrated to work with them there. His two sisters had been left in the household in Japan under the care of his father's widowed sister. After his marriage, Denkichi's wife Fumiyo came to live with him and his parents and worked with them in the store. Although Denkichi's younger brother and his wife also remained members of the household and worked in the grocery store, Denkichi was clearly designated as the successor. After his parents returned to Japan just before World War II, Denkichi sent money regularly to support them and soon provided them with funds for the construction of a larger family home. He also built a smaller *bunke* house for his father's younger brother, whom he had promised his father he would support. As this uncle left no heirs, upon his death Denkichi's widowed sister Mitsu inherited the house and took up residence in it. During the war, Mitsu's only son was killed, and subsequently his widow Fusako and two children came to live with her (see Figure 5). When Denkichi's mother died in 1966, five years after her husband's death, Denkichi inherited the *honke* home and property. As he did not want to return to Japan at the time, however, he

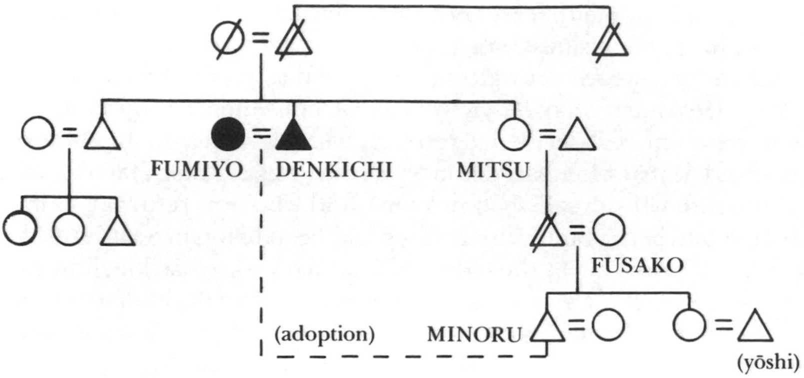

Fig. 5. Succession in the Adachi household. A diagonal indicates that the person was deceased.

allowed Mitsu to move from the *bunke* house into the *honke* house, leaving her son's widow and children in the former.

Denkichi and Fumiyo never had any children. Thus, while Denkichi's status as successor always appeared firm, there was a question as to the eventual transmission of the household. For years he had sent money for the support of his sister's grandson Minoru, as well as the other members of the *bunke*. In 1972, Denkichi and Fumiyo legally adopted Minoru. When Minoru married later that year, Denkichi and Fumiyo stood in as the official parents at the wedding in Tokyo, which cost them several thousands of dollars. Although Minoru and his wife now reside in Tokyo, they will inherit the *honke* house (currently occupied by Mitsu) and its property upon Denkichi's death. Minoru's sister in the meantime was married to a *yōshi* husband; they will inherit the *bunke* house in which they now live with Fusako.

Outcomes of Household Succession and Inheritance

At the time they married, all five of these Issei men were the incumbent successors of their jural parents, whether adoptive or biological. After they married, all five acted to affirm their status as successors, whether by residing with parents and working in the family business (Shoji and Denkichi), by providing money to expand the family's holdings and obtain property for siblings (Senichi and Denkichi), or by sending remittances to the household in Japan (Jisaburo, Bunkichi, and Denkichi).

Four of the five men, in the end, did not succeed to the headship of the household, nor did they inherit the family property. In two of the cases, the problematic nature of the Issei husband's status as successor was already evident at the time of the marriage, if not earlier. When Jisaburo Hayakawa defied his mother's order that he marry his cousin, he knowingly alienated her and risked the same fate as his older brother. His mother did not disinherit him but instead accepted his wife into her home, treating her in every way as a bride of the household. But the tension created by Jisaburo's choice apparently did not altogether dissipate. For quite different reasons, Bunkichi Nakanishi's status as successor was also shaky at the time of his marriage. The unexpected birth of his adoptive parents' daughter threw open the question of whether they would stick to their decision to make him their successor. In the other two cases, the Issei's status seemed more firmly established at the time of the marriage. Senichi Harano, after all, more than met his obligations as first son by supplying money for the family's expanded holdings, and his wedding arrangements and initial postmarital residence conformed to those expected of a successor son. Likewise, although Shoji Yokoi was the adopted son of his older half brother, his work in his adoptive parents' business and his coresidence with them in their apartment building for the four years following his marriage spoke clearly of his status as their successor.

As for the postmarital filial histories of the remaining eight Issei men whom I classified as successors at time of marriage, some resembled the more certain status of Senichi Harano while others displayed from the beginning the insecure status of Bunkichi Nakanishi. In each case, however, the future circumstances of the Issei husband and his kin in the United States and Japan, shaped as they were by unpredicted events (including political developments linking the two nations), altered the relationships between him and his parents in ways not apparent from the circumstances surrounding the beginnings of his marriage. By the time the last surviving parent died, six of the twelve original successors had either ceded their rights to succession and inheritance or had had them taken away. In two cases adoptions had been annulled and replacements found; in another the family home was willed to a young servant. In yet another case, the family holdings had been sold and the money used by a younger brother. Two Issei men had "given"—either of their own volition or in response to family pressure or some combination of the two—the family home to a brother or sister who was residing in it. In an additional three cases, the Issei successor neither succeeded to the headship of the household nor inherited its property, but it was unclear what happened to the family home or whether any existed by the time of the last parent's death.

The transmission of the headship of the household and the devolution of its property onto an Issei successor at the death of the surviving parent occurred in only three cases. In the first of these, the Issei's younger brother remained living in the family home to manage its property. Thus, while the home and property were registered in Katsumi Takitani's name and today are registered in his son's name, it is highly unlikely that the son will claim them. In all but a strict legal sense, then, it was Katsumi's younger brother who inherited the family home and property. In the second case the Issei, Nobuichi Suwa, not only retained the headship but passed it on to a son who had been sent to Japan as a child to live in the family home. As Nobuichi's widowed and childless sister raised this son, she has been allowed to live in the family home. Upon her death, however, there will be no other remaining claims on the home besides that of the Suwas' son. Sachiko Suwa, who has long survived her husband, anticipates that she might return to occupy the home in her last days.

The final case, that of Denkichi Adachi, where the family home and property devolved onto an Issei successor, is one in which succession arrangements continue to link closely together families in Japan. The adoption of Denkichi's sister's grandson has rather obviously done more than provide a successor for the household in Japan and ensure its transmission within the family line; it has also brought about the convergence of what threatened to be the competing claims of an absentee Issei successor, on the one hand, and his resident sister and her descendants, on the other. Just as in the other cases where property actually devolved onto a sibling, the jural rights of the incumbent successor had specific social meaning only within the broader context of the counterclaims of siblings and their descendants. In Denkichi's case, the dynamic and negotiated claims of succession and inheritance characterizing the Issei's past filial relationships are manifest in the present.

The three cases in which Issei designated as heirs at the time of marriage eventually succeeded to the headship of the household and inherited the household property may seem insignificant in comparison to the nine cases in which those so designated did not. Yet the greater frequency of the latter outcome should not lead us to conclude that the Issei anticipated it. For one, such a conclusion would deny the unpredictability of individual and family biographies and the historical events that play so great a part in shaping them. Certainly, many of the actions of successor Issei toward parents, siblings, and other kin in Japan spoke of their investment in a future bound closely to that of their parental households. For another, it must be recalled that the Issei marriage sample does not represent evenly the total population of Issei who came to the United States expecting to succeed to households in Japan. We do not know what proportion of that total were heirs of households in Japan at the time they married; we do not know what proportion of those heirs retained their status as successors. The reason is that the vast majority of Issei who succeeded to a parental household would have returned to Japan, and neither they nor their children were likely to have been members of the Seattle Japanese American community in the 1970's. It seems indisputable that such cases occurred, and with frequency. The Issei's own accounts of friends and relatives who returned to Japan, many to take up residence in their parents' households, attest to this. Indeed, of the twelve Issei nonsuccessor men in the marriage sample, four had older brothers who returned to fill the headship of their parents' household after spending their early married years—which, in two cases, spanned two decades—in Seattle.

This is not to say that all Issei successors continually found the prospect of reincorporation in their parental households attractive, nor that they therefore pursued that prospect consistently during the period before World War II. Some had serious doubts about the desirability of returning to fill the position of successor in a household controlled by a senior couple. In many cases, moreover, the remittances sent by Issei were necessary for the support and maintenance of the household in Japan. Hence, return was not economically feasible until sufficient wealth had been accumulated for a comfortable retirement, the expansion of landholdings, or the capitalization of a business venture in the home community. Issei successors were not in line to inherit substantial property holdings or even enterprises capable of generating enough income to support themselves and their spouses, children, and parents. Indeed, most of them had emigrated because the household's property was insufficient to support its next generation. I do not know the exact size of their parental households' property and wealth. But, when placed in the context of the economic history of Japan at the turn of the century, the Issei's recollections of their parents' occupations provide adequate evidence of their economic circumstances. That not only the Issei but, in many cases, their fathers and brothers emigrated to work in America suggests that they were members of the growing class of Japanese with insufficient landholdings to subsist as full-time farmers. Even those Issei whose parents and brothers never emigrated grew up in households supported in part by petty trade, home craft production, or wage labor.[1]

The Issei, moreover, came from the regions of Japan that were more economically developed, and hence more penetrated by the rapidly expanding monetary economy. These areas were also characterized by high rates of tenancy in the late nineteenth and early twentieth centuries. By the end of the Tokugawa era, there were regional differences in the degree of concentration of landholdings that reflected the differential growth by region of trade and industry (T. Smith 1959, 163). The reforms of the land tax system that began in 1873 and the economic fluctuations that followed led to greater dispossession of peasant farmers and the acquisition of holdings by merchants and moneylenders (Fukutake 1967, 9). Thus, even where the Issei's parents were engaged in farming, it is unlikely that they owned most of the land they farmed. In 1910 tenants, who owned less than 10 percent of the land they cultivated, made up 27.8 percent of farm households in Japan, while part-tenants, who owned between 10 and 90 percent of the land they cultivated, made up 40 percent (ibid., 10). The vast majority of Issei whose parents were "farmers" undoubtedly were members of these two categories rather than the category of owner-farmers, who owned more than 90 percent of the land they cultivated. In short, whatever motives Issei successors of "farm" households may have had to maintain their claims to that status, hope of inheriting the means of production was hardly one of them. In some cases, where the parents were tenant farmers, succession did not even mean inheriting the small plot of land on which the family home sat. Nevertheless, all Issei successors appear to have been interested in keeping the option of succession open. Successors and nonsuccessors alike initially expected to return to Japan.

The economic and political insecurity of the Japanese in the United States reinforced those expectations. If they could not predict the financial losses and personal traumas they would suffer during World War II, the Issei could easily imagine similar misfortunes as they experienced the rise in anti-Japanese sentiment that was conveyed by laws restricting their ownership of land and their business activities, and barring them from U.S. citizenship. Yet more than this lay behind the efforts by successor Issei to strengthen their claims to households in Japan through the contributions of money and, as in the placement of

[1] Between 1908 and 1940, nearly 70 percent of Japanese farmers cultivated less than a single hectare of land (Fukutake 1967, 6). Other sources of income were needed. The landless families, a significant category by the late Tokugawa period, generated some income from tenant farming but most of it from wage-earning jobs (T. Smith 1959, 164).

Kibei children, of personnel. These reasons will become more apparent in Chapter 6, where I examine the Issei's interpretations of filial relations.

At the same time the Issei were reinforcing their claims to succession, however, their absence from parental households undermined those claims. For, as long as they were not present to fulfill the many-faceted duties of a successor—duties that included coresidence, management of the family farm or business enterprise, representation of the household in community affairs, and care of aging parents—the likelihood was great that a sibling would step in to replace them. If at first these siblings were merely temporary substitutes for absentee successors, many soon became permanent replacements.

Postmarital Filial Relationships of Nonsuccessors

I noted earlier that many nonsuccessor sons contributed financially to the support of parental households in Japan, although not as regularly or as greatly as successors. The postmarital relationships of nonsuccessor sons with parents in Japan were limited for the most part to maintaining contact through letters and occasionally contributing money or goods. None of these sons sent children to live in parental households in Japan, and indeed few even returned to Japan for a visit until much later in life. By the time most returned on their first visit, their parents had been long deceased. For a few of these men, the return to their natal household came in the form of the delivery of their ashes by their widows.

Nothing uncovered in the personal histories of the twelve Issei men I classified as nonsuccessors at time of marriage suggests there had been a change in their filial status. If this appears surprising, when so many of the successor Issei were being displaced by younger brothers, it must be remembered that Issei nonsuccessors had little on which to base any claims on their parental households. Where their eldest brothers had died or resigned before succeeding, other siblings who had remained in Japan were closer at hand to replace them.

Time, Indeterminacy, and the Outcomes of Filial Histories

As we have seen, the filial histories of the Issei reveal to us two kinds of successor sons: those who inherited and transmitted to their descendants the property of parental households; and those who did not, but were replaced by siblings or their descendants. These histories disclose the dynamic character of Issei filial relations, which were continually being reevaluated and redefined as parents and children responded to changing circumstances in Japan and America. They also disclose the indeterminate character of Issei filial relations, each of which was but one among several differentiated filial relations in a sibling group.

Such differentiation of filial relations was central to the succession and inheritance practices of the Japanese stem family. Where one child succeeds to the headship of the household and inherits the bulk of the family's property, structurally different relationships are created within a sibling set. But the dynamic adjustments in filial relationships within a particular sibling set were generated by responses of parents and children to unexpected events. In Japan, primogeniture was merely the first preference in a range of legitimate alternative modes of succession and inheritance, as Harumi Befu observes (1963). Yet it was not merely the absence of a rigid rule for the selection of a successor that made succession outcomes indeterminate in any household. Rather, the installation of an heir never eliminated the possibility of his later replacement by another candidate. The status of successor was neither "ascribed" nor "achieved" once and for all, but was constantly negotiated through action. Neither did it entail an exclusive, jural claim on the family patrimony; rather, it was merely the first among many claims of other members of the sibling set, of other kin, and even of nonkin.[2] Moreover, for the Issei as for all successors in Japan, its social significance was also shaped by their relations with their own children. Those relations, then, must now be examined, for, as our cases have already demonstrated, whether or not an Issei provided the next successor had an impact on his own status as successor.

NISEI FILIAL RELATIONS: SUCCESSORS AND NONSUCCESSORS

Prewar Differentiation

Before World War II, the Issei exhibited all the signs of a generation of parents committed to reproducing the stem family and its accompanying system of differentiated filial relations. Some of the actions they took are admittedly rather weak evidence of such a commitment; for

---

[2] Inheritance "rules" are seldom as clearcut as many ethnographic descriptions imply. Undoubtedly, the Issei's status as successors was ambiguous and uncertain, but so was household succession in Japan in general. All studies of Japanese kinship are explicit about the right of the current or even the de facto head of the household to remove and replace the heir at any time. In addition, in areas where primogeniture is the preferred form of succession, there is a high percentage of succession by junior sons (Beardsley, Hall, and Ward 1959, 237).

while these actions were consistent with the formation of stem families, they might well have been more the result of unreflective adherence to custom rather than of conscious strategies for the future. For example, as in the Japanese stem family, the eldest Nisei son usually received special treatment and privileges from his parents. In many families he was the second to be served at meals, after his father, and he was generally indulged by his mother. Younger siblings were instructed to follow his directions, and even older sisters were expected to defer to him. In addition, Japanese terms of address, which reflect the hierarchical distinctions of age and sex among siblings, were taught to the Nisei.[3] Such practices, however, might be attributed to habits not easily altered even where parental plans for future stem families no longer persisted. Likewise, the fact that successor Issei were far more likely to send their eldest son, rather than any other child, to live in his grandparental household in Japan might be attributed to their desire to provide elderly parents with youthful companionship. Finally, the fact that before the war many of the Issei registered their American-born children in the household register of their village or town in Japan may mean only that they expected to return to their natal communities, not that they expected to return to perpetuate its stem-family system.

Other actions taken by the Issei, however, are not so easy to dismiss in this way. For instance, as Nisei sons and their younger brothers reached adolescence and young adulthood, it became clearer that parents expected different things from them. All Nisei children were expected to contribute to the household's economy, whether through work in the family business and home or through the wages they earned in work outside the family, but eldest sons were often groomed to take over the family business. In some cases, only the eldest son worked in the family business, while other sons and daughters were encouraged to find work elsewhere. In other cases, all children worked in the family business as soon as their labor became useful, but only eldest sons were taught about its finances and management. Issei who had hopes of expanding their family businesses or of diversifying into new enterprises sometimes went beyond mere on-the-job training and sent first sons to receive formal training in business, accounting, and related fields. Senichi Harano, for one, in preparation for a move into the import-export business, sent his eldest son to Japan to polish his Japanese

[3] Issei and Nisei usages of Japanese kinship terms of address are the same as described in the literature on Japanese kinship (see, for example, Beardsley, Hall, and Ward 1959, 243-47).

language skills and to learn about Japanese retailing. His other sons, however, he sent to American colleges so that they could earn a living outside the family business. Similar patterns of differential educational and occupational plans were found in other entrepreneurial families for first sons compared with all the rest.

The marriages the Issei arranged for their adult children before the war also provide evidence of parental intentions for relationships with them at this stage of their lives. As I noted in Chapter 3, Issei interest in arranging these marriages was heightened by the fact that so many first sons were marrying in this period. The brides the Issei desired most for their first sons were ones with the desirable characteristics of a *yome* who could be incorporated into their household. Kibei women were particularly desired by Issei parents who wanted a dutiful, "Japanese" bride uncontaminated by "American" ideas. So were Nisei women who brought with them socially useful affinal ties in the Seattle Japanese community. But, given their plans to return to their home communities in Japan, the Issei were at the same time interested in arranging marriages that created or reinforced *shinrui* (kinship) ties with households in these localities.

Prewar marriages arranged between Nisei—neither of whom may ever have set foot in Japan—often evidenced Issei strategies for household continuity. This was true of Henry and Bessie Funada's marriage.

Case N.13a. Both Henry and Bessie were Nisei from early birth cohorts: she was born in 1911 and he in 1904. Bessie was the eldest of three daughters of an Issei widower who operated a flourishing greenhouse business. When Bessie was twenty-two years old, her father and Henry's parents arranged to have Henry enter her household as a *yōshi*. Both parties to the marriage agreed that Henry, who was a second son, would join his father-in-law's household and gradually take over his greenhouse business. As a concession to American custom, Henry kept his surname and Bessie gave up hers for his. Bessie's father and Henry's parents initiated the marriage arrangements and negotiated all the details of the marriage contract through a *baishakunin*. At the engagement party, attended by close relatives and the *baishakunin*, Henry presented Bessie with an engagement ring in private. Aside from this private act affirming the personal relationship of the couple, all other aspects of the engagement and wedding celebration emphasized incorporation of the *yōshi* groom into the bride's household and the affinal relationship established between the two households. Because Henry came as a *yōshi*, his father-in-law presented his parents with a marriage payment of two hundred dollars, half of which was given back as a return gift. Likewise, it was the bride's father, as head of the receiving household, who paid all the wedding costs, including those of a dinner party for a hundred people.

As was seen in Chapter 3, not all Nisei marriages before the war were arranged by the Issei. But even where the Issei had not initiated the marriage or chosen the spouse, they soon became active participants in the marriage arrangements. In Chapter 3, I mentioned that sooner or later a formal meeting between the parents of the bride and groom would take place, attended by the *baishakunin* from both sides. I found it difficult to uncover the details of the marriage agreements negotiated during the formal meetings following upon Nisei-initiated marriages. From the Nisei's perspective—at least as articulated today—these meetings were mere formalities, lacking any social consequence other than promoting the goodwill of parents. The Issei today tend to support this interpretation by claiming that when their children chose their own spouses they "stayed out of their marriage." Yet it is difficult to believe that the Issei were willing to forfeit all claims to their prerogatives as Japanese parents simply because their children were choosing their own spouses. As the Nisei often were not present at these formal meetings—certainly not at the private meetings between their parents and the *baishakunin*—and as the Issei are now, and even then were, fully aware of Nisei resentment at parental intrusion in children's marriages, I suspect much more was discussed and agreed upon by Issei parents than they now admit. The tendency for Issei parents to pay the wedding costs of Nisei sons whose brides they had not selected was probably, at least in part, a parental strategy for establishing future claims on the couple. Prewar Nisei marriages, then, ranged from those arranged by parents in ways that indicated their unequivocal intention of treating Nisei marriage as an event in the perpetuation of a household, to those initiated by the Nisei and followed up by parental involvement in ways that left this aspect of Nisei marriage ambiguous.

Postwar Filial Relations: Postmarital Residence Histories

The historical events described in Chapter 3 proved equally critical for filial histories. The incarceration and its aftermath coincided with the period in which most of the Nisei were reaching adulthood and marrying. Their relationships with their Issei parents, then, were greatly complicated during a critical phase in the development of filial relationships. The unstable and complex nature of filial relations during and after the war is perhaps most starkly displayed in the residential histories of Nisei couples.

At first glance, the postmarital residence patterns of first Nisei sons and junior sons seem to conform to the Issei's prewar expectations. Table 18 shows that two-thirds of Nisei first sons and their wives lived vi-

TABLE 18

Frequency of Virilocal Residence of Nisei Couples
During First Ten Years of Marriage, by Husband's Birth Order

Extent of viri-local residence	First sons		Junior sons		All sons
	Number	Percent	Number	Percent	
Virilocal residence for at least one year	12	67%	8	28%	20
No virilocal residence	6	33	21	72	27
TOTAL	18	100%	29	100%	47

NOTE: Mean number of years of virilocal residence: first sons, 6.8 years; junior sons, 4.2 years.

rilocally for some period of time during the first ten years of marriage. Later birth-order sons and their wives, in contrast, did so in less than a third of my cases.[4] The mean number of years of virilocal residence, moreover, was greater for first sons than for other sons. But not all first sons and their wives matched this pattern. More importantly, most of them did not spend the entire first ten years of marriage living virilo-cally. Indeed, there were considerable shifts in the composition of households in which Nisei couples lived, whether the husband was a first or a junior son. These shifts are apparent in Table 19, which displays the combinations of residence types experienced by Nisei couples during those years. Slightly more than a fifth of first sons lived virilo-cally for the entire period, while a larger percentage lived neolocally. But even more frequent among first sons was some combination of two or more residence types. Junior sons exhibit a similar and slightly larger frequency. They differ from first sons in that they were just as likely to live uxorilocally and neolocally as they were to live virilocally and neolocally, while first sons and their wives tended toward a combination of virilocal and neolocal residence. Among *both* first sons and junior sons, however, almost half of the couples changed residence type at least once during the first ten years of marriage. These shifts did not follow uniform directional sequences. Some couples started marriage living neolocally and then moved to uxorilocal or virilocal residence, and in some cases back to neolocal residence; others moved from an initial virilocal pattern to uxorilocal residence or from virilocal to neolocal residence.

[4] The lower frequency of junior-son virilocal marriage is not attributable to the death of parents before the marriage of junior sons. Only 4 of the 29 junior sons had no surviving parent at the time of marriage as compared with 1 of the 19 first sons. The difference is too small to account for the much larger difference in frequency of virilocal residence.

TABLE 19

*Types of Postmarital Residence of Nisei Couples
During First Ten Years of Marriage, by Husband's Birth Order*

Type of postmarital residence	First sons		Junior sons	
	Number	Percent	Number	Percent
Virilocal only	4	22%	0	0%
Uxorilocal only	1	6	2	7
Neolocal only	5	28	13	45
Two or more residence types:	(8)	44	(14)	48
Virilocal and neolocal	5	28	6	21
Uxorilocal and neolocal	0	0	6	21
Virilocal, uxorilocal, and neolocal	3	16	2	7
TOTAL	18	100%	29	100%

A breakdown of Nisei postmarital residence on the sole basis of husbands' birth order characteristics falls short of displaying the changes that were occurring in residence patterns and the social consequences of those changes. In Chapter 3, I showed that stem-family households did not occur at equally high rates in the different marriage cohorts during the first ten years of marriage. In addition, changes occurred over time not only in the rate of coresidence with parents but in the form of that coresidence. To comprehend more fully the implications of these postmarital residence histories for Issei-Nisei filial relations we must look more closely at those histories over a period of time.

Prewar cohort: 1925-1940. The 8 couples in the Nisei marriage sample who married before the war exhibited everything from virilocal to uxorilocal and neolocal residence. Five of the 8 couples spent at least half their first 20 years of marriage living with the same set of parents. In 4 of these marriages (3 of which involved first sons), residence was virilocal, and in 1 a *yōshi* couple lived uxorilocally. The remaining 3 couples—all of whom were first sons married to first daughters—lived neolocally except for brief periods (under a year) in which they resided with the husband's parents. Thus, only half of the 6 first sons fulfilled the customary expectation of virilocal residence. Even before the war, then, there was evidence that not all first sons would bring their brides into their parents' households. Yet the 4 couples who lived virilocally and the *yōshi* couple who lived uxorilocally had stable, long-term residence in stem-family households. Four of the couples started their married lives as members of stem-family households and 3 of them continued to live with the husband's or wife's parents until the latter's death—an average coresidence of 26 years. The other 2 couples each shifted to neolocal residence after 10 years with the husband's parents.

War cohort: 1941-1945. In contrast to the couples in the previous cohort, those who married during the war years exhibited a shifting pattern of short-term coresidence with parents. As was shown in Chapter 3 (see Table 14), a phenomenally high proportion of the couples in this cohort sample lived for at least a year in a stem-family household. But only 1 couple remained in such a household for 10 or more years. None of the couples continued to live with either set of parents until the latter's deaths. The average amount of time a couple spent living with the parents of either spouse was 4.1 years.

This pattern of temporary coresidence with parents was accompanied by three other features that differentiate this cohort from the prewar one. First, almost all the couples in this cohort began their marriages in neolocal residence. If they were in an internment camp, the camp administration assigned them their own room in the barracks; if they were "on leave" from the camp, they were separated from parents. Second, when they later resided with parents, almost as many of the couples—4 as compared to 5—lived uxorilocally as virilocally before shifting back to neolocal residence. Third, 3 of the 12 couples who lived in a stem-family household lived successively with *both* the wife's parents *and* the husband's parents—sometimes with an interim period of neolocal residence.

Resettlement cohort: 1946-1955. The postmarital residence of couples who married during the 10 years after the war contrasts in turn with that of the previous cohort. Although there was a higher proportion of first sons in this cohort sample than in the war cohort sample (47 percent as compared to 23 percent), there was a lower incidence of virilocal residence, as well as of uxorilocal residence or a combination of the two. After 20 years of marriage, still more than half (8 of 15) of the couples had never resided either virilocally or uxorilocally. The 7 couples who did, lived either virilocally (4 couples), uxorilocally (1 couple), or both (1 couple), for an average of 3.3 years. In all but one case, the couple shifted to neolocal residence before the death of the parents. Of the four marriage cohorts, the resettlement cohort—which significantly was the cohort that experienced the greatest occupational mobility *after* marriage—had the lowest incidence of residence with parents. Those couples in this cohort who lived with parents, moreover, did so for the shortest period of any cohort.

Post-resettlement cohort: 1956-1970. In three ways the post-resettlement cohort recalls the postmarital residence patterns of its most temporally distant counterpart, the prewar cohort. As in the prewar cohort, by the twentieth year of marriage 7 out of 12 couples had resided in stem-family households for a year or more. Moreover, these households were more enduring than the short-lived ones of the war and resettlement couples. The post-resettlement couples, of course, had been married for much fewer years than those in the other cohorts at the time of my study. Yet already the 7 couples who had lived with parents had done so for a mean period of 9.5 years. Only 1 couple had shifted from coresidence with parents to a nuclear family household while the parents were still alive. The other 6 couples—although they did not all begin marriage living with parents—either had continued to live with one set of parents or a widowed parent until the latter died, or they were still living with them at the time of my study. Finally, like the prewar cohort, none of the couples who married after 1955 lived successively with the husband's parents and the wife's parents. Over time they may have shifted from neolocal to uxorilocal residence or vice versa, or from neolocal to virilocal residence or vice versa, but never from virilocal to uxorilocal or vice versa, whether with or without an interim period of neolocal residence.

While this last cohort, in the stability and length of its coresidence with parents, resembles the prewar cohort, in other aspects of coresidence the two cohorts differ considerably. First, as might be expected given the late age at marriage of this cohort, as well as its high proportion of junior daughters and sons, these couples resided with much older parents than the first sons and first daughters in the prewar cohort. Second, whereas in the prewar cohort 4 couples resided virilocally and only 1 couple uxorilocally (and they were a *yōshi* marriage), in the post-resettlement cohort 5 couples resided uxorilocally and only 2 virilocally.

Changing Households, Changing Filial Relations

The four Nisei marriage cohorts differ not only with regard to the *incidence* of coresidence with parents, but in the *stability* of that coresidence over time; they also differ in the ratio of uxorilocal to virilocal residence. When we consider, furthermore, the decline in the occupational and economic position of the Issei in relation to the concurrent social mobility of the Nisei (see Chapter 3), it is rather obvious that the relations of dependency that existed in prewar stem-family households no longer characterized those of the 1950's and 1960's.

By the end of the war, the majority of Issei men in my sample were over fifty-five years old; the majority of Issei women were in their late

TABLE 20

Postwar Occupational Shifts Among Issei Men

| | Prewar occupation (1941) | |
Postwar occupation (1946)	Self-employed	Wage work
Self-employed, same business	5	-
Self-employed, new business	2	0
Wage work	5	4
Unemployed/retired	4	0
Deceased	1	0
TOTAL	17	4

forties and early fifties.[5] Many Issei couples who had small family businesses before the war did not have sufficient savings to start new businesses or reopen old ones. Given the lingering anti-Japanese sentiment, neither could they count on attracting enough customers to support a hotel, restaurant, greenhouse, or laundry. Moreover, as Edna Bonacich and John Modell have noted (1980, 97), the vertical integration of the Japanese American produce industry, which before the war had linked Japanese American truck farmers with Japanese American wholesalers and retailers, had been destroyed. The skills these Issei had acquired managing family businesses did not bring them comparable jobs with white employers. Instead, after the war, many entrepreneurs were forced back into the unskilled, low-paying jobs in which they had begun.[6] Less than a third of the men in the Issei marriage sample who had been self-employed entrepreneurs at the outbreak of the war were in the same line of business in 1946, one year after the war had ended and the camps had closed (see Table 20). Another 2 men had started new business ventures. Four men were unemployed and remained unemployed for the rest of their lives, and 5 had taken wage-earning jobs. The kinds of work these 5 men did, in all but one case for the rest of their working lives, display starkly the reversion to their earliest, and lowest, occupational levels. The 2 men who had been hotel and apartment owners became janitors and handymen. Two others who had operated grocery stores found work as a kitchen helper and grocery clerk. Finally, a former owner and manager of a laundry

[5] S. F. Miyamoto and R. W. O'Brien (1947) report that the average age of Issei returning to Seattle immediately after the war was sixty-one.

[6] The dramatic decline in the number of Japanese American businesses in Seattle and the corresponding rise in employment of Japanese Americans by white employers and government agencies has been documented in Miyamoto and O'Brien 1947.

TABLE 21

Postwar Occupational Shifts Among Issei Women

Postwar occupation (1946)	Prewar occupation (1941)		
	Self-employed	Wage work	Housewife
Self-employed, same business	5	-	-
Self-employed, new business	0	0	0
Wage work	7	2	1
Unemployed/housewife	4	0	5
TOTAL	16	2	6

business became a houseboy. Issei women who had worked in family businesses before the war experienced the same shift to wage work after the war. Again, less than a third of the women who had been self-employed were occupied in the same business in 1946 (see Table 21). Almost as many were unemployed or housewives. But the largest number were found in wage work. Women who had worked with husbands to run hotels, grocery stores, and laundries became domestic servants, chambermaids, seamstresses in garment factories, and cannery workers. Although a couple of them later changed jobs, none moved back into business. In contrast, the men and women who had been wage-workers before the war returned to wage work after the war. Tables 20 and 21 reveal that none of the 4 Issei men and 2 Issei women working for wages in 1941 were in business or unemployed in 1946. Likewise, all but 1 of the 6 women who were housewives before the war remained in this category.

The occupational decline of so many Issei, especially Issei men, to just those jobs from which they had struggled to escape in the first two decades of the century, when combined with their increasing rate of retirement, brought a comparable decline in their economic power in the community and in their power over their children. Not only did most Issei no longer have economic resources to offer these children, but many felt socially dependent upon their American-educated children, who they felt had better linguistic and cultural skills for dealing with people and institutions outside the Japanese American community. If they were not yet financially dependent on them, they could see that such a time was drawing near.

The return to war-devastated Japan where siblings and other relatives were struggling to survive was no longer a viable alternative for any but a few Issei. For most successors, then, the filial claims, discussed in Chapter 2, that influenced Issei conjugal relations were severely un-

dermined. Before the war, Issei couples saw themselves located in a social world that included both the Seattle Japanese American community and their natal communities. Issei successors in particular
provided their families with a place in communities in Japan. After the
war, Issei couples saw themselves located in a Japanese American community surrounded by an American society to which their children
provided the links. The increasing power and autonomy reported by
Issei wives after the war resulted not just from their Issei husbands' decline in economic status, since they provided less income, but also from
the decline in their social status, since they were less able to provide a
place in society.

Much more happened between 1946 and 1960 than a mere decline
in the percentage of Nisei couples living with parents. By 1960 both the
genealogical and the social relationships of the community's stem-family households had changed. Couples who had just married, if they
were not residing neolocally, were more likely to be living with the
elderly parent or parents of the wife. They were not, like the prewar
cohort, starting marriage as the junior, subordinate members of the
husband's parents' household, but rather as the main couple of a
household that they were willing to allow the wife's parents to join. In
between these two cohorts, the war and resettlement couples had
passed through a shifting pattern of short-term coresidence with either
or both sets of parents.

Postwar Filial Relations: Economic Histories

Residential arrangements alone, of course, tell us nothing of the social organization of residence units or their ties with other units. The
most notable feature of households after the war was that they were
accompanied by a wide range of economic and social arrangements. Although some first sons and their wives both lived and worked with the
husbands' parents in a family enterprise, most Issei and Nisei members
of stem-family households worked at separate wage-earning jobs. And
while they shared in the cost and preparation of meals, they did not
always pool all their earnings and savings into a common fund. Instead,
in many households each couple contributed toward some portion of
the household's operating expenses, keeping the rest of their earnings
in separate bank accounts. At the time of residential separation, each
couple took their own conjugal fund with them.

Just as residential units were not necessarily productive units, so productive units were not necessarily residential units. A few Nisei first
sons and their wives worked with the husband's parents in a family

business but resided neolocally. Edward and Carol Harano, for example, never lived with his parents, yet they worked continually after the war in the family hotel and apartment business. Younger sons and their wives too were involved in a range of different residential and economic arrangements with Issei parents. Some, like Junji and Minako Motoyama, were tied to the husband's parents in what appeared to be primarily residential arrangements, but which had some economic entailments. Shortly after their marriage in 1947, the Motoyamas moved into his widowed mother's house. Junji was working only part time while he studied engineering at the university; his wife also worked for a year until the birth of their first child. After five years, Junji's mother moved to California and left Junji and Minako in the house, which she owned. Two years later she returned to live with them again, and she continued to do so until, after several years as an invalid, she died. Junji retained the house, which had already been transferred to his name. Other second sons had even stronger economic ties with parents.

Case N.19a. Toru Iida and his wife not only lived with his parents for a while, but were involved in a restaurant business with them. After they married in camp, the couple lived next door to Toru's parents and his older brother. When they left camp, Toru and Chizuko joined her parents in the eastern Washington town in which she had been raised. After living with her parents for a year, the couple found their own apartment. But soon after this move, Toru's parents came to live with them while his older brother was in the army. Two years later the older brother returned to Seattle and his parents joined him. Together they bought an apartment house and began to rebuild the apartment business they had before the war. Shortly thereafter, Toru and Chizuko also moved to Seattle, where Toru worked in a series of wage-earning jobs. Subsequently, Toru joined his father in a restaurant venture that they jointly managed for twelve years. When his father sold the business, Toru took his portion of the proceeds and opened his own janitorial business. When his parents died, all their holdings went to their eldest son.

Even where second sons never lived with their parents after marriage, they sometimes were tied to them economically. Thus Masaru Arashi's wife Grace worked for years in his mother's restaurant after the war along with Masaru's older brother's wife. As the older brother and wife were living with Masaru's mother, the three of them had a common budget. Masaru and Grace lived apart from them and had their own expenses and savings. Yet Grace was treated as a family "helper" in that she was paid intermittently and in varying amounts depending on the business profits.

Finally, after the war Nisei couples had a range of residential and economic ties with the wife's parents. Some lived for long periods of time with them, a few permanently. Again, the social and economic accompaniments of coresidence varied. Although the members of these uxorilocal extended households rarely worked together in a common business enterprise or pooled their earnings into a common fund, they sometimes jointly purchased the home in which they lived. In one case, the Issei couple provided the down payment for the house and the daughter and her husband assumed the mortgage payments. In another, the Nisei couple lived rent-free in the home owned by the wife's parents, but paid all the daily expenses of food and utilities. In yet other cases, the Issei couple or widowed parent was an economic dependent in a home owned and maintained by the daughter and her husband.

THE AMBIGUITY OF FILIAL HISTORIES

Just as time and historical circumstance raised fundamental questions about Issei successorship, so they raised questions about the Issei's relationships with their children. The predominance of family business in the community before the war had provided the Issei with an economic basis for the stem-family system of differentiated filial relations. First sons could be groomed to work in the family business, assume its management, and eventually support elderly parents with the proceeds from an enterprise they had themselves worked to build. The wives of first sons could be incorporated into the household as useful productive workers as well as reproducers of the next generation. Second sons and daughters could be "married out" of the household to create a ring of affinal ties with other households in the community.

The incarceration swept away the economic foundation of the Issei's filial expectations. The return to Seattle at the closing of the "relocation camps" was less a process of reconstructing family and community than a process of constructing them anew. What had been a community of households engaged in production as well as consumption was now one of households whose members relied primarily upon earnings from jobs outside the family and, indeed, outside the community. Many first sons had no family enterprise to which to succeed, and so most became salaried workers like their younger brothers. The differentiation in the economic ties linking parents to first sons as opposed to second sons disappeared in many families. Even where businesses were started after the war, second sons and now daughters were pulled in as workers—sometimes in addition to first sons, sometimes without them.

Many Issei parents returned to Seattle without their eldest sons. The relocation program that had placed Nisei in jobs and colleges in mid-western and eastern states had thinned the ranks of first sons as well as those of second sons and (though to a lesser extent) daughters. As more Nisei trickled back to Seattle after college, work, and marriage in other cities, many Issei parents became involved in a succession of residential and economic arrangements with different children. I have already described the postwar diversity in forms of coresidence, the instability of residential units, and the varying economic arrangements linking parents and married children. All these challenged the cultural order that had structured the Issei's relations with children before the war. If before the war the virilocal residence of a Nisei couple could be read as a statement of the husband's status as successor, after the war it could be interpreted in a variety of ways. Postmarital residence could no longer be read as an unequivocal statement of successor status—not when married second sons and married daughters were moving in and out of their parents' homes at a phenomenal rate. Certainly, uxorilocal residence did not mean, as it had before the war, that a *yōshi* marriage had been agreed upon. Hence, the social meaning of coresidence had become ambiguous. So too had the meaning of work in a common family enterprise.

Considered together, the cases described in this chapter reveal the Issei's filial histories in the Japanese stem-family system to have been no less indeterminate and unstable than the Nisei's filial histories in a changing Japanese American family system. Both sets of filial histories—those linking the Issei to parents and households in Japan and those linking them to children and households in Seattle—display the questions raised over time about the meaning of parents' and children's actions. If we are to know the answers to those questions, we must turn to the Issei and Nisei interpretations of these actions.

CHAPTER 6

The Interpretation of Filial Relations

As with "Japanese marriage" and "American marriage," relations between "Japanese" parents and their children are construed by both Issei and Nisei as opposed to an "American" form of parent-child relations. Here, too, the Issei and Nisei disagree on their evaluation of these contrasting cultural types, and on how to classify their own relationships. In contrast to their marriage relationships, however, the filial relationships that Issei and Nisei categorize differently are the ones they share. Thus, while their respective interpretations of these relationships are structured by different systems of symbols and meanings, they are also shaped by each other through a dialogue in which action is negotiated and evaluated.

ISSEI INTERPRETATIONS OF FILIAL RELATIONS

The "Japanese Past"

To the anthropologist interested in reconstructing the normative structure of Japanese filial relations at the turn of the century, the Issei would seem the ideal informants. For, when asked about their relations with parents, they typically respond with accounts abounding in normative prescriptions and ideals. Filial relations in Japan, in general, and their own relationships with parents, in particular, are described in terms of unambiguous statuses with attached rights and duties—language of reassuring familiarity to the social anthropologist and one that presents a rather tidy model of Japanese kinship.

According to the Issei, a person in Japan had a clear set of rights and duties to his or her parents, depending on that person's birth order and sex. In Japan, the Issei say, you were raised as a member of your parents' household and you obeyed them and worked for them as long as you remained a member. Filial relations in adulthood, particularly after marriage, are uniformly described as having been governed by a coherent set of rules that distinguished a successor's relationship with his parents from that of his siblings. Characteristic statements made by the Issei include the following:

"In Japan the first son always takes over his parents' household and lives with them and inherits their property."

"It was the system for parents to live with their married first son."

"When I lived in Japan, sure first son must take care of parents and live with them. And [his] wife has hard work."

"As a second son, I didn't have to stay with my parents."

"Daughters went to live with their husband's family when they got married."

"I grew up thinking only of the Japanese way as regards my relationship with my parents."

The above statements and many more like them were not Issei responses to inquiries about the "rules of the Japanese family," but were volunteered by them in accounts of their relationships with parents. When, for example, I asked Issei men who were junior sons whether after marriage they had lived with their parents, a common answer was "No, in Japan it's the first son who must live with his parents."

In this rule-focused account of their filial relations, the Issei depict the "Japanese way" as having little ambiguity, inconsistency, or indeterminacy. In Japan—at least when they lived there—there were clear, easily articulable criteria for determining one's filial status and equally clear, articulable rights and duties attached to that status, whatever it was. If you were the first-born son you became the *atotori*, that is, the heir and incumbent successor, and took on the indivisible bundle of rights and obligations of that status. You lived with your parents and brought your wife into their household, inherited the household enterprise and property, and took care of your parents in their old age. If you were a younger son, you left the household to marry and start your own household, whether in the same community or not. You were not expected to live with your parents, nor were you responsible for them in their old age—for that was your eldest brother's task. If your eldest brother should die without producing an heir or your parents found themselves lacking a successor for some other reason, you might have to assume the position of successor. But aside from your being a potential replacement for the successor, your relationship with the parents whose household you had left was governed by only diffuse expectations of affection and solidarity. Of course, you were expected to "be nice to them" by maintaining close communication with them, visiting them when possible, and sending gifts as tokens of your affection and enduring gratitude. If they were financially needy, you should try to help them. But that, as one Issei put it, depended on "how much you have and how much they don't have." Thus, in contrast to the specific rules governing the successor's relations with his parents, the filial commitments of a nonsuccessor, once he or she was no longer a member of their household, are portrayed by the Issei as having fallen in a realm of vague altruism.

The parents to whom one was tied by these normative prescriptions could be any of the following persons: (1) one's biological parents, to whom one was related by "blood" (*chi*) and in whose household one was registered as a member; (2) one's biological parents, in whose household one was not registered; (3) one's adoptive parents, in whose household one was registered; or (4) one's spouse's parents, in whose household one might or might not be registered as a member.

Any potential normative ambiguity or conflict arising from the existence of several kinds of parents is minimized, however, by the Issei's hierarchical ordering of filial relations. The parents to whom one had primary and specific obligations and on whom one, in turn, had primary and specific claims were those in whose household one was registered as a member. The filial relations that superseded all other such relations one might have were based, therefore, on household membership rather than on consanguinity, fosterage, or affective ties. Issei who had been adopted out as young children said it was made clear to them that their obligations, as well as their claims, rested with their adopted parents rather than with their biological parents.

Although a person's primary filial responsibilities and claims lay with his or her jural parents, this did not mean that biological parenthood had no social meaning. To the Issei, biological parents and child share "blood" (*chi*), by which they mean common biophysical—or, in the case of some well-read Issei, genetic—substance. Both parents transmit to their biological children physical and psychological attributes and tendencies. Thus, a son can inherit a strong character or an aggressive personality from his mother as well as from his father. A blood tie is unconditional. In other words, regardless of what changes occur in the social relationship between parents and their biological child, they remain tied by the fact of shared blood.

Biological parenthood also transmits racial identity—in other words, both the observable and the imputed physical, mental, and personality characteristics that the Issei identify as "Japanese." The precise nature of these racial characteristics is not something the Issei agree upon. For some it includes such personality characteristics as *gaman* (perseverance, forbearance). Other Issei claim that such characteristics are learned rather than inherited, but at the same time admit they consider high intelligence an inherited Japanese trait. Regardless what a particular Issei believes Japanese racial identity consists of, for all Issei racial identity comes from one's biological parents. But biological parenthood in and of itself does not entail any specific jural relationship between parents and children in Japanese kinship, according to the Issei, who are able to recount cases in their family histories that illustrate the absence of specific rights and duties between biological parents and child where the latter had been adopted out. The Issei also point out that a woman who had been sent back home had no legal claim on the children she had borne for her husband's household.

Just as blood in and of itself did not bring a jural relationship, so it did not bring a status or social position. Instead, membership in the household of one's jural parents brought one a place in society.[1] In tracing genealogical ties the Issei used either or both biological ties and adoptive ties. Thus a man whose father was adopted included both his adoptive grandparents and his biological grandparents in his genealogy. That one's social standing was derived from one's jural parents did not mean that it was absolutely unchangeable. To the contrary, according to the Issei, a person could alter his status through his achievements or failures. Given the shared social identity of members of a household, however, the achievements or failures of individual members affected the status of the entire household. Consequently, while children received a social status from their jural parents, they could also transmit a social status to their parents. For example, when the children of poor, uneducated parents attained high educational and occupational levels, this raised their parents' social standing in the community because it

[1] None of the Issei I interviewed attributed their social status to a grandparent or earlier ancestor. Indeed, they placed no emphasis on descent (that is, on a series of filial links) and only one man was able to trace his ancestry past his great-grandparents. When asked about their earlier ancestors the Issei either pled ignorance or responded with statements such as "we came from a long line of farmers" or "our family had been there [in that village] for generations." While several of the Issei who were practicing Buddhists had *butsudan* (household altars) in their homes, none had tablets in it for ancestors other than parents.

was seen as manifesting the family's true qualities and, hence, its proper place in the community.

Biological parenthood and any blood relationship brought a recognition of shared biological substance and a vague sense of attachment even when there was little social basis for the bond. For example, after she was adopted out of her biological parents' household, Matsue Kusumoto maintained communciation with them. When her father died and her older brother became disabled, she began sending her mother a small sum of money every other month. She sent it neither because she felt she "had to" nor because she "felt like it," but because she felt sorry for her brother's wife, who was living with Matsue's elderly mother. Matsue emphasized that she did not owe her biological mother anything, because "she never did anything for me." By this she meant not only that she resented being adopted out but that she had not been raised by her biological mother even before the adoption. As she was born prematurely, and her mother did not have sufficient milk to nurse her, Matsue had been sent to live with another family in which the woman had lost her own infant and had abundant milk. Later she lived with her father's sister. Yet, while she minimized the affective, personal bond with her biological parents, Matsue still admitted to some enduring attachment to them, however weak and ambivalent.

Where one's blood parents had raised you as a child, however, the bonds were stronger. Adoption still entailed the transference of the jural aspects of parenthood, and one's first and foremost obligations and claims rested with one's adoptive parents. But the Issei said the experience of being nurtured and raised by one's biological parents created a lasting emotional commitment to them. Thus, although Bunkichi Nakanishi said that after he was adopted by his father's brother he knew he had to do everything for his adoptive father that he would have done for his "own father," he still maintained close communication with that father and sent him spending money and gifts on special occasions such as the New Year and Bon Odori, the annual Buddhist festival celebrating the return of the spirits of the dead. Like the relationship of a nonsuccessor son to his parents, Bunkichi's relationship to the biological parents who had raised him and then adopted him out of their household was described by him in terms of a personal, affective bond and an enduring, though nonspecific, commitment. Finally, if a woman married into a household by marrying a successor son, her primary obligations were transferred from her own parents to her husband's parents. The same was true for a *yōshi* husband who married into his wife's parents' household. Thus, according to Rentaro Kusumoto, when he came as a *yōshi* to his wife's adoptive parents' household, he was bound to them by the same obligations as was his wife. Again, the relationship with his own parents, like his wife's relationship with her biological parents, became secondary, being relegated to a realm of vague altruism.

While the Issei's accounts of their "Japanese" filial relations with their parents manifest a rule-focused character, the Issei have no difficulty recounting, and accounting for, deviations from the rules. When asked what parents did when they had no son or no children, the Issei readily list a range of alternative modes of succession, including adoption, *yōshi* marriage, and second-son succession. Succession by the first son was preferred and was the "best way," they say, but it did not always work out in every household. In other words, it was merely the first choice in a complex set of contingent alternatives. Moreover, when asked to reconcile the actual outcomes of succession in their own natal households in Japan with this rule-focused description of "Japanese" filial relations, the Issei cite idiosyncratic circumstance as requiring adjustments in specific cases. If an Issei man who was the first son and incumbent successor at the time of his marriage was later replaced by his younger brother, it was because it was more convenient for the younger brother who had remained in Japan to manage the family property. If an Issei successor's widowed sister had moved into the family home in Japan and her son later inherited it, it was because the sister and her son had needed a place to live and the Issei could not afford to return to Japan. In short, economic constraints, geographic distance, the unexpected impact of historical events, and people's changing circumstances—the kinds of "exogenous" factors that anthropologists recognize as preventing social relationships from mirroring ideal models of society—are offered by the Issei as explanations of the diverse outcomes of filial histories.

The existence of the desires, emotions, and motives of individuals is not denied in the Issei's accounts of what they called Japanese filial relations. Ideally, a person's relationships with parents—whether blood parents, adoptive parents, or spouse's parents—entailed a harmonious integration of social rules and personal feelings. Parents and children took certain actions not just because there were rules that directed them to do so, but often because they also wanted to do these things. A man sent money to his parents in Japan not merely because he was expected to, but because of his emotional commitment to them. An Issei widow lived frugally for years in order to save enough money to return her husband's ashes to his parental home not solely because of duty, but as an expression of her deep affection for him.

But the Issei also described situations in which personal feelings were not congruent with the prescriptions of Japanese kinship. And, they explained, it was inevitable that there were situations in which you did not want to do what you were supposed to do. In such situations, however, duty (*giri*) took precedence over your personal desires and feelings (*ninjo*). When Bunkichi Nakanishi described his relationship with his adoptive father, for example, he emphasized the *giri* dimension of the relationship. He explained that he fulfilled all his obligations to his *giri no otōsan* (literally, "father by duty" and the Japanese term of reference for a father-in-law or adoptive father) out of "respect," even though he did not "feel" that way toward him. Similarly, Matsue Kusumoto said she sent money regularly to her adoptive parents after they returned to Japan because "that was the rule; not because I wanted to." Several Issei women claimed they fulfilled all their obligations to their husbands' parents even though they had never met them and so had no feeling for them. Other Issei wives explained that they would rather have sent their meager earnings to their own parents, but their obligations to their husband's parents came first.

Not only did people often have to set aside personal desires and emotions in Japanese filial relationships, but the priority of duty over individual wishes was already written into the rules supposedly governing filial relations. Personal feelings and emotional attachments had already been subordinated to jural considerations in the rule that gave jural parents the prior claim on adopted children and in-marrying spouses. Similarly, the selection of one's spouse, the Issei say, had little to do with "how you felt" and everything to do with your obligations to your parents. Thus, the desires and feelings of individuals, having already been written into the rules of Japanese kinship and assigned a low priority, did not belong in the domain of factors that lay between rules and outcomes. Instead, the factors constraining people's actions and modified outcomes were those that lay *outside* individual control. These external constraints arose from unexpected historical events such as wars, government policies, economic depressions, illnesses, deaths, births—in short, from the changing circumstances of people's lives. Individual "choice," the Issei claim, had little or no place in "Japanese" filial relations. One did not "choose" to live with one's parents or not to live with them; nor did one "choose" to send them money or not.

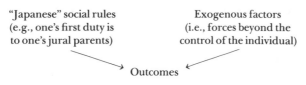

Fig. 6. Issei model of "Japanese" filial relations. Written into the "Japanese" social rules is the precedence of duty over personal wishes, feelings, and desires.

One did these things because, whether one felt like doing them or not, those were the rules. If one did not follow these prescriptions it was because circumstances beyond one's control made it impossible to do so.[2]

The Issei interpretation of their relations with parents is but one illustration of an interpretive model they employ in describing and interpreting Japanese social relationships in general—including, as we saw in Chapter 4, marriage. It can be represented as an ethnotheory of action according to which people's behaviors are the result of normative prescriptions (rules) constrained by exogenous factors beyond the control of individual actors (see Figure 6). It is a model of action in which forces—whether these are social rules or social events—*outside* people prevail over the forces (feelings, motives, desires) *inside* them. Moreover, though circumstances might require some adjustment in one's behavior, the rules themselves were not thereby adjusted. In other words, the fact that there was a range of outcomes in relations between successors and their parents as well as in those between non-successors and their parents did not undermine the rules, nor does it appear to hamper the Issei's current rule-focused interpretation of Japanese filial relations.

The "American" Present

When they first arrived in America, some Issei say, they thought their future relations with their adult children would be much the same as their relations with their parents. After all, they had been taught "traditional ideas," including the expectation that the first son would "stay in the family." Other Issei claim they never entertained such ideas. When they left Japan, they assert, they knew that living in a new coun-

[2] Noticeably absent from the Issei's list of such circumstances is any form of individual motivation. Whenever individuals enter into the discussion, it is in the form of personal attributes, such as physical and mental handicaps or major character flaws, that made attainment of the ideal impossible.

try would mean new circumstances and new ways. As one Issei woman put it, "When I came here, I wasn't thinking about the old system; so I never expected my first son to live with me [after marriage]."

Whether they admit or deny having held "Japanese" expectations about filial relations, the Issei uniformly claim that they do so no longer. If they had in the past, they soon "gave up the hope" when they realized it was "not the American way." A few admit but many deny that they still expected more from their eldest son than from other children. Most insist that they treated all children equally. Issei women, in particular, are adamant in refuting any suggestion that they might have shown a preference for their eldest son. But having left behind the "old system" of filial relations, the Issei are rather vague about the new one. Indeed, where "Japanese" filial relations are portrayed by the Issei as having been governed by unambiguous rules agreed upon by all people, "American" filial relations—in which they include their own relationships with adult children—are depicted as bereft of rules. In America, one Issei woman said, "everybody has [their] own ideas and likes to live [their] own way; so they should live their own way." Given this diversity of ideas and life-styles, it is fruitless to try to control your children.

Whenever I asked Issei whether they expected ever to live with their adult children, they tended to deny such expectations. Any Issei who was living apart from his or her children expressed ambivalence about the desirability of living with a married child. As long as they were healthy they would rather live alone. Living alone, they opined, is much easier because you have your privacy and you do not have to adjust to other people's schedules. Besides, it is "painful" to live in the same household with grandchildren with whom you cannot communicate because of language differences. And, in general, circumstances are different in America today, so the old rule of living with your eldest son does not apply any more. As one Issei widow put it, "Now we have social security, so we don't have to live with [our] eldest boy." The Issei admit there still are some of their generation who think their eldest son should take care of them and who would like to live with him. These Issei complain to each other about their dissatisfaction with their sons. But such people are said to be foolish. Issei informants also observe that some Issei live with eldest sons or with other married children. Some of these Issei are very happy, they say, but others are not so happy because it is hard to live with a married child and his or her family. There are cases too where an unmarried son or daughter has stayed with a widowed mother. While it is nice to have such a son or daughter, the mother must feel guilty about that person never marrying.

Questions about financial help or personal care in the event of sickness or disability brought even vaguer answers. Many Issei said they had no idea who should or would take care of them if they became sick; probably they would go into a nursing home. Some said they supposed it would depend on whether any of their children had the time or the inclination to take on the responsibility. Others said they did not think about such things, or they simply "trusted in God, and didn't worry." In their discussions of contemporary relations with their adult children, therefore, the Issei do not articulate any specific normative expectations—short of a very diffuse commitment by children to help their parents if they can—to replace the "Japanese" expectations they disavow.

The absence of rules in "American" filial relations is nowhere more clearly expressed by the Issei than when they are asked about inheritance. Although in the past, they explain, many Issei adhered to the "Japanese rule" of inheritance by the first son, now there are "no rules" for its distribution. There are a number of alternative ways of handling inheritance that are mentioned by the Issei, but none is considered satisfactory. Most Issei informants offer several different, and conflicting, options for distributing parental wealth and property. The most commonly mentioned ones are: (1) to give equal shares to all children; (2) to give all, or a major portion, to the child who cares for you in old age; (3) to give all, or a major portion, to the child with whom you reside; and (4) to give all, or a major portion, to the child with the greatest financial need.

None of these options is without its limitations and problems. Equal distribution is considered unfair because usually one child has taken more responsibility for the parents' care than his or her siblings. Parents cannot know when drawing up their will which of their children will help them when they become seriously ill. Furthermore, dividing parental property and cash is "meaningless" because in the end their children "will have nothing to show for it."

The Issei's claim that there are no longer any rules of inheritance or any satisfactory options for handling it is borne out by their inability to resolve the issue in their own wills. A couple of Nisei lawyers who have many Japanese American clients reported that a good many Issei (exactly what percentage they could not tell) die intestate, leaving many Nisei sibling sets with a legacy of conflict.

In contrast to their rule-focused interpretation of past relationships with their parents, therefore, the Issei's interpretation of present relationships with their children emphasizes the absence of rules and, indeed, the absence of shared normative expectations. To the Issei, the actions of the parties to what they call an "American" filial relationship are the unpredictable outcomes of an unstructured amalgam of personal inclinations, desires, and circumstances. No rules exist to tell such people how to order their feelings of duty and obligation to their parents. Nor is it clear to them how personal circumstance should enter into the shaping of action. In place of the orderly model of Japanese filial relations, the Issei model of American filial relations is one in which the outcomes are determined by a host of factors, all blended together in a disorganized mass. These outcomes may be satisfactory or unsatisfactory, surprising or not surprising, but nevertheless they are outcomes one would be foolish to try to control or predict.

It is not that the Issei claim their children lack any sense of duty, respect, or loyalty to parents, but rather that duty, respect, and loyalty no longer exist outside individuals, constraining and predominating over feelings and wants. Their children feel a sense of duty and want to help their parents, but they feel and want many other things at the same time. Above all, there simply are no rules directing them to give priority to some feelings as opposed to others.

NISEI INTERPRETATIONS OF FILIAL RELATIONS

The "Japanese" Past

Like the Issei, the Nisei conceptualize past and present filial relations in terms of contrasts between cultures. But, unlike the Issei, they see the Japanese past as extending further into the present. For the Nisei, the Japanese system of filial relations did not end with the Issei's relationships with parents in Japan but continued to shape the filial relations of both Issei and Nisei—at least while the Nisei were growing up, and to some extent to this day. The agreement among the Nisei—with the exception of a few who say they had unusually "progressive" or "modern" parents—is near absolute that their upbringing was governed by the "old rules" of the "Japanese family."

The filial relations that the Issei constructed, or at least attempted to construct, were based on strict discipline. Fathers were authoritarian figures whom one obeyed without hesitation unless one was willing to accept the unpleasant physical consequences. Because of his position of authority, an Issei father was often emotionally distant from his children—although sometimes he had a close, affectionate relationship with a favorite daughter. Issei mothers are described as having more intimate and less authoritarian relationships with their children. A mother often mediated between father and children, who could negotiate with her in a way that they could not with the father. Still, she was a parent whom one was expected to obey.

According to the Nisei, the expectations of obedience and duty were not communicated so much by what the Issei said as by what they did. In describing their upbringing, the Nisei emphasize the low level of verbal communication between parents and children. Some Nisei claim they know very little of their parents' backgrounds because such topics, as well as many others, were not discussed in the family. Others simply explain that "we didn't talk to each other very much." Many Nisei informants cannot recall ever having participated in a sustained discussion with either parent or having observed one between them. One Nisei man stated: "There was not much communication in those days. You just did what they told you and there was no talking back. I never had an extended conversation with either my mother or father. The contact between us was based on strict discipline." Several Nisei attributed this lack of communication to the "language barrier," referring to the fact that most Issei spoke little English, while many Nisei spoke little Japanese. Others think their parents were too busy working to have much time for talk with their children. Nevertheless, as regards their parents' expectations, the Nisei assert that "very little was said, but you just understood." You learned what was expected of you merely by observing parents and "the way they lived."

The low level of verbal communication and the absence of physical demonstrations of affection are interpreted by some Nisei as evidence of the "lack of love" in their natal families. Issei parents, they complain, never hugged them or verbally expressed affection, and hence they never felt much "human warmth" in their relations with them. Other Nisei, however, explain the absence of physical affection as a consequence of "Japanese restraint" and "stoicism." Their Issei parents, they say, may not have lavished hugs and kisses on them as *hakujin* (white) parents might have done, but they did express love and affection in their own way.

Little disagreement exists among the Nisei, however, about the Issei's expectations of first sons. Parents are said to have been firmly committed to "Japanese rules" of succession, inheritance, and filial obligations. First sons were expected to succeed to their parents' businesses, to bear the major financial and social responsibility for parents in later years, and to live with them. Representative statements made by the Nisei include:

"My mother is of the old school, where the eldest son takes over the family and everything." [*A Nisei first son*]

"The responsibility of the eldest son was strongly emphasized." [*A Nisei first daughter*]

"I was raised to follow the Japanese way; so I always felt it was the [first son's] responsibility and so I never thought about it [living with parents]. It was definitely thought that the eldest son is responsible for carrying on the family name and for taking care of the parents." [*A Nisei fourth son*]

Where the Nisei do express different views here is with regard to the different treatment the first son received. Some Nisei, among them first sons, feel that the first son suffered from even greater disciplinary control than his siblings; others, particularly junior sons, feel he was spoiled and favored by Issei parents. All express at least mild disapproval of this differential treatment, but the younger sons' disapproval is the strongest. Many of them, in particular the second sons, admit they still feel hostility toward the eldest brother who bullied them while receiving special treats and license. In the words of one Nisei second son: "The first-son thing was the worst disaster in family history. It creates many family problems, and I've seen too many brothers and sisters fighting over it. The Issei favored their first sons and even today still favor them. That favoritism is extremely bad."

To the Nisei, particularly younger sons who resented this "favoritism," their differential status as children exemplifies the impersonal, rigid rules of the Japanese family as followed by the Issei. The "Japanese way" they see their parents as attempting to instill in them—in some cases, so successfully that even today they cannot entirely free themselves of it—corresponds to the Issei model of Japanese filial relationships. It is, as we have seen, a model in which there are unambiguous rules one must follow unquestioningly, subordinating personal desires, feelings, and goals; one in which external forces beyond one's control may modify outcomes, but in which internal feelings may not. One man, when I asked him whether he had considered pursuing his own career rather than managing his parents' business, perfectly conveyed this conception of filial relations by replying, "Haven't you heard of *giri?*"

The "Japanese American" Present

Much as they still feel the tug of the past, the Nisei do not accept "Japanese rules" as appropriate for Japanese American filial relations. Rather, they have their own ideas about the correct relationships between parents and children. Like the Issei, the Nisei construe biological parenthood as transmitting biological substance or, in their own words, "blood" or "genes." Physical as well as mental and psychological characteristics are inherited from one's biological parents—although the Nisei, again like the Issei, are not in complete agreement as to which characteristics are inherited. In comparison to the Issei, the Nisei place more emphasis on environment in the shaping of a child's intelligence and character, but at the same time they believe temperament and certain tendencies, including a proclivity for mental illness or alcoholism, may be biologically transmitted. Furthermore, like the Issei, they view racial identity as transmitted through the blood and genes one receives from biological parents. What makes a person racially Japanese is substance rather than conduct. Hence, even the Sansei (third-generation Japanese Americans) whom the Nisei view as "very Americanized" and as exhibiting almost no "Japanese" social conduct and interactional styles, are considered fundamentally, and in essence, "Japanese." As one Nisei man put it, "They may not act Japanese, they may not speak Japanese, they may not even hang around other Japanese, but inside they are Japanese."

The Nisei, however, do not differentiate biological parenthood from jural parenthood the way the Issei do. For the Nisei, one's "real" parents are one's biological parents; it is they who should raise you and with whom you should live. In the event of adoption, the filial relationship is transferred to the adoptive parents, of course, but this is considered an exceptional situation by the Nisei. In their minds, parents should not give up their "own flesh and blood" but should raise all biological children in their own "family." Nisei say that they would give away a child for adoption only under the most dire circumstances ("if we were starving"), and only in the case of infertility would they adopt a child. Even then, they say, adoption is problematic because the child often has "identity problems." In accord with this emphasis on biological filiation, the Nisei construe their family line and ancestry as a series of biological filial links rather than of jural filial links.

While biological parenthood gives one a place in a "family" and so a social identity, it does not and should not transmit social status—in particular not one's social status as an adult. The Nisei believe each individual should achieve his own status in American society based on his individual achievements. Children can have a different "class" status than their parents and siblings, although the Nisei recognize that the resources parents offer children play a large part in determining that status. At the same time, the Nisei say the individual's achievements reflect on his parents and his siblings. It is not only that an individual's achievements manifest his family background in the sense of the treatment, discipline, moral training, and love he received from his parents; they also evince the genetic inheritance he received from them—an inheritance that he shares with his siblings and, to a lesser extent, his more genealogically distant relatives. Thus, in this sense, the achievements of individuals are interpreted as the expression of inherited family traits. Furthermore, in spite of their emphasis on individual achievement, the Nisei concede that biological filiation transmits social status insofar as it assigns you a racial identity from which you can never escape. In short, no matter how much you try to "act like a *hakujin*," and no matter how successful you may be at it, you will always be "Japanese" and treated as such. Thus, while individual achievement can drastically alter one's class status and even raise the class status of one's family, it can never alter one's racial identity—a fact that the Nisei say was an inescapable lesson of the World War II imprisonment.

Normative Components of the Filial Relationship

What the Nisei have to say about the contemporary norms governing filial relations is surprisingly clear when contrasted with what their parents say about those norms. It should be immediately apparent that the five components of filial relationships discussed below are former components of the Japanese successor son's relationship with his parents.[3]

Component 1: Representation of the family. Given the expectations of Issei parents and the social requirements of membership in the Japanese American community, the Nisei feel one member of each Nisei sibship should assume the position of family representative. This individual represents the family unit of siblings and their parents in certain kinship and community affairs, and takes the lead in decisions concerning parents or the entire family unit. As a kind of chairman of the sibling set, this individual bears the primary responsibility for managing the financial and legal affairs of elderly parents. When aging Issei parents need advice, when important decisions must be made or implemented, they should be able to turn to this child. Finally, upon the death of a parent, this child should take charge of funeral arrangements. He should receive the mortuary offerings (*koden*) and the record of contributors, and should reciprocate these payments on behalf of his parents and siblings (see Chapter 8 for further discussion of *koden* reciprocity).

[3] For an earlier analysis of the Nisei division of these components of the filial relationship, see Yanagisako 1975b. In the present discussion I have made a couple of revisions: the first component has been relabeled "representation of the family" rather than "leadership of the family"; and the explication of the gender constructs underlying the assignment of components to sons and daughters has been refined to include both the Issei's sociospatial gender domains and the Nisei's functional gender domains.

The Nisei say that, because of parental expectations, the eldest son is the best candidate for this position. An eldest son should assume these responsibilities unless circumstances make it impractical for him to do so. If the eldest son does not live in the Seattle area, the day-to-day local duties may be assumed by a younger brother, a sister, or a sister's husband. But, on important occasions such as a parent's death, an eldest son living as far away as the East Coast or Hawaii is expected to fly in to assume this role. Even if the task of reciprocating mortuary offerings is handed over to a sister or younger brother who lives in Seattle, the eldest brother should be the official receiver of *koden* at his parent's funeral.

Component 2: Financial responsibility for parents. One of the core values the Nisei say their parents transmitted to them is that of family self-sufficiency, which precludes any reliance on extra-familial financial aid. Although social security benefits are welcome, welfare or any form of "charity" is unacceptable as a source of economic support. A parent who must resort to financial help from "outside the family" is pitied and his or her children considered a disgrace to the community. As social security is inadequate to meet the material requirements of the Issei, if parents do not have some other means of support or savings, their children should provide the balance of money needed to maintain them at a comfortable standard of living. Children are not expected to support their parents at exactly the same standard of living they themselves enjoy, but any noticeably large discrepancy between the material comforts of Issei parents and their Nisei children occasions criticism in the community. It was "disgraceful," one of my Nisei informants declared, that the Issei mother of a successful Nisei physician had furniture that appeared to have come from a Goodwill store, while her son was taking trips to Europe.

All Nisei informants agree that sons should take responsibility for their parents' financial support. Daughters should neither have to ask their husbands for money nor seek employment to support their parents. "Work" (that is, earning an income) is, after all, men's responsibility. Only in exceptional situations is it considered appropriate for a daughter to support her parents. In the two cases where an informant's parents were being supported by a daughter, the daughters were widows who had acquired sizable amounts of money upon their husbands' death. As these daughters did not have to work to earn money, it was acceptable for them to support their parents. In both cases, moreover, the widowed daughters and their parents resided together and were considered one family unit.

The Nisei feel strongly that all sons should share the responsibility of providing for their parents. An exception is made, however, if one son has taken over his parents' business and acquired all or most of their wealth. In such a case, this son is expected to assume all the components of the Japanese successor role, including financial support of his parents. Otherwise, the Nisei expect each son to contribute an "equal share" or a "fair share" to parental support. What constitutes a fair share is ambiguous, however, and often there is disagreement and resentment between brothers as to the exact amount each should contribute. Some Nisei feel a man who has a significantly larger income than his brothers should contribute a proportionately greater amount of money. Others argue that all sons should contribute an equal amount regardless of the size of their incomes. There is no question, however, that it is the sons' responsibility to support parents, and not that of their sisters or sisters' husbands.

Component 3: Coresidence with parents. As we saw in Chapter 3, there is total unanimity among the Nisei that living with one's parents after marriage is an undesirable burden to be avoided if possible. Nisei who have lived in three-generation households after marriage describe them as tolerable, but undesirable, arrangements that intrude on personal "privacy" and "independence." "Two families," they say, cannot live together happily under one roof. Yet the Nisei also agree that some circumstances require coresidence with parents. If financial resources are inadequate to support parents in a separate household, if parents require physical care, or if they simply cannot manage living alone, then they must be taken into a child's home. Few Nisei are willing to send their elderly parents to a nursing home if they can provide them with adequate care at home. To send one's parents to an "institution" is "heartless" if you have the resources to care for them in your home, especially as nursing homes are managed by *hakujin* and parents would feel uncomfortable surrounded by people who do not understand them.

If a Nisei sibling set has an unmarried member, he or she is considered the best candidate for coresidence with parents. Such a residential unit, the Nisei reason, can be a comfortable arrangement as it does not interfere with a conjugal relationship. If all children are married, the Nisei say it is better for the parents to live with daughters rather than sons. The closer emotional bond between mother and daughter makes it easier for them to get along on a daily basis. Having been brought up in her mother's household, a daughter already understands her temperament, housekeeping styles, and kitchen practices. And, as women "stay at home more" and "run the household," the relationship between the two women is considered more critical than the relationship between the two men. According to the Nisei, a household can survive a distant relationship between an Issei father and his son-in-law, but friction between an Issei mother and her daughter-in-law will make life miserable for everyone. Men are viewed as less likely to openly express their hostility, and tension between father-in-law and son-in-law is considered less likely to erupt into open conflict. Moreover, the Nisei point out, it is generally widowed Issei mothers who have to be taken into a married child's home. Because of the large age difference (averaging ten years) between Issei husbands and wives and the longer life spans of women, there are few Issei husbands who do not have a younger and still physically fit wife to care for them. Hence, it is the Issei woman who is left alone in old age to be taken into a child's household, and it is her relationship with the married couple that must be considered.

The Nisei feel that the burden of coresidence with parents should be shared equally by all married daughters. Accordingly, Issei are often sent to live with one daughter for a year or two and then transferred to a second daughter's household. The Nisei recognize that this practice has serious drawbacks—especially in the case of senile or disabled Issei—as it is often detrimental to their physical and mental state. Consequently, one daughter often ends up bearing the primary burden of coresidence. This inequity generates resentments among sisters, as does the parallel problem of equal division of financial responsibility among brothers.

Component 4: Personal care of parents. Parents who may not require placement in a child's household may still have other physical and emotional needs that their children are expected to meet. Taking care of parents in the event of prolonged illness or any physical condition requiring attention is considered more appropriate for daughters than for sons. Nisei agree that "women seem to be made to care for people" because of their nurturant, mothering capacities. It is also more "practical" for women to care for parents as men are "busy working." As in the case of coresidence, a daughter rather than a daughter-in-law is preferred to fulfill personal care functions because parents are emotionally closer to their daughters than to their sons' wives. Again, daughters should share equally in helping their parents, dropping in on them to see if their needs have been met. One daughter, however, often does more than her sisters, who explain the inequity as due to "practical" considerations: they work full-time while their sister does not, they live farther away from the parent than their sister, or they have young children to reckon with while their sister's children are grown-up, so that she has more "free time."

Component 5: Inheritance. Where the eldest son has taken over his parents' business and assumed all the duties of the successor, including co-residence with parents and financial responsibility for them, the Nisei accept his right to all or a major portion of his parents' wealth. If he has taken on all responsibilities of the Japanese successor, he deserves to inherit all his parents' property and assets. In such a case, inheritance is construed by the Nisei as an accompaniment to the status of successor. Few eldest sons, however, are such open-and-shut cases. The great majority have fulfilled some of the successor's duties, but not enough for their siblings to grant them legitimate claim to their parents' entire inheritance or even the greater part of it. Where there is no succession by the eldest son, both eldest sons and their younger siblings feel the inheritance should be distributed equally among all the children. In contrast to their parents, the Nisei do not express any indecision or ambivalence as to the proper way to handle inheritance. Just as all children (according to their appropriate sex roles) should share the burden of taking care of their parents, so they should all share in any of their deceased parents' remaining wealth.

Even when they complain about siblings who did not contribute their fair share, the Nisei discuss coresidence and responsibilities for personal care with little emotionality. Not so, however, when they discuss inheritance. Some assert that the unequal distribution of parental wealth has been the greatest source of familial conflict in the Japanese American community. Complaints are most often—and most strongly—expressed by men whose eldest brothers were willed or simply took possession of all or most of their deceased parents' property. A typical account of an inheritance dispute among Nisei siblings was given by a Nisei fifth (and youngest) son. When his father died leaving no will, the eldest brother took control of all assets, including the family home and several pieces of land, without consulting any of his siblings. The eldest brother had not lived with his parents after marriage and his siblings felt they had worked just as hard for many years to help their parents financially. "We always felt it was an injustice," the fifth son explained, "but we said let's not cause a disgrace by squawking. The Issei never said anything [about conflicts within the family] and so the Nisei don't talk much either. The children said to each other, let him have it, it's not important. But there was ill feeling." The ill feeling, which this infor-

mant and his siblings kept from being known "outside the family" so as
to avoid *haji* (disgrace), continues to this day to divide the sibling group
(in this case a rather large sibship of ten children) into those who speak
to their eldest brother and those who do not. Generalizing from his
own family and from conflicts over inheritance in other Japanese
American families, this informant—who is one of the siblings who still
refuses to speak to his eldest brother—commented:

"Human nature being what it is, in most cases the eldest son takes all the family
assets but leaves the responsibility to others. . . . Human nature being what it
is, the first son, who could share it, keeps it all. . . . I've seen cases where the
injustices [in inheritance] are so apparent, it's amazing that the [Nisei] children
don't go to court. Because people don't want to bring it out in public they let the
older brother take it all, but the family feeling is destroyed."

The only way to avoid conflict and the destruction of "the family feeling," and the only "fair" decision, according to the Nisei, is for parents
to divide all their wealth and personal belongings equally among all
children.

Core Constructs and Situations

Nisei discussions of the claims and obligations linking parents and
adult children reveal that they have teased apart and distributed
among members of the sibling group the bundle of rights and duties
that their parents at least initially attached to the successor son (Yanagisako 1975b). Underlying these norms for filial relationships are several core constructs.

First, the division of components of the successor role and their assignment to sons or daughters employs both Issei and Nisei *gender constructs* (see Chapter 4). In matters linking their parents to the community, the Nisei have accepted the Issei's assignment of family leadership
to the eldest son. *Koden* reciprocity, funeral arrangements, and financial and legal affairs all involve relationships between parents and people or institutions outside the family. Primarily because of Issei expectations, the first son is conceived to be the best candidate to lead the
family unit of parents and siblings in these kinds of affairs. The assignment of financial responsibility for parents to sons rather than daughters, on the other hand, is congruent with both Issei and Nisei gender
constructs, since it requires going "outside" the family to "work." Likewise, the assignment of personal care and coresidence responsibilities
to daughters speaks of women's symbolic placement "inside" the
home—their fulfillment of and suitability for housekeeping and nur-

turant functions. Hence, the Nisei's division of the successor role is congruent with both Issei sociospatial gender domains and Nisei functional gender domains.

Second, what the Nisei say about filial relationships, and indeed all family relationships, evinces a concept of *family love*. To the Nisei a strong family is unified by love and the expression of love rather than merely by rules and obligations. For this reason, they say, they try to openly demonstrate their affection for their children, as difficult as it is to overcome their "Japanese" inhibitions. Furthermore, they emphasize the affective basis of cooperation within the family and of actions toward family members rather than the "duty" their parents stressed. At the same time, the Nisei tend to interpret the actions of family members toward each other as the expression of "feelings" as well as of obedience and loyalty.

Third, and closely linked with the construct of the family, is a belief in *sibling equality*. When the Nisei assert that sisters should share equally the burden of taking needy parents into their homes and that brothers should contribute an equal or "fair" share to the support of their parents, they are speaking of a general commitment to the absence of differential treatment, hierarchy, or any form of inequality among siblings. Although they may disagree, in any particular case, over what exactly constitutes "equality" in the distribution of responsibility and claims among siblings, all of them—older and younger siblings, brothers and sisters—say they are committed to the equality of siblings. Siblings are, in the minds of the Nisei, inherently equal human beings, and any attempt to undermine this equality leads to dissension and the destruction of the family. For in the family there is one, and only one, legitimate vertical relationship and that is the one between parents and children. Parental love must therefore be distributed equally among all children regardless of birth order or gender. Not only parental affection and attention, but any commodity that passes from parents to children must be equally distributed. A parent who has willed all his or her wealth, however paltry, to one child is a parent who did not love all the children equally. Those Nisei who received smaller shares or no shares of parental wealth thus feel unloved and rejected by their parents. The brother who appropriates more than his equal share of parental property symbolically hoards his parents' love and denies it to his siblings. Having destroyed by his greed the very substance of family unity, little wonder that he is ostracized by his siblings.

The "natural" and the "practical." Except with regard to the distribution of inheritance, the normative expectations the Nisei apply to contemporary filial relations generally are not phrased as rules or prescriptions. Although they sometimes say brothers "should" provide for their parents and that an eldest brother "should" arrange for his parents' funerals, they often qualify these statements by saying there is no "rule" that requires it to be this way; it is just "better" than other options. Other expectations—particularly those attached to daughters—are phrased not as rules or prescriptions but as the outcomes of people's inherent tendencies or attributes. Nisei informants rarely assert that daughters "should" or "must" take parents into their homes; and they never claim there is a "rule" that daughters assume the responsibility of personal care for parents. Instead, they phrase their expectations in terms of the inherent attributes and inclinations of women and the nature of people's circumstances.

"It always falls on the girls in the family to take care of the parents; it ends up when parents are old that they live with daughters—probably because women seem to be made to care for people. The parents don't want to have daughter-in-law take care of them." [*A Nisei man*]

"We [siblings] feel that it's better for our mother to live with our oldest sister [the only sister who lives in Seattle] because there would be least friction between a mother and daughter. She [oldest sister] agrees that that's the best alternative." [*A Nisei man*]

"My wife didn't want to live with my parents, and I felt it was natural that she didn't want to live with my mother. She wanted to run her own house. And anyway girls are closer to their own mother." [*A Nisei man*]

"It seems to work out better for parents to live with a daughter. Most of the time the husband is gone working and if they [parents] are home with the daughter-in-law all the time it's tough." [*A Nisei woman whose father lived with her and her husband for several years*]

Likewise, when Nisei spoke of their preference for living in nuclear-family households, they explained it was "better" and "more comfortable" given a couple's desire for privacy and independence.

References to "human nature," people's "natural" wants, and the "natural" inclinations of men and women are common in Nisei interpretive remarks about filial relationships and relationships in general. For example, several said that "it is only natural for married couples to live by themselves." What they mean by "human nature" and what is "natural" is, however, not entirely clear. In the case of gender constructs, for example, there is ambiguity as to whether women's "natural" inclinations to care for people are biologically given, culturally constructed, or a combination of both. To some extent Nisei belief in the natural basis of gender attributes and tendencies derives from their observation that these are not limited to Japanese or American culture. As one informant stated, "It's not just Japanese who feel this way [that women are better at nurturing and taking care of people]. *Hakujin* feel the same way." Generalizing from a sample of two cultures, the Nisei seem to have concluded that these gender attributes, if they are pan-cultural, must therefore be "natural." Yet, at the same time, most Nisei do not claim these things are biologically determined. When asked what they mean by "natural" they answer, "It's just normal," "People are just like that," or "It's understandable that people feel that way." A couple of informants made clear they did not mean that these tendencies and attributes of men and women were "inherited"; it could have been otherwise, but given how people were raised, that was how they felt.

What is most salient in the Nisei's usage of the terms "natural" and "human nature" is not a symbolic opposition between biology and culture, but rather a more loosely construed set of oppositions between what, given people's common experience, is understandable, and what requires explanation; what people do because of internal feelings and inclinations, and what they do because of external prescriptions; what is statistically frequent, and what is not. If there is any lack of specificity in the Nisei's concept of nature, there is no lack of clarity in its normative implications. What is natural is what is expected of people, and to do otherwise is to call attention to the idiosyncratic, uncommon feelings and motives behind one's actions as opposed to the shared and therefore culturally legitimate reasons for action. And that, the Nisei know, is an open invitation to public scrutiny and criticism.

People's actions, however, cannot be read as direct expressions of their feelings and inclinations. Circumstance and what they consider "practical" play an important part in the Nisei's interpretation of filial relationships. Which daughter takes elderly parents into her home depends on "practical" factors such as space, people's schedules, and resources. One Nisei married woman explained that her parents came to live with her rather than one of her siblings because she does not work (whereas her older brother and his wife are very busy with their business), and because she knows how to drive (whereas her older sister does not) and so can chauffeur her parents. Another woman took her parents into her home because she had a larger house than any of her sisters. A second son became the main financial adviser to his parents because he was an accountant, while his older brother had no expert knowledge of finances.

The Nisei's interpretive model of their relations with parents is one

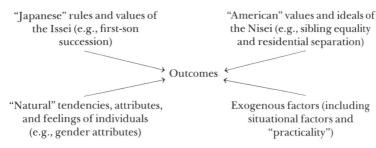

Fig. 7. Nisei model of Japanese American filial relations

in which an amalgam of elements combine to produce outcomes. There are the "Japanese" rules and expectations of the Issei, which still influence Nisei behavior, but there are also such "American" ideals and values of the Nisei as sibling equality and individual freedom, which often conflict with them. There are the "natural" feelings and tendencies of people, including gender attributes, and there are exogenous circumstances and "practicality." People's actions are therefore negotiated compromises between the two cultures, between Issei and Nisei, between what is given in people and what they confront outside themselves.

Moreover, the Nisei model (Figure 7) is one in which no fixed hierarchy of elements prevails. Instead, individuals must decide in each *situation* which actions are best given the universe of considerations. In some contexts, the Nisei feel the "Japanese" expectations of the Issei should be deferred to if circumstances permit and if they do not tread too heavily upon one's own beliefs and feelings. So at funerals or an Issei wedding anniversary it is appropriate for the eldest son to represent the sibling group, because it is a "Japanese" context of importance to the Issei. In other situations, such as decisions about coresidence, the Issei's expectations must be overriden by Nisei desires for an independent family life or because of the "naturally closer" bond of mothers and daughters. In yet other situations, "practical" considerations may override all others.

GENERATIONAL DIFFERENCES IN INTERPRETATION

As we have seen, the Issei and Nisei share the same conception of "Japanese" filial relations. But they disagree on when relations of this type existed. The Issei allege that their own relations with parents and very young Nisei children were the last. If there is some fuzziness

among all concerned as to when "Japanese" filial relations ended and
"American" ones began, to the Issei there is at least no doubt that the
fuzziness does not extend to the present or even the recent past. The
Nisei, however, do not portray the Issei as so readily acceding to the
"American way"; rather, they represent them as continuing advocates
of a "Japanese system." Furthermore, while the Issei concede the "old
rules" are no longer socially appropriate, many Nisei also consider
them inherently flawed and contrary to "human nature."

The Issei and Nisei, however, do not share the same conception of
contemporary Japanese American filial relations. The American present in which the Issei place their relations with Nisei children is one in
which no rules exist to direct people's actions, and in which outcomes
are made unpredictable by the disorderly array of competing feelings
and interests experienced by individuals. Not only is it impossible to
count on any pattern of action from one's children, but there are also
(as in the case of inheritance) no rules to direct one's own decisions and
actions toward them. The best stance in such an unpredictable social
world, therefore, is to stay healthy, entertain minimal expectations, and
trust in God or accept one's fate. The Nisei, in contrast, articulate a specific set of norms for the distribution of filial obligations and claims. In
spite of the absence of rules like those governing "Japanese" relations,
for the Nisei contemporary filial relations have a normative order that
can be articulated through constructs such as gender, love, equality,
and duty.

Why do only the Nisei articulate a set of norms guiding filial obligations and claims in the present? If the Nisei can find normative order
in their relations with parents, why can their parents not do the same
of their relations with children? Do the differences between the normative statements of the Issei and Nisei mean that they do not share a
system of symbols and meanings pertaining to filial relations? If so,
how can they participate in such relations?

It can hardly be that the Issei's rule-focused account of their relations
with parents and their rule-free account of their relations with children
is an accurate description of the predictability of the former and the
unpredictability of the latter. For such a conclusion rests on the assumption that the Issei's relationships with parents were as tightly
bound by prescriptions as their interpretation implies. The Issei filial
histories reviewed in Chapter 5 disclose too many incumbent successors who did not inherit parental property or succeed to the headship
of the parental household, too many nonsuccessor sons who did, and
too many cases where components of the successor role were divided

among siblings. Nor can it simply be that the Issei's account of contemporary filial relations reflects accurately the fact that the goals and strategies of individuals now shape outcomes, whereas in the past outcomes were determined by rules and forces that overrode individual motives. The actions of the Issei, their parents, and their siblings demonstrate their continual reassessment of filial relationships—reassessments that generated significant alterations in the relations among people on both sides of the Pacific. Admittedly, the histories of the Issei's relations with their parents and their rule-focused accounts of these histories might be said to illustrate the truism that all human relations deviate to some extent from rules and normative expectations without necessarily subverting them. But this truism does not explain why the Issei can so readily make normative sense of their filial relationships with parents while making so little normative sense of their filial relationships with children.

The Issei's failure to articulate a new normative order in filial relations might be attributed to the truth of their claim that there are no "rules" governing the relationships of parents and their adult children in the United States. The Issei may be speaking of the fact that Nisei normative expectations are often not phrased as rules, but rather as natural outcomes of the feelings of individuals and the practical constraints of their situations. But both the Issei's rule-focused accounts and the Nisei's expectations are normative. Consequently, it is only the difference in their mode of discourse that gives Issei actions the appearance of being generated primarily by forces that exist outside people and Nisei actions the appearance of being governed by forces that exist inside them.

There are other reasons why this variance in the way in which norms are expressed cannot be used to explain why the Issei keep silent about the Nisei's new norms. For one, it casts the Issei as a generation of immigrants so wedded to a "traditional" system of rules that the norms their children have constructed—norms that are not phrased in the form of rules—appear to be just so many fragmented feelings lacking structure and culturally rooted meaning. Such an explanation rests on the rather dubious depiction of the Issei as cultural creatures so reliant on explicit rules that they are incapable of recognizing more subtle guidelines for behavior—a portrayal rather incongruent with extant descriptions of Japanese cultural styles. Moreover, to attribute the Issei's failure to recognize Nisei norms to the way in which the Nisei express themselves would be to wrongly assume that because the "Japanese" normative system is expressed predominantly through specific, unambiguous rules, and because the Nisei's normative system is expressed predominantly through vaguer constructs, the Issei are incapable of recognizing the normative implications of anything other than rules. This could not be the case, however, for the Issei are also guided by normative constructs—for example, the sociospatial gender constructs of "inside" and "outside" (see Chapter 4). And some Nisei norms—for example, equal inheritance of siblings—are expressed as explicit rules for behavior.

Finally, such an explanation implies the Issei are unaware of the norms the Nisei articulate for filial relationships. Yet this cannot be the case. That the Issei understand these norms and the cultural constructs behind them is evident from their denials about their present and past expectations of their children. The actions of the Issei described in Chapter 5 leave little doubt that they expected, at least before the war, to reproduce in their families the differentiated filial relations that are the basis of the stem family. The Issei's denials that they held such expectations, except perhaps in their very first years in the United States, and their adamant refutation of any suggestions that they treated their sons differently, are strong evidence that they know about the Nisei's condemnation of such practices. They recognize the Nisei tendency to interpret the actions of family members as expressions of "love" and the Nisei equation of the differential treatment of children with the differential distribution of parental love. Hence, they realize that to admit to "Japanese" practices would be, in the eyes of the Nisei, to admit they had not loved all their children equally.

AMBIGUITY AS STRATEGY IN THE NORMATIVE DIALOGUE

If, as I contend, the Issei are more cognizant of Nisei norms and constructs of filial relations than their statements about the disorder of contemporary filial relations imply, this suggests the need for a rather different analysis than the ones we have been considering. That analysis, which is the one I propose here, treats the disparate accounts of the two generations as elements in a continuing dialogue of negotiation between them. When the Issei say there are no longer any "rules" governing filial relations and that they have no specific expectations of their children, they are speaking both *about* their children and themselves and *to* their children. Likewise, when the Nisei locate the order in people's actions not in rigid prescriptions, but in situational configurations of gender, equality, love, and the family, they are speaking *about* themselves and their parents and *to* their parents. Both are participating in a normative dialogue—a dialogue that does more than interpret action, but that is itself an integral part of the negotiation of action. It is within the context of this ongoing dialogue, moreover, that we must place the Issei's rule-focused accounts of "Japanese" filial relations. For there is a crucial difference between the Issei's relationships with their parents and their relationships with their children, namely, that while their parents are dead, their children are alive. Put another way, the Issei are no longer engaged in a negotiation with their parents, but they are most certainly engaged in one with their children. Any normative dialogue they had with their parents will likely remain unknown to us, for it is too problematic a task to reconstruct a dialogue by listening to a monologue—a monologue delivered self-consciously to an audience peopled by the Issei's children and grandchildren. If, as I submit, normative statements and accounts of expectations are elements in a dialogue of negotiation, then the Issei's "just-so" accounts of relationships they had with parents must be seen as further elements in a continuing dialogue with their children. The Issei, after all, no longer have any stake in the ambiguities of the past, but rather a living concern with the ambiguities of the present.

This is not to say the Issei have invented the "rules" of Japanese filial relationships for use in negotiations with their children. To the contrary, it seems clear that the Issei learned these rules in Japan—specifically from the standardized lessons in ethics and the Japanese family system they learned in the national public school system (Dore 1958). Yet, if the ideology of household and nation taught to the Issei explains how they acquired such a rule-focused model of filial relations, it does not help us understand why they continue to describe in these terms a set of relations, namely those with their own parents, that never conformed to those rules. Nor does it help us understand why the Issei do not acknowledge and, indeed, reify into "rules" their children's norms for organizing filial relations.

The Issei failure in this respect, and their portrayal of a disorderly social universe of parents and children, stem not from confusion and indecision about what is good, correct, and desired by them, nor from inability to comprehend the norms of the Nisei. Rather, they stem from what I propose to call an Issei strategy of ambiguation in the negotiation of their filial relationships. At the same time that they comprehend Nisei notions about filial relations and their norms for distributing responsibility for parents among the sibling group, the Issei have their own preference. That preference is to have one child, often an eldest son but sometimes an eldest daughter or other child, assume all components of the successor role. This desire is not something the Issei openly express; indeed, as we have seen, it is something they deny. But, if they deny it of themselves, they do not hesitate to attribute to other Issei the hope for such a "Japanese" outcome.

The Issei prefer succession by one child for several reasons. For one, they recognize that the division of filial responsibility entails an inherent disadvantage for a parent. And they know this from experience. As was shown in the previous chapter, after the war the Issei entered into an assortment of economic and residential arrangements with a succession of children. They lived with married second sons and daughters as well as with first sons, operated businesses with some children, and pooled their earnings with others. Through their experimentation with varying alternatives to first-son succession, they came to recognize the inherent instability and hence the insecurity for parents of such arrangements. A married daughter who lived with her parents one year might go to live with her husband's parents the next year; the same was true of a married son. The postwar residential histories of Nisei couples show that this indeed was a common occurrence. The sharing of filial responsibility among siblings also entails negotiation among siblings. Although parents may be consulted as to their wishes, there is no assurance that their children's negotiations will yield results satisfactory to the parents. Of course, despite the clarity of normative expectations in the case of succession by one child, parents would still have to negotiate their claims on that child in any specific instance. But with the division of filial responsibility parents often became the objects of the negotiation rather than one of its participants. If today the Issei prefer the undivided commitment of one child, it is partly because their experience has taught them that a single, primary commitment by one child can be better controlled by parents than the divided commitments of several.

But more important—and more problematic—is the fact that the division of filial responsibilities is accompanied by considerable ambiguity as to which Issei parents a Nisei couple is succeeding and, therefore, as to whose social identity the couple is perpetuating. Not that the Issei today have any desire to reproduce stem-family households that can be traced to distant ancestral pasts. For (as I said in Note 1, above) the Issei lay no claim to such family histories. Neither do they desire a successor who will continue their business enterprises or even one who will live with them. What they hope for is an unequivocal successor who is recognized as perpetuating their social identity in the Japanese American community. Such a successor, while he may have an entirely different occupation and reside in a different part of town from his parents, not only represents them in important business and social affairs but extends their participation in community activities and organizations into the future. In so doing, he establishes for them a continuing place in the community and, by extension, the United States.

That the Issei would rely on their children for the establishment of such a claim to a place in American society is understandable, particularly in light of their marginal status in a country that denied them citizenship for so many years. That they would be averse to the Nisei's division of the responsibilities and claims of the successor also must be traced to their own histories rather than to any alleged Japanese tradition. For many of the Issei, the demise of their natal household in their natal community in Japan was preceded by just such an ambiguous division of elements of the successor role among siblings. As the filial histories of successors in Chapter 5 revealed, most successors who emigrated from Japan to fulfill their financial duties, leaving their siblings to fulfill other components of their role, eventually had no household to which to return, and hence no place in their natal community. Even those who had not seen the end of their own natal household in Japan had seen households disappear from communities through the migration of its children. For the Issei, those households generated not only offspring without filial pasts in new communities, but parents without filial futures and, therefore, without a continuing social identity and place in the community. Division, whether of duties, rights, or inheritance, symbolizes for the Issei a social demise they have already had to bear in one community and one country.

At the same time that they strongly prefer succession by one child, the Issei are acutely aware that the Nisei are strongly committed to the division of the successor's responsibilities and claims. Indeed, in this continuing dialogue what the Nisei are committed to is readily comprehensible because it is directly expressed. If what the Issei say is more opaque, it is because today they are in a weaker position to negotiate with their children, whose voices dominate in the normative dialogue. Hence, if the Issei speak vaguely about the claims and obligations of parents and children, it is because they realize that to communicate openly their hope for the assumption of the successor role by one child is to risk alienating their children and creating dissension within the sibling group.

Although they recognize the dangers of betraying their desires by speaking openly about them, the Issei are unwilling to echo their children's normative reorganization of filial relationships because to do so would be to legitimize it. They are engaged in a dialogue with their children in which their statements about the absence of rules and priorities are elements in a strategy of passive resistance to a normative order that they still hope to subvert. Their classification of present relationships with their children, like their classification of Nisei marriage as "American," is a thinly veiled accusation that their children have failed to follow "Japanese tradition." The Nisei classification of both their marriages and their filial relationships as "Japanese American" is a rejoinder.

Although I have argued that their refusal to articulate the Nisei's norms is a conscious strategy of resistance, this ambiguation has another consequence—one rather favorable for the Issei—of which they may be less aware. That is, by denying any specific expectations and desires for the assumption of filial responsibility by their children, the Issei strengthen their claims rather than weaken them. For, as we saw earlier, their children equate the nonverbalization of desires and the demonstration of self-reliance with "Japaneseness." Thus, the denial of expectations by parents casts filial relations into the domain of "Japanese" relationships—a domain in which both Issei and Nisei agree that rules prescribe the priority of duty over individual feelings and wishes. Were they to openly voice their hopes, the Issei would risk not only alienating their children, but transforming a "Japanese" dialogue into an "American" one, for it is considered "American" to display one's feelings at the risk of conflict. Once the dialogue has been transformed into an "American" one, "American" values and norms would likely prevail. By the very form of their dialogue with the Nisei, therefore, the Issei communicate the "Japanese" expectations that they verbally deny.

Inheritance is a central issue in the normative dialogue between Issei and Nisei because it is a key symbol of filial transmission. For the Issei, inheritance is the central component of the complex of rights and duties that make up the successor's role. It is, in a sense, the distinctive feature of succession. So when the Issei recount the succession histories of their natal households, the person who eventually inherited parental property and transmitted it in turn to his or her children is the person whom they identify as the successor. But inheritance is a problem because for the two generations it is at once a symbol for the same thing and for different things. On the one hand, both Issei and Nisei construe inheritance as symbolizing whatever it is that parents transmit to children. For both, as I have explained, parenthood is more than biological and true parents transmit to their children more than genetic material, physical traits, and personality dispositions. On the other hand, the Issei and Nisei have different notions of what the more-than-biological content that parents transmit to children should be. For the Issei, the stuff of which families are made and that parents should transmit to children is a social identity and claim to a legitimate place in a community. The community can be in Japan or the United States and the social identity flows not only from parents to children but from children to parents as well. The desire to maintain such a claim to a rightful place in their natal community in Japan motivated the Issei attempts to buttress their claims to succession that were described in the previous chapter.[4] Today, however, the vast majority of the Issei no longer have such a claim to a place in a community in Japan; thus, as I have argued, only their children can provide them such a legitimate claim to a place in the United States. For the Nisei, however, the stuff of which families are made and which is necessary for fashioning emotionally complete individuals is the filial love parents transmit to children who then return it to them.

An appreciation of the symbolic power of inheritance in both Issei and Nisei conceptions of the filial relationship renders the dilemma of wills more understandable. I have already described the emotionality of the Nisei's statements about wills and inheritance. The Issei indecision as to the devolution of property and belongings, however small, and the intestate deaths of many Issei now are more comprehensible given that wills have one unavoidable feature: namely, that they are read by survivors as unambiguous statements of the deceased's conception of his relationships with other people. One cannot consider ambiguous the meaning of a will that gives everything to one child. Yet, at the same time, the Issei are caught between two different systems of meanings. For the equal division of inheritance, which symbolizes the equal and just division of parental love for the Nisei, symbolizes the division and demise of a social identity to the Issei. To leave everything to one child, therefore, is to leave your other children only a legacy of resentment. On the other hand, equal division would be a statement of one's lack of a successor and so the end of one's social identity—an end that most Issei cannot bring themselves to canonize in their last testament to family and community.

The normative dialogue about inheritance, like the broader dialogue about filial relations that it encapsulates, appears to be an argu-

[4] It is not that a nonsuccessor son or daughter could not return to the natal community and establish a household and a respectable social identity there. Indeed, that was the goal of many nonsuccessor Issei. But the symbolic security of this possibility was nowhere near as reassuring as that of returning as the successor of an already established household, with a recognized place and social history in the community.

ment over the rules for distributing what parents transmit to children. But, at a deeper level, it is an argument over the *content* of what should be transmitted from parents to children and from children to parents. To put it another way, the argument over two different systems of meanings about parenthood and filiation is being conducted through a shared system of symbols and meanings in which norms for the distribution of inheritance and filial duties are symbols for the content of filial transmissions and, by extension, the entire relationship. The Issei-Nisei dialogue about the content of filial transmission goes on between the lines of a dialogue about how it should be distributed.

PART THREE

SIBLINGHOOD AND KINSHIP

*The strength and extension of kinship ties in the Seattle Japanese American com-
munity is of just the sort that invites attention from researchers who argue for the
continued importance of "extended families" in industrial-capitalist society. In
the past two decades a good many such researchers have contested the Parsons-
Redfield-Durkheim model of the evolution of the family in modern society. In particular, they have contended that industrialization and urbanization have not
weakened what they call "extended kin networks" or "extended families" in all
sectors of these societies. But although these researchers have provided a necessary corrective to the excessively ambitious hypothesis that with so-called modernization all kinship relations and groups outside the conjugal family decline, they
have more often than not exacerbated the confusion by using the same murky
terms, such as "extended family," in discussing kinship relations. Precisely how
the families of so many ethnic groups in the United States and other advanced
industrial-capitalist societies are "extended" usually remains unspecified, but the
extensions are assumed to follow "traditional" family patterns.*

*In this section my analysis reveals that, far from replicating a "Japanese family
tradition," the inclusiveness of Japanese American families and the extension of
Japanese American kin networks are transformations of the past. I begin with the
culturally unelaborated sibling relationship in order to display aspects of change
that have been overlooked. Just as the sibling relationship is a boundary issue in
the perpetuation of stem families, so it is a boundary issue in the creation of independent conjugal families. Consequently, in the movement from one family system to another, conceptions of siblinghood have been transformed. An important
aspect of this transformation has been the change in people's notions of the place
siblings occupy over time in the kinship universe. The expected movement of sib-*

lings over the life cycle in relation to the Issei categories of kazoku *and* shinrui, *which is described in Chapter 7, differs from the expected movement of siblings over the life cycle in relation to the corresponding Nisei categories of "family" and "relatives," which is discussed in Chapter 8. Underlying these different expectations are different concepts of the family.*

Issei Siblings, *Kazoku*, and *Shinrui*

THAT DISCUSSIONS of Japanese American families have paid scant attention to sibling relationships is understandable in light of two facts. First, in both a stem-family and a conjugal family system, the sibling relationship is the structural basis for neither the formation of families nor their continuation. Hence, in studying change from stem families to conjugal families, inattention to the relationship seems justified. Second, in neither Japanese kinship nor American kinship nor Japanese American kinship is the sibling relationship as culturally elaborated as the conjugal and filial relationships. That is, people have much less to say about siblings than they do about parents, children, and spouses.

These facts, however, do not justify the prevailing inattention to sibling relationships.[1] Even when a relationship does not provide the basis for the formation or perpetuation of identifiable kinship units and is not culturally elaborated, it may be of considerable importance in shaping the dynamics of those units. Indeed, my argument in this chapter and the next is that change in the sibling relationship among Japanese Americans has been central to alterations in the boundaries of households and families and their articulation with other kinship relationships. In this chapter, I lay the ground for that argument by outlining the history of Issei sibling relations and Issei conceptions of those relations. In order to understand Issei conceptions of siblinghood, however, it is necessary to push beyond the confines of that relationship itself and locate it within a larger system of relations. I therefore go on to

[1] See, for example, Kitano 1976, Miyamoto 1939, Bloom 1943, Bloom 1947, Broom and Kitsuse [1956] 1973, and Johnson 1973.

explicate the categories through which the Issei organize their kinship universe and the place of siblings within it.

ISSEI SIBLINGS

The Japanese adage "The sibling is the beginning of the stranger" (Nakane 1967, 7) appears an incisive summation of an observable social fact. That fact, in turn, seems consistent with a household system in which the basic units of production, consumption, and residence are perpetuated through single, exclusive vertical links of filiation at the expense of horizontal links of siblinghood. Not only does utrolateral household succession and inheritance necessarily separate the one sibling who remains in the natal household from those who leave it, but the latter also are separated by their incorporation into different households or their formation of new ones.

Yet, as we saw in Chapter 5, Issei men who were designated successors at the time they married might remain linked with siblings in Japan long after immigration had physically separated them. Indeed, the siblings of Issei successors played a critical role in the ambiguities surrounding succession claims and in the eventual resolution of those ambiguities. Whether they eventually succeeded to the headship of the household and transmitted it to a child or not, eight of the twelve designated successors had some kind of postmarital financial and residential arrangement with a sibling or siblings in Japan.[2] In four of these cases, a younger brother or sister of the Issei successor had continued to live with their parents after marriage (see, for example, the first three case histories in Chapter 5) and thus had shared in the benefits of the financial contributions sent by the Issei. In three more cases, the siblings in Japan were widowed sisters who had returned to the parental home with the permission of their brother in Seattle. One of these cases—that of Denkichi Adachi and his sister, her children, and grandchildren—was also described in Chapter 5. Another Issei invited two of his widowed sisters to return to the natal home and sent his eldest two children to live with them. This Issei also contributed substantially to the support of his sisters, in this instance through the money he sent for the living expenses and care of his children. Although the Issei's eldest son inherited the home, his surviving aunt and her stepson's son continue to live in it rent-free. The third Issei successor, whose widowed

[2] Of the four designated successors who did not, one was a *yōshi* whose siblings had no stake in the household into which he had been incorporated upon marriage. The other three had no siblings who remained in or returned to the parental household in Japan.

sister returned to the family home, signed the property over to her after their parents' death. In the final case, that of Shoji Yokoi (see Chapter 5), the Issei successor's relations with his siblings were complicated by his adoption by his older half brother. Although for four years after he married, Shoji lived with this half brother and worked in his hotel business, he was later replaced as successor by his younger sister and her husband. As a result of this temporary business partnership with his half brother, Shoji was able to acquire sufficient capital to open his own business.

Just as the presence of financial and residential transactions linking Issei successors with siblings in Japan manifests the successors' commitment to and claims on parental households there, so their relative absence in the case of Issei nonsuccessors manifests the weakness of any such ties. Once they emigrated, the twelve nonsuccessor Issei men's transactions with siblings in Japan were limited to letter writing, the exchange of small gifts, and, on rare occasion, some financial aid. No doubt their siblings, as long as they lived in the parental home in Japan, benefited from the remittances these nonsuccessors sent to parents. But, as I have said, their contributions were less substantial and more occasional than those sent by Issei successors. None of the Issei nonsuccessors made regular financial contributions, either directly or indirectly, to siblings of the sort that Issei successors made to siblings living in the parental home. After World War II, when the Issei's siblings and their families in Japan were experiencing the deprivations shared by much of the Japanese population, many Issei—successor and nonsuccessor alike—sent goods and money to them. But again these were short-term (and often one-time) donations.

Issei women by and large kept in close written communication with their siblings in Japan, particularly their sisters. Indeed, women tended more than men to follow consistently the lives of their siblings and their children through the exchange of letters and, when they could afford them, small gifts. They also sent money and goods to needy siblings after World War II. But as women who had married out of their parental households, they, like nonsuccessor men, had little claim on those households and hence no significant economic or residential involvement with them after marriage. Before they had married, three of the twenty-four Issei women in the marriage sample had made substantial financial contributions to their parents and siblings in Japan. All three were the eldest children in sibships where there were no males (in one sibship because of the early death of the eldest brother) old enough to earn money for the household at the time the

Issei women reached young adulthood. Hence, in each case the Issei woman worked before marriage for several years to help support siblings as well as parents. After their marriages, however, none of these women had any greater involvement with siblings in Japan than did other Issei women. Although several of the Issei women's eldest brothers had been involved in their marriage arrangements, acting as representatives of the women's natal households, their involvement in their sisters' lives after marriage was minimal. A few older brothers in Japan took some interest in their emigrant sisters' marriages and their financial and personal well-being; when two of the Issei women became widows, for example, their successor brothers wrote offering help in the form of passage back to Japan. Aside from these offers, however, the associations that Issei women had with siblings in Japan were restricted to those already mentioned, plus an occasional visit.

Issei men had stronger economic and residential connections with brothers who had also emigrated to the Seattle area than did Issei women. Brothers predominated heavily among immigrant siblings. Half of the 24 Issei men in the marriage sample had at least 1 sibling emigrate to the Seattle area, in comparison to 4 of the Issei women in the same sample. In all, 26 siblings of 45 Issei emigrated to the Seattle area and 23 of the 26 were brothers. Of these siblings, half returned to Japan and half remained in the United States or Canada.[3] The 6 successor Issei with immigrant brothers all had some economic or residential tie with a brother during their initial period of residence in the Northwest. As long as they were unmarried, these brothers usually lived together. They often did so even after one married, with the unmarried brother joining his married brother's household. If both were married, however, they kept separate residences unless one was separated from a wife who had remained in Japan.

Brothers were commonly instrumental in helping each other get a start in Seattle. Most of the men who were engaged in wage-earning jobs found similar jobs for their brothers, often with the same employer. Only the Kusumoto brothers, of whom there were four, never worked together. Yet these brothers lived together at times before they married. Five of the Issei men in the marriage sample cooperated in a business venture with a brother. At the least, these men provided some of the labor for the brother's business. One man did not himself work

[3] The Issei in my marriage sample had a mean sibship size of 5.2. This figure is based on the number of live-born *and* adopted children in the Issei's *natal* families. Since it includes half siblings who were members of the Issei's natal household as well as any siblings transferred in by adoption, it should not be mistaken for a measure of fertility.

in his brother's barber shop as he was busy with his own hotel business, but he sent his wife to work there daily for a couple of years without pay. Other Issei brothers helped each other start greenhouse businesses and then exchanged labor and supplies. Another pair of brothers did the same with vegetable stands. Two other pairs of brothers were involved in joint business ventures. The Yashima brothers and the Adachi brothers operated grocery stores together, and in both cases their fathers were also involved in the business. In the Yashima case, however, a younger brother and father had been called from Japan to work in the elder brother's expanding grocery store. In the Adachi case, the father and two sons had initially cooperated to start three separate but interlinked vegetable stands and eventually joined forces in a store.

In spite of these work associations and joint business ventures, however, brothers maintained separate financial accounts both before and after they married. They did not pool their earnings into a joint fund from which they then paid common expenses. Even when they lived together they kept separate their earnings and savings and each contributed to their common living expenses. So, for example, when Rentaro Kusumoto's brother came to live with him and his wife, he paid a monthly sum to cover his share of the rent and food. The same arrangement held for the Adachi brothers after their parents returned to Japan. So long as their parents lived with them, the two brothers, their wives, and the parents formed a single budget unit with the father managing the finances. But after the parents returned to Japan, the two brothers kept separate conjugal funds even though they continued to operate the store together and live together.

During their initial years in the United States, as we have seen, these immigrant brothers tended to form important economic and residential connections. Over time, however, almost all of them took divergent paths. Except for the Adachi brothers', all the Issei fraternal business associations ended after a few years when one of the brothers died, returned to Japan, or took up a different line of work. Nine of the Issei men's brothers returned to Japan, all but one of them before 1940. Three more moved to other areas of the United States, and two died only a few years after immigrating. By the outbreak of World War II, only 3 of the 24 Issei men in the marriage sample had a brother remaining in Seattle. Again, except for the Adachis, these brothers had no business ties, nor did they engage in the same kind of work. The few brothers who continued to live in geographic proximity still got together on festive occasions and visited each other occasionally. But the rest who were now separated by great geographic distance did no more than exchange letters and small gifts.

As only one of the Issei men and two of the Issei women in the marriage sample had an immigrant sister, not much can be said of sisters and cross-sex siblings in Seattle. It appears, however, that although these siblings were in regular contact and participated jointly in holiday and life-cycle gatherings, they had little to do with each other's financial, occupational, and residential affairs. The difference between the brother relationship, on the one hand, and the sister relationship and the brother-sister relationship, on the other, is well illustrated by the largest immigrant sibship in my Issei sample, which included three brothers and two sisters. The brothers cooperated closely in starting their greenhouse businesses and farms on the outskirts of Seattle. But aside from arranging their sisters' marriages to Issei men in the Seattle area, they did not have financial or business dealings with their sisters or sisters' husbands. Besides regular visiting, there were several family gatherings each year that all the siblings, their spouses, and children attended. In later years, when the brothers' wives and the sisters had all outlived their husbands, a sort of sisterhood of widows was formed of the sisters and sisters-in-law. Until widowhood brought these women into more frequent contact, however, the Issei sisters generally led rather separate lives.

The Agnatic Bias of Kinship Relations in Japan

Relations between sisters played a lesser role for the Issei than relations between brothers because the same was true of sibling relations in Japan. There, the virilocal postmarital residence of successors inevitably created an agnatic bias in the membership of stem-family households in Japan. Moreover, because nonsuccessor sons often took up residence in their natal communities, while daughters more often married out of the community, an agnatic bias also characterized local, interhousehold relations between kin. I take the time here to describe briefly this agnatic bias because in Chapter 8 I shall point to an emerging uterine bias in Japanese American kinship.

Eight of the 20 Issei in my marriage sample grew up in stem-family households in which their fathers' parents and unmarried siblings also resided for some period of time. In all these cases, the Issei's fathers were the successors to the household, whether through birth or adoption. The other 12 were raised in nuclear-family households or, if the father was deceased or had emigrated to the United States, incomplete nuclear-family households.

TABLE 22

Frequency of Issei Contact with Paternal and Maternal Kin in Japan

Frequency of contact	Father's parents	Mother's parents	Father's brother	Mother's brother	Father's sister	Mother's sister
Seven or more times a year	11	3	10	3	5	3
One to six times a year[a]	1	5	2	6	3	5
Less than once a year	0	2	2	2	3	2
Unsure	2	5	4	4	5	6
Deceased or none	6	5	2	5	4	4
TOTAL	20	20	20	20	20	20

NOTE: Frequency of contact with parents' siblings is based on the individual in the kin category with whom ego had the most contact; e.g., if there were two mother's brothers, the one whom ego saw most frequently is used.

[a]Festivals and life crisis ceremonies.

Even where they did not reside in stem-family households, these Issei tended to live in closer proximity to agnatic kin because of the greater frequency of residence in the father's natal village or town as opposed to the mother's. Of 18 cases where it was clear in which parent's natal village or town the Issei had been raised, 12 involved the Issei's father's natal community, five the common natal community of both the Issei's parents, and only one the Issei's mother's natal community. Hence, except in the last case, the kinship character of the communities in which the Issei were raised conformed to one or another of two basic types: communities in which many of the households surrounding the Issei shared the same surname and an identity of agnatic descent; and communities in which the Issei grew up surrounded by a dense network of both paternal and maternal kin. Given the predominance of virilocal residence, the Issei generally had greater contact with paternal grandparents, uncles, aunts, and cousins than their maternal counterparts (see Table 22). Although the natal households of half the Issei's mothers were within eight miles of the Issei's natal household, the absence of modern transportation was a constraint on frequent visiting over such a distance.

Despite the density of kinship ties among the households in their natal communities, the Issei did not have important economic ties with kin outside their own household. If there were significant economic transactions between their parents and kin outside the household, the Issei were unaware of them, although they knew the genealogical links between households and a bit of their inheritance histories. After the Issei emigrated from Japan, these kin also had very little part in their lives. If they made any noticeable contribution it usually came early when they participated in the Issei's marriage arrangements. But after marriage the Issei were too far away for kin in Japan to keep up the relationship as before.

Prefectural Associations as Replacements for Kin

In the absence of sufficient kinsmen in the Seattle community, the Issei formed voluntary mutual aid associations based on their prefecture of origin in Japan. Each Issei joined the association of the prefecture in which he or she had lived in Japan. In the few cases where a husband and wife came from different prefectures, the couple tended to join the husband's association. These *kenjin-kai* (prefectural clubs) provided assistance to members in the event of illness, death, or other crises. Funeral arrangements, which in Japan were usually handled by neighbors and kin of the deceased, were handled by the Issei's fellow *kenjin* (prefectural person). The annual summer picnic and New Year's Day party organized by each *kenjin-kai* replaced the celebrations in Japan that brought kin and neighbors together. The shared regional identity of fellow *kenjin* also provided an interpersonal network for the recruitment of business partners, for economic and social aid, and for friendship. Issei were sometimes recruited into trades that had proven successful for fellow *kenjin*, and were able to obtain financing through rotating credit associations based on prefectural ties (Miyamoto 1939, 74-75). Fellow *kenjin* patronized each other's businesses and tended to show greater concern for each other than for non-*kenjin*. But again, like the relationships among genealogically linked households in the Issei's natal communities, relationships among *kenjin* were for the most part confined to informal socializing, life crises and ritual celebrations, and short-term mutual aid. Fellow *kenjin* had little more claim on each other, aside from a diffuse expectation of greater trust, cooperation, and friendliness, than they had on any fellow countryman.

ISSEI CONCEPTIONS OF SIBLINGHOOD

What the Issei have to say about their relations with siblings bears little resemblance to their rule-focused accounts of filial relations. Rather than specific rules guiding action, for the most part there are only diffuse norms of solidarity. Biological siblings share blood and therefore common substance, but as in biological parenthood blood alone brings no specific rights and duties. The experience of a shared childhood creates a more meaningful bond between siblings, but that bond is not always one of enduring loyalty or altruism. Some Issei express continuing strong affection for siblings, including those they may not have seen for several decades. Others express a detached indifference toward them.

Whether one felt close to one's sibling as a child or not, however, one's obligations to a sibling as an adult are vague, contingent on a host of factors, and secondary to one's obligations to a parent, child, spouse, and any other member of one's current family. Indeed, according to the Issei, after they left their common natal household they had no specific obligations to their siblings nor any specific claims on them. While it was good to help one's siblings, it was not at all required. Even after the war, when many siblings in Japan were financially needy and some were poverty stricken, sending money and goods was considered an act of altruism rather than the fulfillment of an obligation.

Unlike filial relations, in which rules *should* determine actions even though exogenous factors may subvert them, in sibling relations actions are interpreted as the outcome of circumstances and of intentions ranging from strong loyalty to casual concern. Whereas in filial relations how one feels is said to be irrelevant to what one does, in sibling relations action is contingent on how one feels. So, for example, a sibling of whom one has fond memories will regularly be sent small gifts, while a sibling who was "like a stranger" will be sent nothing. If a sibling does not respond in kind with letters and gifts or an adequate expression of gratitude, then the Issei feel less inclined to be generous. One woman explained that she used to send money to her brother and his wife and children, but they ungratefully asked for more. "I sent them money because I knew they had a hard time and because I felt sorry for them. Otherwise, I don't have to send. If they complain then I'm through. I told them off [when they asked for more] and so from that time they don't ask for anything." The mistake committed by this brother and his wife was not simply ingratitude, but the treatment of a voluntary act of personal generosity as if it were the fulfillment of an obligation.

The denial of obligations to siblings also manifests itself in the way Issei talk about their financial contributions to kin in Japan. Issei who sent contributions of money that helped support both parents and younger siblings represent them as fulfillments of filial obligations. Even when these contributions clearly benefited siblings—and, in some cases, the spouses and children of siblings—they were described as being sent to help parents. One woman, who for all the years she taught school sent most of her earnings home to support her parents and eight younger siblings, spoke of her willingness to make the personal sacrifice of postponing marriage only in terms of filial responsibility. The fact that several of her younger sisters married before her did not prompt her to mention the sacrifice she had made for them.

The closest the Issei came to articulating a specific obligation toward siblings was when a couple of Issei successors explained that they had invited their widowed sisters to take up residence in the parental home because, being successors, they were obliged to help their siblings. But, although they phrased this obligation in general terms, in both cases they cited a very particular circumstance, namely, one in which their physical absence from the parental home and their sister's widowhood made her return home feasible and even convenient. Other Issei, including one of those men's wives, denied that a successor was obligated to take back a widowed or divorced sister into the parental home. A successor, they said, had a greater obligation to help a needy sibling than did a nonsuccessor or a sister, but how he helped them depended on his resources and what prior claims to these resources existed. After all, his duties to parents, spouse, and children took precedence over any desire to help his siblings.

The absence of any consensus about the obligations and claims of siblings is an aspect of the general lack of interest in the content and meaning of the sibling relationship. The Issei had little to say about what the relationship between adult siblings should ideally be like except that they should try to help one another and should maintain communication. In addition, siblings play a rather insignificant role in Issei narratives of their lives both before and after marriage and departure from the parental home. Even when they had joined a brother in America and spent the first years of immigration working and living with him, the Issei often failed to mention him until I specifically asked whether any siblings had also immigrated. The impression conveyed by these men's accounts of their immigration was that of a solitary young man's struggle for survival and advancement. Issei men who had lived with both brothers and father in America spoke only of emigrating to join the latter.

For the Issei, the histories of sibling relationships are mere conjunctions of independent life histories. Whether they are describing relations with siblings left behind in Japan or with those still living in Seattle, the Issei tend to portray these relations as the outcomes of forces and decisions external to the relationship itself. The separate developments in the lives and families of individual siblings might have brought them temporarily into closer proximity and made it convenient for them to cooperate in wage work or business, but other developments just as easily separated them from each other. Whereas a parent and child lived together to fulfill filial norms, siblings cooperated in business because it was convenient and beneficial to do so.

The Issei's rather thin explication of siblinghood can be fleshed out by examining the units into which they conceptually organize their kinship universe and their placement of siblings within it.

KAZOKU AND SHINRUI

The most fundamental distinction the Issei draw among categories of kin divides *kazoku* from *shinrui*. All the Issei I interviewed translated *kazoku* as "family" and *shinrui* as "relatives," and all claimed that the distinction is equivalent to the one that Americans draw between "family" and "relatives." The Issei's enumeration of the membership of the *kazoku* in which they lived in Japan, however, indicates that they are households rather than residentially dispersed families. The Issei include in their childhood *kazoku* all individuals who resided under one roof at the period of time in question. For almost all of them, this included only kin with whom they were connected by blood, marriage, or adoption. If they were raised in a stem-family household, they include as members of their childhood *kazoku* (in addition to parents and siblings), their father's parents and any of his siblings whom they remember as residing in the household. If they were raised in a nuclear family household, they include only parents and siblings. Issei who had unrelated servants or farm workers living in their homes also include them as members of the *kazoku*. For most Issei their childhood *kazoku* was not, however, a strictly residential unit. Several include in it fathers who were overseas for long periods of time.

When asked to list the current members of their *kazoku*, the Issei respond in a couple of ways (Figure 8). The great majority list their spouse (if surviving), any surviving children and their spouses, and grandchildren. A few of these Issei also include their grandchildren's spouses. Coresidence is not a requirement, and indeed is irrelevant to the way most Issei define their contemporary *kazoku*. A couple of Issei women, however, did use residence criteria in their definitions. Both were widows living with a married daughter and her spouse and children. Each widow included in her *kazoku* only the daughter, her husband, and their children. Unlike Issei living apart from their children, they excluded all their other children and grandchildren.

Siblings are included as members of their childhood *kazoku* by all Issei. But once a sibling, or one of the Issei in the sample, has married and left the household, that person is classified as a member of a differ-

CHILDHOOD KAZOKU IN JAPAN   PRESENT KAZOKU IN U.S.

A. *Stem-family household*

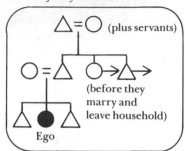

A. *Residentially dispersed inclusive conjugal family (reported by a majority of Issei)*

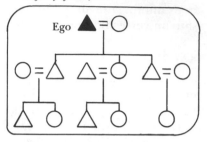

B. *Conjugal family household*

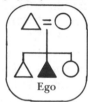

B. *Reported by two widows living with married daughters in stem-family households*

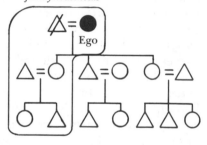

Fig. 8. Membership of Issei *kazoku*. Perimeter lines denote boundaries of ego's *kazoku*.

ent *kazoku*. The Issei say that all siblings except the incumbent successor "marry out" of the *kazoku*. Hence, two married siblings can never be members of the same *kazoku*. So although Denkichi Adachi and his brother have always lived together and jointly operated a grocery business, Denkichi excluded his brother, his brother's wife, and their children from his present *kazoku*. Even though they live together, he explained, "we are two separate families." Instead, he included, besides his wife, his adopted son and adopted son's wife in Japan. In this instance, as in many others, the Issei informant used the terms "family" and *kazoku* interchangeably. Another example illustrates the Issei insistence on the equivalence of these terms. When Mr. Yokoi was asked to list the members of his present *kazoku* (in which he included his wife, his three married daughters, their husbands, and all his grandchildren), he excluded his younger sister who also resides in Seattle. In response to my question, "What about your sister?" he replied, "That's outside my family." When I reminded him that I was interested in his *kazoku*, he replied, "It's the same thing."

Where an eldest brother had married and brought his wife to live in his parents' household before his Issei sibling had departed, the Issei say they were all then members of the same *kazoku*. At the same time, however, the Issei stress that a *kazoku* composed in this way was short-lived. After an Issei successor married, any unmarried younger siblings who continued to reside with parents in Japan are also said to have remained members of the Issei's *kazoku*. But again, the temporariness of such a *kazoku* is emphasized by the Issei.

The Issei are correct, of course, in pointing out the transitory nature of a *kazoku* that includes both married and unmarried siblings. But as any composition of a *kazoku*, like that of any domestic group, is transitory, I take their point as indicating something other than a keen awareness of developmental cycles. It appears, rather, to reflect the Issei's construct of the *kazoku*—a construct in which the core relations are filial and conjugal. Sibling relations, though secondary, are included as long as all siblings remain unmarried. But as soon as one sibling marries, the Issei tend to foresee the movement toward the new *kazoku* that will consist only of one married sibling, his wife, children, and parents.

It is possible that this tendency expresses a more general inclination to think of adult siblings as members of different *kazoku*. Thus an Issei's brother who was not the successor and who had gone to work in the United States was described as "outside" the *kazoku* even while he was still unmarried and officially registered in the household. Even when the brother had been called to America by his father and was working with him to support the household in Japan, the Issei excluded him from the *kazoku*, explaining that this contribution was only temporary; soon, they said, he would start his "own *kazoku*." In turn, Issei nonsuccessors defined themselves as "outside" their childhood *kazoku* once they emigrated even though they were still unmarried and officially registered in it.

Once an Issei and his siblings are married, the sibling falls into the category of *shinrui*. The term *shinrui* as well as the term *shinseki* are used by the Issei to refer to what they say Americans call "relatives."[4] Accord-

---

[4] Most Issei used the term *shinrui*, but several used the term *shinseki* to refer to what they said Americans call "relatives." When asked about the difference between these terms, the Issei explained that they had the same meaning. Several added that *shinseki* was the proper written term, but *shinrui* was used in speaking. A couple claimed that *shinrui* was "common" language, and *shinseki* was used only by "high-class" people, a category from which they excluded themselves.

ing to the Issei, *shinrui* include all people with whom one recognizes a connection by blood, marriage, or adoption. Like the American category of "relatives," *shinrui* denotes an ego-centered kindred based on cognatic kinship. In listing the *shinrui* they had known in Japan, the Issei exhibited no unilineal descent bias except for a slight agnatic bias resulting from the predominance of virilocal residence. However, the Issei claimed that father's kin were no different from mother's kin as far as both being *shinrui* was concerned.

Few of the Issei could trace genealogical relations further back than two ascending generations and only one man was able to go back more than three generations. This Issei had made family history a hobby of sorts and whenever he visited his natal village in Japan would collect information from relatives and off gravestones. As a result he could trace the genealogical relations of a large number of agnatically related households with the same or related surnames in his natal village. Although he said that the members of this localized set of households considered themselves to be "part of the same family, because we all came out of the same family tree," there was no special term for the set, nor did they have any special economic or social relationship aside from the general expectations of cooperation and mutual aid among *shinrui*.

All the Issei knew the succession histories of their parents' natal households and, in some cases, those of one or two of their grandparents' natal households. They used the term *honke* to refer to the household of the successor in their parents' sibship, and the term *bunke* to refer to branch households formed by his brothers.[5] But these terms referred only to the genealogical relations between households rather than to any special economic or social relations between them. Several of the Issei used the term *bunke* in a very broad sense to refer to any household established by a nonsuccessor son or daughter of a household, regardless of whether it had received any land from the *honke* or whether it was located in the same community as the *honke*. Two Issei men called their own households in Seattle *bunke* households, and an Issei woman said that her father's brother had "made a *bunke*" in an adjoining prefecture. In their usage, then, the requirement of residence within the original community was ignored. Other Issei, however, employed the criterion of location within the same community and said households in the United States could not be considered *bunke* households. *Honke* was also used loosely to refer to any household in

[5] The Issei from Aichi Prefecture used the terms *honya* and *shinya* to refer to main and branch households.

Japan that was considered the successor to the Issei's natal household. The Issei referred to such a household as *uchi no honke* (our main household), despite the absence of any economic relationship with it. Even where the present successor possessed neither the house nor the land of the original household, the Issei referred to it as the *honke*. Thus the Issei's usage of the terms *honke* and *bunke* was based either solely on the genealogical criterion of branching or on the two criteria of genealogical branching and common locality. If there were any vertically structured, patron-client relations between these *honke* and *bunke* households on the order of *dozoku*, the Issei were unaware of them.[6]

Just as there are no specific functional criteria for a *shinrui* relationship, so there are no specific genealogical criteria. Inclusion in the category depends on whom the Issei recognize as connected to them through blood, marriage, or adoption.[7] A few Issei said that beyond first cousins the relationship is rather "distant," but they admitted you might have a *shinrui* relationship with such kin if they lived near you. Several informants even classified as *shinrui* individuals to whom they could not trace a specific genealogical connection, but whom they knew to be somehow genealogically connected to them.

The Issei include affines as well as consanguines in the category of *shinrui*. A few said that there was a special term for people related by marriage, but none could recall it.[8] The distinction between affines and consanguines was in any case considered unimportant and, according to one Issei, just a "technicality" as far as *shinrui* relations were concerned. Chie Nakane, in a study of rural Japanese kinship, has emphasized the affinal aspect of the relationship between *shinrui* households

[6] The kinship units called *dozoku* (Befu 1963; Brown 1968; Nakane 1967; S. Kitano 1962) were not part of the Issei's background. *Dozoku* could develop when a household, whether *bunke* or *honke*, had sufficient resources to give the younger son(s) a portion of the household property on which he could establish a branch household. In the succeeding generation the newly created *bunke* would be succeeded by its first son and might even redivide its land holdings to establish yet another *bunke* household. In relation to the latter, the former would now be a *honke* household, although it retained its status of *bunke* to the original *honke*. In general, strongly corporate and hierarchically structured *dozoku* were found in the less economically developed areas of northeastern Japan. In the more economically developed southwest they were nonexistent except among wealthy land-owning families.

[7] According to Nakane (1967, 27), the range of *shinrui* normally includes first cousins. However, the Issei usage of *shinrui* is more consistent with Befu's conclusion that "there is no limit to the extension of the kin (*shinrui*) relationship except the inability to trace the genealogical connection" (Befu 1963, 1331). Not even the specific genealogical connection need be known, however, for the Issei to classify an individual as *shinrui*.

[8] It is highly likely that the term they could not recall was *inseki*, which means an affine or a relative by marriage.

by stating that "a shinrui arises through the marriage of a member (kin) of ego's household" (1967, 27-28). She cites the local term "enka," used for *shinrui* in Kumamoto Prefecture, as evidence of the affinal content of the Japanese conception of *shinrui*; the literal meaning of *enka*, she says, is "affinal household" (ibid.). However, in a footnote she also states that "the term shinrui (or shinseki) which is now standard Japanese and has been used widely all over Japan was originally derived from Chinese. Indigenous terms for shinrui are itoko (*cousin*) or oyako (*parent-child*) which are still used in many parts of Japan." (Ibid., 26-27; my italics.) If, as Nakane claims, *shinrui* relationships are traced through individuals even though the functions of *shinrui* are carried out by household units, it seems just as reasonable, moreover, to characterize *shinrui* as arising out of cognatic kinship ties. Although a marriage may have been the event that created a *shinrui* relationship between two households, the relationship was not only one of affinity but of consanguinity, since the receiving household was connected to the sending household by the consanguineal tie between the bride and her parents. In the next generation, the bride's son was connected to his mother's natal household by a cognatic tie with his mother's brother and his children. Similarly, in the case of adoption, the receiving household was connected to the sending household by the consanguineal tie between its new member (and his or her children) and the members of his or her natal household. The point is that what defined *shinrui* relationships was not genealogical criteria, whether consanguineal or affinal.

In my sample, the affines commonly included by the Issei as the *shinrui* they remembered from their childhood in Japan were their parents' siblings' spouses and their parents' siblings' spouses' parents. Later, after the Issei and their siblings married, siblings' spouses, spouses' siblings, and spouse's siblings' spouses were added. When listing their current *shinrui*, the Issei include any of the aforementioned affines who are still alive, as well as their children's spouses, children's spouses' siblings, and children's spouses' parents. In some contexts the Issei treat individuals as the units of a *shinrui* relationship without including the other members of their households or families. In other contexts, the Issei treat families as the units.[9] For example, in the exchange of obitu-

---

[9] In this the Issei appear to share the concept of *shinrui* described in the literature on Japanese kinship. Thus according to Nakane (1967, 27), "for the understanding of this Japanese concept of shinrui, the unit of the household is of prime importance. Though a shinrui is recognized in terms of kinship relations and with reference to a single person, the function of shinrui is carried out on the basis of household units. A shinrui is recognized as a set of households, not simply as an aggregate of kin. A kinsman who is a member of ego's own household is not called shinrui."

ary gifts called *kōden*, the Issei consider the reciprocating parties to be family units of parents and their children rather than individuals. Thus, when any one member of a family gives such a gift, the deceased's family unit is expected to reciprocate upon the death of any of the members of the giver's family. It is the family, however, that is responsible for reciprocating and not its individual members. As long as any of them reciprocates at the death of a member of the giver's family, the family as a whole is deemed to have fulfilled its obligations.

Regardless of whether in any particular context the Issei's units of *shinrui* relations are individuals, families, or both, the Issei are in firm agreement that *kazoku* and *shinrui* are mutually exclusive categories. Hence, there is no overlap between the Issei's lists of current *kazoku* and their lists of current *shinrui*. There are, however, some obvious differences between the units the Issei identify as their past *kazoku* and the units they identify as their present ones. First, the genealogical compositions of these two sets of *kazoku* are different. The *kazoku* of the Issei's childhood and early adulthood never include married siblings; indeed, the Issei insist that married siblings are by definition members of two different *kazoku*. In contrast, except for the two widows living with married daughters, the Issei list all their children, married and unmarried, and their spouses and children as members of their present *kazoku*. In doing so, they greatly expand the lateral genealogical range of *kazoku* membership. The change, however, does not indicate a change in the Issei conception of *kazoku*, but rather reflects a change in their position from members of a junior generation to members of a senior generation. When the Issei claim that *kazoku* and "family" are the same, and that for them *kazoku* is to *shinrui* as "family" is to "relatives" for Americans, it is because they perceive a common meaningful opposition in these categorical distinctions. That opposition, for the Issei, lies neither in genealogical nor residence criteria, nor in any specific set of functional characteristics. Rather the distinction between *kazoku* and *shinrui*, like that between "family" and "relatives," differentiates those upon whom one can, or at least should be able to, depend for enduring, unconditional loyalty and support, and those who fall outside this domain of primary obligations. In the Issei's eyes, the people upon whom one can legitimately make such claims today in America are one's children and their spouses and even perhaps one's grandchildren.

Kazoku and "family," moreover, are construed as units in which long-term reciprocity operates. That is, one is not concerned about immediate repayment or return of what one has given or received, lent to or borrowed from, a member of one's family, because one can rely upon a similar loan or aid from them if necessary anytime in the future. Neither should there be concern for balanced, symmetrical exchange. Parents, after all, give much more to their children than they can ever be repaid. Thus, one does not keep a mental ledger sheet of the flow of money, materials, and labor between oneself and members of the *kazoku*. Relations with *shinrui*, on the other hand, fall outside this realm of generalized, long-term reciprocity. One may be able to count on *shinrui* for certain kinds of help, but that help comes with obligations of repayment in kind in the near future. Certainly, loans between *shinrui* must be repaid as soon as possible. If one brother loaned another capital to start a business, or tools and materials to expand it, or simply offered his labor, he expected the same or the equivalent in return. When brothers worked together in a common enterprise, it was as partners to a quasi-contractual relation from which each expected to gain proportionally to what he put in.

Finally, for the Issei, *shinrui* blend into neighbors and *kenjin*. Several Issei said that in Japan your neighbors were the people you felt closest to and upon whom you depended for help outside your *kazoku*. As they had been living next to you for generations, one Issei explained, your neighbors were like your *shinrui*. Similarly, the relations among *kenjin* during the early years of immigration were commonly described as like those of siblings. In portraying *kenjin* in such terms the Issei intended to convey the closeness of that relationship while revealing that siblings, like all other *shinrui* but unlike *kazoku*, were only potential helpers. Given this sharp difference between the conception of *kazoku* relations and of those outside the *kazoku*, it is not surprising that only the Issei who live with a married child employ residence criteria to define their present *kazoku*. The ones who do not live with their children—and they comprise the majority of their generation today—are understandably unlikely to employ criteria that would exclude all their children from the domain of primary relations to which unconditional, enduring loyalty is attached. None, not even an Issei widower who lived alone in an apartment and only rarely saw his three sons, said they had no *kazoku* or "family."

FROM KAZOKU TO SHINRUI

Issei sibling histories display a greater range of diversity than is intimated by the adage that "the sibling is the beginning of the stranger." While among them are siblings who did little more than keep each other informed of the barest outlines of their distant lives and families, there are also those who more than fifty years after their departure from the natal household are still engaged in financial and residential arrangements centered on the parental home. The timing of important transactions between siblings was also far from uniform. For although most siblings went their separate ways, some did so much earlier than others. Cooperation and mutual aid by immigrant brothers in the formation of what in the long run proved to be independent careers and families occurred largely in the first two decades of the twentieth century, when the Issei were embarking on married life. The transactions and negotiations between successors in Seattle and siblings in Japan, however, span a much broader period of historical time and life stages. For the Issei, siblinghood is a relationship that is born in the *kazoku* but moves inexorably outside it. Even while they were members of the same *kazoku*, siblings anticipated the secondary, short-term character of their relationship. The cooperative business ventures, shared residences, and mutual aid of immigrant brothers were experienced as, and so became, transitory arrangements. These joint ventures were never more than interim phases in a sustained movement toward financial and social separation.

CHAPTER 8

Nisei Siblings, Family, and Relatives

I N THIS CHAPTER, I discuss the variations in contemporary Nisei sibling relations and the terms in which the Nisei interpret them. Once again, I locate my analysis of siblinghood within my analysis of a broader system of kinship categories—in this case, the "family" and "relatives"—in order to display the link between the changing location of a relationship and the transformation of its meaning.

NISEI SIBLINGS

Nisei in Seattle are rarely without any siblings in the area. The Nisei in my sample had a mean sibship size of 5.1, and between 60 and 70 percent of their generation returned to Seattle after the war. By the 1970's, they had an average of 2.2 siblings residing in the Seattle area (for my definition of "Seattle area" see the Appendix).[1] The postwar geographic spread of the Japanese American population from its original concentration in what today is known as the International District has increased the spatial distance between Nisei siblings and their parents.[2] Some Nisei reside within a few blocks of their siblings and par-

[1] This mean sibship size is derived from a sample of 92 Nisei, which includes the Nisei from my marriage sample plus an additional 8 Nisei for whom I had sibling information. To avoid counting any sibship twice I have excluded 3 of the Nisei from the marriage sample (whose siblings are also in the marriage sample) from this figure. The mean number of surviving siblings (both in Seattle and elsewhere) of the Nisei in this sample is 3.6.

[2] The geographic concentration of the Japanese American population *within* Seattle has decreased since 1930. Although in 1950 the distribution of the population resembled the highly concentrated settlement pattern of the 1920 immigration period, this was a temporary phenomenon generated by the postwar housing shortage, economic hardship, and lingering anti-Japanese sentiments. The occupational mobility and rising income levels of the Nisei in the 1950's and 1960's coincided with their movement out of the original residential area.

ents, but this is not usual; the majority live between two to ten miles from siblings and parents. In terms of driving time, however, the community is not widely dispersed. People commonly say that a sibling lives "only a five-minute drive away" or "eight minutes down the freeway."

Variations in Sibling Relations: Sisters and Brothers

Contemporary relations among Nisei siblings run the gamut from affectionate intimacy to reserved distance, from near-daily communication to as little as an annual contact. The diversity of relations among siblings is the outcome of a range of factors, including geographic distance, available time, comparative education and occupation, and the degree to which interests, tastes, and life-styles are shared. None of these factors, however, orders the variations in sibling relations more than gender.

Nisei sisters are in much more frequent contact than brothers. Many sisters see or telephone each other two or three times a week. Some are in daily contact with at least one other sister, and a woman with three sisters in the area may speak to all three in one day. Sisters do not hesitate to telephone each other on the spur of the moment or to drop in on each other without advance notice. During my interviews, Nisei women frequently called their sisters and mothers to check on the accuracy of some piece of information, such as a marriage date. Spontaneous acts such as these provided evidence of women's accessibility to their sisters and mothers, and their willingness to phone or visit each other for no other reason than to "keep in contact."

In contrast, few Nisei men visit or telephone their brothers more than twice a month, and the average appears to be closer to once every other month. Many men see their brothers, even those who live within a couple of miles of them, as infrequently as three or four times a year—in other words, at holiday gatherings and life-cycle celebrations. Brothers tend to telephone or call on each other, moreover, only when they have a specific reason, for example, to discuss a decision concerning parents or to request the loan of a tool. Unlike women, Nisei men were reluctant to call their brothers and fathers to obtain any information about the family.

The greater frequency of interaction among Nisei sisters is, as I have pointed out elsewhere, but one component of the women-centered character of Nisei kin networks (Yanagisako 1977). Nisei sisters and, if she is alive, their mother not only engage in frequent interaction but manifest a close, affective solidarity. Most women feel they can always rely upon their sisters and mother for emotional support and help. As there is no *enryo* (reserve, holding back) with one's sisters, mother, and daughters, they are asked to baby-sit at a moment's notice, invited over for lunch minutes in advance, or asked to pick up an item on their way to the grocery store. If a woman is ill or recovering from childbirth, her sisters or mother comes to help with the household chores without having to be asked.

Nisei women with no sisters in the Seattle area sometimes develop a "sister" relationship with a female cousin or a sister-in-law. But, because her husband's sisters, husband's brothers' wives, and brothers' wives are themselves part of a consanguineal sister set, a woman finds herself only a peripheral member of her affinal kinswomen's solidary group. A close relationship usually develops among female affines or cousins only when neither of the women has sisters in the area. For example, two women who had been raised in other Japanese American communities but who married brothers from Seattle developed a "sister" relationship because neither had any consanguineal kin in the area. Furthermore, because she had no daughters, their mother-in-law was included in this female sodality.

Men not only see less of brothers and fathers, but they also tend to feel emotionally and socially distant from them. Fathers and sons and brothers are not the foci of kin networks, but rather are drawn together by female relationships. Brothers rarely seek each other's companionship or participate in joint recreational activities. A Nisei man whose brother belonged to his skiing club told me it was purely "by accident" that they ended up on the same slope every other Saturday. Where sisters feel no hesitancy in requesting help from each other, brothers are more reluctant to make such requests. Some brothers lend each other tools and occasionally help each other with repairs and small projects. But these exchanges are infrequent and in many brother relationships they never occur. Where a woman confides in her sisters before anyone else—aside from her husband—a man confides in his friends or his affines before his brothers. Men commonly say they feel closer to their wives' brothers and their wives' sisters' husbands than to their own brothers, and would go to them for help first.

Relations between cross-sex siblings fall somewhere between those of sisters and brothers in both frequency of contact and affective solidarity. Although most brothers and sisters generally do not visit or phone each other regularly, they tend to do so more frequently than brothers. Communications with siblings who live in other areas of the country are equally women-centered. Sisters write each other and call long distance more than brothers. Those who live in some other area of the West Coast and even in the Midwest visit each other annually or at least every other year, often accompanied by their husbands and children. Brothers residing at similar distances rarely visit each other unless they have an additional reason for coming to town, such as business or a visit to parents or their wife's family.

Sisters, moreover, are the kin keepers who facilitate communication, coordinate gift exchanges, and bring kin together. When children are young and birthday parties are attended by cousins and other relatives, for example, sisters not only plan the party but decide how much should be spent for presents. Gift-exchange plans among sisters sometimes approach the elegance of structuralist solutions.[3] Nisei sisters and their mothers are also the organizers of what are referred to as "family gatherings." Because these gatherings involve rather large assemblages of kin, they require considerable planning. Although sisters do not necessarily cohost these gatherings, nor do they always decide jointly when and where one will be held, they do negotiate their composition with each other and with their female affines.

FAMILY GATHERINGS AND SIBLING SETS

Family gatherings are one of the ways in which Nisei siblings affirm their solidarity and so make known their continuing presence as a family in the community. In this section, I analyze the composition over time of these gatherings to illuminate the central role of the sibling relationship in the larger structure of kinship relationships.

The Nisei consider certain holidays and life-cycle events as occasions for bringing together "family" and "relatives." Later in this chapter I will explain what the Nisei mean by these terms. On some of these occasions friends and acquaintances are also included. On New Year's Day (Shōgatsu), for example, friends and even work associates are invited to "drop by" for a buffet of specially prepared foods that is set out for most of the afternoon and evening. This New Year's buffet is a modification of the Japanese custom by which the mistress of the house prepared food and remained at home to greet and serve guests, while her

[3] For example, one set of sisters and their mother decided that it was too costly for each to buy Christmas presents for every member of the others' conjugal families. First, they tried a form of direct exchange in which the three sisters and their mother paired off into two exchange dyads. Not having read Lévi-Strauss's (1969) analysis of patrilateral cross-cousin marriage, they took two years to recognize the limitations of an arrangement in which each woman was exchanging gifts with only one other woman. They then shifted to indirect exchange, wherein A gives to B who gives to C who gives to D who gives to A. By giving gifts in a circle, each woman was giving or receiving from two other women, making this a more effective plan for promoting family integration.

husband visited the homes of kin, neighbors, patrons, or clients (Embree 1939). Although, in the earlier days of the community, the Issei continued this practice, among the Nisei husband and wife either both stay at home to receive guests or both go visiting. People have contact with a wide range of kin and nonkin on such occasions, as the flow of people allows a host to invite a large number of guests. Because people can attend two or three of these gatherings during the course of the day, moreover, the problem of competing invitations is minimized.

Weddings and funerals, the two life-cycle ceremonies that entail the largest assemblages of kin in the Japanese American community, are also attended by nonkin. Marriage and death are considered events of significance to more than what the Nisei consider the "immediate family," and it is rare that either event does not include a wide range of kin as well as friends and associates.[4] When a wedding, or more so a funeral, is restricted to a narrow range of kin, the Nisei consider it strange and embarrassingly ungenerous. In both ceremonies the attendance of kin is more important, and kin play a more central role than friends and associates. The two events are shown to be radically different, however, when the procedures by which people—both kin and non-kin—come to attend them are considered. At weddings a set of people (the bride and groom and their respective parents) decide whom to invite; at funerals those in attendance have invited themselves. Funerals are unique in this regard. They require that not ego, but his or her kin, friends, and acquaintances, decide whether attendance is appropriate. The strong obligation to attend the funerals of one's kin, friends, and acquaintances, as well as of those who have attended the funerals of one's family members, creates large funerals in the Japanese American community. An average funeral is attended by a hundred and fifty people or so; many include two to three hundred mourners. Like New Year's Day, however, weddings, funerals, and other life-cycle celebrations do not require people to choose between competing family gatherings. Because of this, they do not throw into relief the outlines of families and their structural core in the way that the following occasions do.

[4]The minimal range of consanguineal kin whom the Nisei expect to be invited to a wedding are the bride's and groom's grandparents, parents, parents' siblings, first cousins, siblings, nieces, and nephews. As few Nisei have genealogically distant consanguineal kin in the Seattle area, the range of such kin is generally restricted to these kin types, all of which are within five civil degrees of removal. If more genealogically distant consanguines are known and live near enough to attend the wedding, they may or may not be invited. Most weddings are also attended by affines of the same kin types so often found at Christmas and Thanksgiving gatherings. (For an example of the kin present at a Nisei wedding, see Yanagisako 1975a, 235-38.)

Thanksgiving and Christmas

In order to celebrate Thanksgiving or Christmas, people have to assemble at a particular time and place. On Christmas Day they may visit elsewhere before and after dinner to exchange presents and greetings, but a "sit-down" dinner is eaten at only one gathering. As on Thanksgiving, it is the group of people with whom they ate dinner that people say they "spent Christmas with."

In Figure 9 I have diagrammed 12 assemblages of kin who participated in Thanksgiving and Christmas celebrations in 1972 and 1973.[5] The shaded persons are those who hosted each gathering. The first assemblage (*A*), which includes only a conjugal family, is of a type rare in the Seattle Japanese American community. This particular gathering took place in an East Coast city where the Nisei couple and their young children were temporarily residing and so were isolated from their kin. It was experienced in just the way other informants imagined such a Thanksgiving gathering would be, that is, as a "lonely" affair. Assemblage *B* might be labeled an example of the "ideal American" Thanksgiving gathering, as it is the one commonly depicted in the popular media and appears to be the ideal among many middle-class white Americans. It includes a conjugal family in its later stage of development to which have been added the spouses and children of the junior members. This particular dinner was held at the Issei couple's home, but assemblages such as this are more likely to be hosted by one of the Nisei couples. Assemblage *C* is merely a variant of the "ideal American" gathering. It lacks the senior Issei couple, who happened to be deceased. Note that although assemblages *B* and *C* each include more than one sibling set (who are first cousins to each other), each is restricted to one set of *married* siblings.[6]

As long as only one set of married siblings or one set of parents and their married child (or children) are present, as in *B* and *C*, the assemblage retains a single conjugal family as its core. This type of assemblage, which I will refer to hereafter as an inclusive conjugal family, is one of the more genealogically restricted of Thanksgiving and Christmas gatherings among Japanese Americans. It is also not a common

[5] Occasionally, one or more nonkin may be present at a Christmas or Thanksgiving gathering. But these people are considered peripheral to the celebration and only are included because they have "no family" in the area. Furthermore, they are rarely present more than once. I have therefore excluded them from my description.

[6] I use the term "sibling set" rather than the term "sibship" to refer to the siblings present at a family gathering because the latter implies that all members of the sibship are present, which is often not the case.

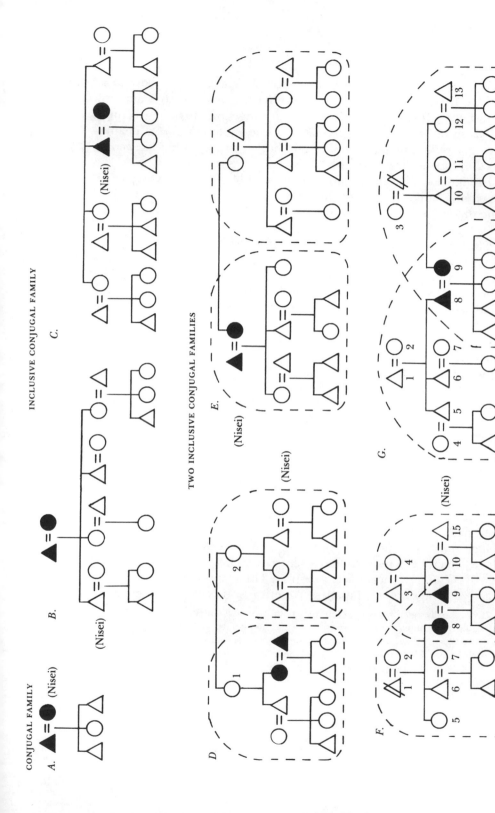

CONJUGAL FAMILY

INCLUSIVE CONJUGAL FAMILY

TWO INCLUSIVE CONJUGAL FAMILIES

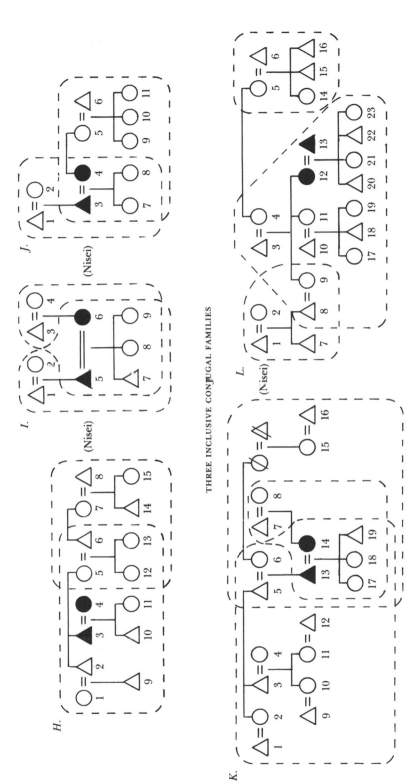

THREE INCLUSIVE CONJUGAL FAMILIES

Fig. 9. Kin assemblages at Thanksgiving and Christmas. Solid symbols denote the host couple.

assemblage on either of these holidays; only 4 of the 15 gatherings for which I obtained attendance lists conformed to this genealogical type. Most common are Thanksgiving and Christmas gatherings that bring together two inclusive conjugal families. Examples D through J are variations of this type of assemblage. They can be further subdivided according to the character of the genealogical link between the two inclusive conjugal families. Thus D and E are both linked by a sister tie in the senior generation; the only difference (aside from the number and sex of the middle-generation siblings and of their children) is that the husbands of the linking sisters in D were deceased. In addition, in D the gathering was held at the home of the Nisei daughter of one of the linking Issei sisters, whereas E was held at the home of one of the linking Nisei sisters.

Whereas in D and E the two inclusive conjugal families are linked by a female sibling tie in the senior generation, in F, G, and H they are linked by a marriage tie in the middle generation. In both F and G the Nisei couple who hosted the gathering invited both the husband's and the wife's parents, siblings and their spouses, and children. Hence, two overlapping, affinally related inclusive conjugal families attended the celebration. Assemblage H differs in that none of the parents of the two Nisei sibling sets participating in the gathering were alive. In this case, moreover, the Nisei couple (5 and 6) who provided the affinal link between the two sibling sets did not host the gathering. Assemblages I and J also include two inclusive conjugal families linked by a marriage tie, but in both cases the presence of only a small subset of the members of each inclusive conjugal family renders these gatherings rather different from the three preceding ones. In I, because none of the siblings of the Nisei host couple (5 and 6) participated in the gathering, they were the only members in the middle generation of the two overlapping, affinally linked families. In J, the husband's parents on the one side and the wife's sister and her husband and children on the other were brought together by the host couple (3 and 4) whose marriage linked the two families.

Finally, the most genealogically complex assemblages are K and L, each of which includes three inclusive conjugal families. In K, a Sansei couple (13 and 14) hosted a gathering in which they included the wife's parents (7 and 8) as well as the husband's parents and their respective siblings, spouses, and children. The assemblage combined two inclusive conjugal families linked by an affinal tie in the senior generation with the parents-in-law of one of the sibling's children. If this last couple (7 and 8) had been excluded, K would have been equivalent to F, G, and *H*. Assemblage *L*, in turn, would have replicated *D* and *E*, had not individuals 1, 2, and 7 been included. The addition of the parents and brother of the husband of one of the senior sisters, however, extended the gathering to include a third inclusive conjugal family. In both *K* and *L*, the combined use of a sibling tie in the senior generation, to link two consanguineally related inclusive conjugal families, and a marriage tie in the junior generation, to link two affinally related inclusive conjugal families, resulted in the presence of three inclusive conjugal families.

Obviously, the genealogical range of kin participating in any family gathering depends on the nature of the links between the inclusive conjugal families that have been brought together. If the two inclusive conjugal families are linked by a sibling tie in the senior generation (*D* and *E*), then the assemblage includes second cousins as well as first cousins and their spouses. If the two inclusive conjugal families are linked by a marriage tie in the middle generation (*F* through *J*), then a wider range of affines rather than consanguines is included. That the range of kin at these assemblages is more affinally than consanguineally extended is not surprising given the genealogical shallowness of the community. Recall that, although many Issei had siblings and parents who also emigrated to Seattle, most of them returned to Japan before World War II. Today, therefore, few Nisei have aunts, uncles, or cousins in the community. Among those who do, moreover, these parents' siblings and their spouses and children are often not close acquaintances. The increasing divergence of Issei siblings' lives described in the previous chapter has, for many, been accompanied by minimal contact between their families. Issei sisters, such as the pair in assemblage *D*, are uncommon in the community. Issei brothers are commoner, but they do not bring their respective families together for annual celebrations like Thanksgiving and New Year's.

Rather than consanguineal depth, then, it is primarily lateral, affinal breadth that is responsible for the size and genealogical complexity of these assemblages. The affinal extension, in turn, is an outcome of attempts by Nisei couples (and an ever-increasing number of Sansei married couples) to bring together in one gathering both their respective "sides of the family"—that is, each spouse's parents, siblings, and their spouses and children, or what might be called their inclusive natal conjugal family. In 7 of the 12 assemblages (*F* through *L*) in Figure 9, one couple per gathering had members from both the husband's and wife's inclusive natal conjugal families present. With the exceptions of assemblages *H* and *L*, that couple hosted the gathering. As no more than one married couple, however, has both sides of the family present at any

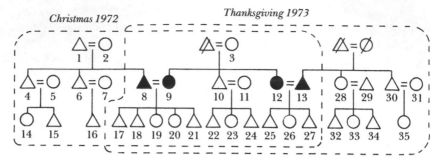

Fig. 10. Christmas and subsequent Thanksgiving kin assemblages hosted by two Nisei couples

particular gathering, the other married siblings must either arrange to spend the next holiday with their spouse's side or arrange to host a celebration combining both sides. Thus, kin assemblages are not stable but fluctuate from one celebration to the next. Figure 10 represents the kin invited in 1973 to Thanksgiving dinner by a Nisei couple (12 and 13), as well as the kin with whom they attended Christmas dinner the previous year. At Christmas dinner in 1972, this couple attended gathering *G* in Figure 9, which had been hosted by the wife's sister and her husband (8 and 9). The host couple had included both their respective sides of the family, but the other Nisei couples present fulfilled only their obligations to one spouse's family. At Thanksgiving dinner the following year, couple 12 and 13 hosted the gathering and invited both *their* sides of the family. Consequently, the Thanksgiving assemblage was a genealogical mirror of the Christmas dinner except for the change in the host couple whose marriage connected the two inclusive conjugal families.

Genealogical restrictions and the equality of sibling sets. None of the Nisei articulated any special rules for restricting the genealogical range of kin participating in Thanksgiving and Christmas gatherings where people have to assemble at a particular time and place. When I asked the Nisei why they did not invite both sides of the family of more than one married sibling, they replied that there should be an upper limit to the size of a gathering or "things get out of hand." Space was another consideration; few homes can accommodate over thirty people at a sit-down dinner. Occasionally, a gathering will be held at a rented hall, but the additional expense and public nature of the setting discourage people from doing this often. After a certain point, anyway, the Nisei say, "the relationships get too distant" and the gatherings include people who "have nothing in common." Yet more than sheer size and social

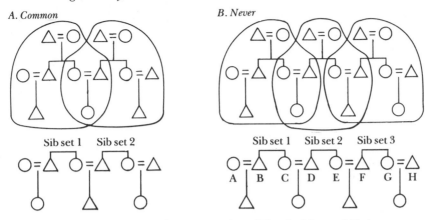

Fig. 11. Restrictions on the genealogical extension of Thanksgiving and Christmas gatherings

and genealogical distance lie behind the composition of kin assemblages at family gatherings. The fact that in none of the assemblages in Figure 9 did more than one married couple have both sides of the family present suggests an unstated rule that no more than two affinally connected, inclusive conjugal families participate in a single gathering. In other words, while *A* in Figure 11 is common in the family gatherings of Seattle Japanese Americans, *B* rarely occurs. This means that cograndparents may be included in the same gathering, but no more than two pairs of them. Likewise, two sibling sets linked by marriage commonly participate in one gathering, but not three sibling sets linked by marriage. Although assemblages *K* and *L* in Figure 9 comprise three inclusive conjugal families, each is restricted to a pair of affinally connected sibling sets. This restriction stems from the fact that while married couples are the acknowledged hosts of Thanksgiving and Christmas gatherings, adult siblings and their parents are the implicit family units participating in them. As will become clear when I examine the Nisei conception of siblinghood, adult siblings are considered the members of an enduring and identifiable "family" that has a biography, a reputation, and a set of obligations in the community. When a sibling set and its surviving parent or parents gather at the home of one of its members for a Thanksgiving or Christmas dinner, it affirms its continuing existence as a family in this sense. When the sibling set of the spouse of the sibling at whose home they gather is also present, affinal bonds are also affirmed. As they gather at what is for each sibling set the home of a sibling, each can claim to have spent Christmas with "our family" (i.e., their inclusive natal conjugal family).

Because the Nisei married couple that provides the affinal link between the two families hosts the gathering, moreover, these families do not stand in the relation of host and guest to each other. Rather, they meet on equal footing and mutual territory, although given the Nisei's conception of the "home" and "family" as women's domain, the wife's kin may feel a bit more "at home." Such equality would be undermined if three affinally connected, inclusive conjugal families were present at the same gathering, for then one of the sibling sets would be guests in the home of an affine. In Figure 11, if couple C and D were the hosts, sibling set 3 (individuals F and G) would be attending a gathering at their sister-in-law's home. More significant and more problematic, at such a gathering one sibling set (sibling set 2 in Figure 11) would be the obvious center of a gathering into which they had pulled two affinal sibling sets. This sort of asymmetry is common and expected at life-cycle celebrations such as weddings where there is a focal "family" whose affinal ties are being displayed and affirmed. But it is unacceptable at Thanksgiving and Christmas gatherings, when every "family," and therefore every sibling set, can be making itself known.

The centrality of sisters. The changing composition of Thanksgiving and Christmas gatherings over time, furthermore, reveals the centrality of sisters to them. While the Sansei children of a Nisei sibling set are unmarried, gatherings center around the Nisei sibling set. Even though sisters may be more involved in planning these affairs, their brothers also participate in them and even host them. With the marriage of the Sansei and particularly with the birth of their children, there is a tendency for the Nisei sibling set to divide. At some point, usually when more than one of the Nisei siblings has grandchildren, the Nisei's inclusive procreative family becomes the core of these gatherings. This inclusive family now joins with the inclusive natal families of the Sansei offspring's spouses. Over time, then, Nisei couples participate less in family gatherings with their siblings' affines and more in family gatherings with their children's affines. Yet most continue to attend some gatherings with their siblings and spouses. As assemblages E and L in Figure 9 show, Nisei sisters who are grandmothers continue to bring their respective inclusive procreative families together.[7] On this evidence, however, it appears that Nisei brothers who are grandfathers never do.

Even though brothers do bring their spouses and children to gath-

---

[7] Assemblage K could also be considered such a case. Here, one of the sisters is deceased but her daughter continues to be included in her mother's sister's family gatherings.

erings planned by their sisters and do host gatherings for their siblings and their families, men tend to participate more frequently in the gatherings arranged by their wives and their wives' sisters. Because of this, Sansei are more often better acquainted with their uterine cousins than with their agnatic cousins. Sisters' husbands also develop close relationships with each other. That the Issei and Nisei are aware of this uterine bias is evinced by their frequent observation that at marriage "a man is lost to his family" and is drawn into his wife's family.

Kōden and Sibling Sets

The exchange of mortuary offerings known as *kōden* is another medium through which sibling sets affirm their continuing presence as a family in the Japanese American community. As I mentioned earlier, the Japanese custom of exchanging *kōden* has persisted, with some modifications, in most Japanese American communities (see, for example, Johnson 1973). In contrast to the practice in rural Japan, where *kōden* consisted of fixed quantities of rice or other edible goods, in Japanese American communities *kōden* consist of relatively fixed amounts of money that is used to pay the costs of the funeral. In Seattle, *kōden* reciprocity has always involved friends and associates as well as kin. The categories of people involved in *kōden* reciprocity in the Seattle Japanese American community differ from those described by Nakane for rural Japan. In rural Japan, *kōden* were given by all *shinrui* households to the household of the deceased. According to Nakane (1967, 32) the degree of commitment between *shinrui* households was reflected in the different amounts of *kōden* given. Since the beginnings of the Seattle Japanese American community, friends and acquaintances as well as kin have given *kōden* on the death of a community member. Nakane claims that the giving of *kōden* by nonrelatives is a recent phenomenon in Japan, but other evidence suggests that this may not have been true in all areas of the country. Both John Embree (1939, 130) and Tadashi Fukutake (1967, 104) report the giving of *kōden* by neighbors in rural areas of Japan, and neither suggests this is a recent phenomenon. Several Issei informants claimed it was the custom in their natal villages to give *kōden* to neighbors as well as kin. The majority of the Issei interviewed, however, could not recall the custom in their natal villages.

In the Seattle community, as many Issei do not have the usual complement of *shinrui* present, prefectural groups and other voluntary associations fulfill some of the traditional *shinrui* functions of mutual aid, including giving *kōden*. At every funeral a list of all persons who have given *kōden* is recorded and kept by a member of the deceased's family.

This is usually a spouse or, if there is no surviving spouse, one of the deceased's children. The holder of the *kōden* list is expected to reciprocate *kōden* on the death of any contributor or any member of the contributor's family (that is, his parents, siblings, spouse, or children). In Chapter 6, I explained the Nisei conferral of this responsibility on the eldest son as part of his chairmanship of the sibling set. *Kōden* reciprocity, however, is conceived of as an exchange between families rather than individuals. Later in this chapter I will examine more closely the Nisei definition of these families and its place in a system of kinship categories. Here it is relevant to point out that although the eldest son (or his substitute) may be the official keeper of the *kōden* list and the one who signs the *kōden* offering card, the local sibling set cooperates with him to fulfill *kōden* obligations arising from their parents' funerals.

The only way for a sibling set to ensure the fulfillment of their *kōden* obligations and thereby to affirm their continuing unity as a family in the community is by coordinating their efforts to maintain a close watch over deaths in the community. If a hundred mortuary offerings were given at a parent's funeral, it is unlikely that any one of the siblings will be aware of all the names of the members of each contributor's family. Personal communication networks are not always adequate, so many Nisei systematically peruse the funeral announcements in the local newspapers to compare the names of the deceased and their surviving kin with the names on the *kōden* list from their parent's funeral. Often people call friends and relatives to obtain information on the deceased's kin ties to be sure they are not overlooking an obligation. During my research, I was asked several times by Nisei attempting to ascertain if *kōden* should be sent whether I knew the genealogies of recently deceased members of the community. Once a Nisei realizes that a recent death requires a response from her family, she notifies the sibling in charge of sending *kōden*.[8] Here again, although eldest brothers are most often the official representatives of the sibling set, sisters are its most active agents.

NISEI CONCEPTIONS OF SIBLINGHOOD

There is considerable variation in what the Nisei say their relations with siblings are like and what their sibling relations ideally should entail. In some contexts, the Nisei characterize the sibling relationship as

[8] If a Nisei who is *not* the sibling in charge of sending *kōden* has an additional social connection to the deceased or his "family" (that is, other than being a child of a parent upon whose death that family sent *kōden*), he or she will also send *kōden* in his or her own name (and, most likely, his or her spouse's name).

one that continues to demand primary loyalty and a long-term reciprocity that tolerates an imbalance of exchange. Statements such as "What's mine is theirs too; it's all part of the family" and "If we [siblings] need help, naturally we come to each other" seem to assert that, even after they have formed their own conjugal families, adult siblings retain primary claims on each other. In other contexts, however, these same Nisei tend to say that "we [wife and I] would loan them money, but only what we can afford," or that "you should loan each other things you don't actually use or need at the time," or even that "there are limits to what you should ask of a sibling." The last of these statements, it should be noted, is one the Nisei make about all kinship relationships except the conjugal relation, and so does not render the sibling relation uniquely limited in its claims. Similarly, when some Nisei say that it is better not to borrow from or loan money to a sibling, they are airing a general resistance to borrowing money from anyone other than a bank. But the manner in which they express their personal willingness and, indeed, the normative correctness of lending money or other items to siblings implies that the claims of a sibling relationship, though less than primary, are still rather more than secondary. The relationship is an ambiguous one. Although some Nisei speak of the "obligations" between siblings, others are uncomfortable with this term; "obligation," they say, is "too strong." "Responsibility" seems more appropriate, according to them. Put another way, one has an obligation to a sibling only in times of crisis or dire need. At the same time, a sibling is always a sibling, and hence one has enduring, unconditional responsibilities (if not obligations) toward them regardless of how one feels about them. Accordingly, one helps all of one's siblings, even if one does not feel equally close to each of them. On the other hand, the Nisei commonly explain their actions toward particular siblings in terms of how close they feel toward that sibling. So people say, "If a problem arose, I would go to my sister because we're very close," or "I would be surprised if my brother came to me for help; we hardly see each other and we've never been close."

These are the terms, moreover, in which the Nisei explain the differences between the relations of brothers and the relations of sisters. Sisters say they are in more frequent contact and do not hesitate to call upon each other for help because they "feel closer" than brothers, who find it painful to ask each other for help. Why, in turn, brothers do not feel close to each other is attributed to several factors by the Nisei. Men commonly assert they have "nothing in common" with brothers whose occupation, leisure activities, political values, and "life-style" are different from their own. Yet, if today they have nothing in common with them, it is not because what was once a close, affectionate relationship has eroded with the passage of time and the responsibilities of adulthood. Most Nisei men claim they have never felt much in common with their brothers and that this was particularly the case during their adolescence. This early experience of social distance is again commonly attributed to differences in "interests" and attitudes. But the roots of this distance are also traced to hostilities arising out of the unequal treatment of brothers by Issei parents. While all junior sons express some resentment of the eldest son, second sons in particular attribute their alienation from the first son to the preferential treatment he received from their parents. A few junior sons spoke openly of resenting their eldest brother because "mom always liked him better"; but most of them attributed such resentment to the elder brother's character and temperament, which in turn were said to be consequences of his position as successor. Being considered special by parents, assigned authority over younger siblings, and in many cases coddled by a mother, rendered first sons egocentric, spoiled, dogmatic bullies with quick tempers. Junior sons were claimed—that is, by junior sons—to have had easier dispositions and thus more amicable relationships with each other.

Finally, both men and women attribute the distance between brothers to men's less expressive and communicative character. The Nisei do not agree as to whether this male interpersonal style is the outcome of nature ("Men are naturally like that") or culture ("Men are taught to be less emotional") or some combination of the two. Neither is there agreement as to whether men are less emotionally sensitive than women or merely less communicative of their feelings. Whatever reason they give for it, however, people agree that men's uncommunicative interpersonal style contributes to the distant relationship between brothers as well as between fathers and sons. One Nisei third son from an all-male sibship described his experience in the following way: "Being from an all-boy family can be a pretty austere thing. We didn't talk at dinner, didn't give presents at Christmas, didn't have the kinds of feelings that girls have—you know at birthdays, Christmas time. The first birthday party I had was after I got married. Boys just don't talk about anything unless they have to. They just cope with each other."

Sisters also have different interests, attitudes, and life-styles. Many Nisei women described their sisters as holding rather different opinions from them. But at the same time women feel they are capable of transcending those differences. Two reasons are given. On the more positive side, women are said by both men and women to be more openly communicative and tolerant of different opinions than are men. Sisters are able to disagree and even argue without "taking it so personally." If, however, feelings are hurt, women are able to swallow their pride and patch things up. On the more negative side, shallowness of character and superficiality are said to allow sisters to gloss over differences. The wife of the Nisei man from the all-male sibship followed her husband's lament about the austerity of his natal family experience with this comment about her all-female sibship: "There are a lot of petty things my sisters go through; the brothers [referring here to her husband's brothers] just grunt, but they feel strongly; there is a real loyalty there. The girls like my sisters chatter away, but there are hidden feelings. I can't say that I could be cruel toward my sisters, but I don't know about them. I really don't know how deep their feelings go; it's rather superficial." In other words, if in Nisei gender caricatures brothers only grunt at each other, those grunts can be interpreted either as evincing a lack of interest and emotional involvement or as conveying deeply felt, but unarticulated, commitments. If sisters chatter freely with each other, the chatter may be the expression of either an uninhibited relationship or a superficial one.

Whether they incline to a cynical or a generous view of men's and women's interactional styles, the Nisei cite women's style as the reason why sisters handle family gatherings and gift exchanges. Both men and women say that family gatherings of all kinds are "run by women," with the husbands joining in. Some people label the situation a "matriarchy"; others say men "let women run the show." It is not just because food is an important part of family gatherings that women are in charge of these events; rather it is because women can negotiate and cooperate with their sisters and mothers much better than men can cooperate with brothers and fathers. Gift-exchange arrangements could never be handled by men, the Nisei say, because men are too "guarded" to discuss such matters openly. Accordingly, it is the ability of women to communicate, whether openly or superficially, to negotiate, and to cooperate, that explains for the Nisei the uterine bias of family gatherings and family relationships in general. It is why, they say, at marriage "a man is lost to his family" and is drawn into his "wife's family." This observation by the Nisei, which reverses the Japanese expectation that daughters are "lost" by incorporation into their husbands' families, brings us to the question of what the Nisei mean by "family."

"FAMILY" AND "RELATIVES"

"Family" for the Nisei does not denote a single genealogically defined group of people or even one whose composition changes in predictable ways over the individual's life cycle. The membership of a person's "family" differs not only over the life cycle, but from one context to another at any particular stage of the life cycle. "My family" may refer to only ego, with his or her spouse and their children—in other words, to ego's procreative family. In other contexts, "my family" denotes ego's natal family (parents and siblings). "My family" may also signify an individual's natal and procreative families in combination. This unit of ego and his or her parents, siblings, spouse, and children is referred to by many Nisei as "my immediate family." In addition, the Nisei usually include their siblings' spouses and children in this "immediate family," which thus corresponds to the inclusive conjugal family that was central to my analysis of Christmas and Thanksgiving gatherings. If a Nisei's children have married and produced grandchildren, moreover, their children's spouses and their grandchildren will also be included. Finally, "my family" may refer to an even larger set of kin including, in addition to the above, any of the following: ego's parents' siblings and their spouses; ego's first cousins; and the members of ego's spouse's inclusive conjugal family.

Which one of these sets of kin is the relevant family in which a Nisei includes him- or herself depends on the occasion or activity the informant has in mind. My request that informants list the members of their families created one such specific context and, indeed, one unlikely to reoccur for most of them. When I asked Nisei whom they included in their "family," the answer that best articulated their shared conception was "It depends on the occasion." Even those who were less acute observers of their usage of the term made it apparent in other ways that family membership depended on the occasion. Statements such as "I include Uncle Henry and his wife because if we had a birthday dinner we would invite them" and "I guess they are part of my family, because we always see them over the holidays" were common.

"Family," if defined by genealogical criteria, shares the polysemous character of many kin categories explicated by anthropologists. Like the Nuer lineage (Evans-Pritchard 1940), the Nisei family exists only in opposition to other units at the same genealogical level. In one context, a Nisei informant will distinguish "my family" from "my sister's family," thus defining his sister and her spouse and children as members of a different "family" from his own. Yet, the same informant will include all the above people in "my family" when, for example, he says "I get together much less with my family than with my wife's family." In this instance, the informant's inclusive natal conjugal family is contrasted with his wife's inclusive natal conjugal family and so includes his sister, her husband, and their children. Hence, as in the case of the Nuer lineage, a person can be both a member of a "family" and not a member of a "family."

A "family" that includes both the informant's and the informant's spouse's parents, siblings, siblings' spouses, and siblings' children may be divided into "sides of the family." What in one context is referred to as a "family" in and of itself ("my wife's family") can be referred to as a "side of the family" ("my wife's side of the family"), the two different sides being connected by an affinal link. Finally, that the polysemous, contextually shifting referent of "family" poses no conceptual confusion for the Nisei is apparent from their ability to use the term to refer to two different, overlapping units in the same sentence. An example of this common pattern of usage is the response a Nisei gave when I asked her who she included in her family. "My family," she said, "includes just my kids and their families."

"Persons" and "Families" as "Relatives"

The Nisei category of "relatives" likewise has no constant genealogical referent. Any person to whom ego can trace a consanguineal or affinal tie may be referred to as a "relative." But someone whom ego classifies as a "relative" in one context may in another context be excluded from that category. If the context is perceived to be an "American" one, the relevant units are "persons"; if the context is perceived to be a "Japanese" one, the relevant units are "families." When I asked Nisei informants to "list for me all the people you consider to be related to you," they construed the context as American.[9] Everything they said to explain their varying lists of relatives was consistent with Schneider's claim that in the United States "the decision as to who is and who is not a relative is made by and about a person" (Schneider 1968, 57). No rules, according to Schneider, require one to include people who fall within a set range of genealogical distance as one's relatives, but rather an individual decides for himself whom to include in this category. The decision depends on ego's assessment of the closeness of the relationship between himself and alter. By closeness or distance, Schneider means the genealogical distance between people, the social distance be-

[9] Following the field procedures of Schneider's American kinship research project, I had asked each informant to "list for me all the people you consider to be related to you." As I argued in my 1978 article, however, this instruction has two critical implications: that individuals are the units in the relationship, since it asks for a list of people related to "you" rather than to your family or household; and that there is some "consideration" and therefore choice involved in the matter. Consequently, the Nisei informants perceived the kin listing to be an "American" procedure involving individuals and choice; one *chooses* which "persons" are one's relatives.

tween them (the "personal relationship"), or both, as assessed by either party to the relationship. Accordingly a specific individual from a kin type such as "uncle" may be included while other individuals who fall in that same category are excluded.

The Nisei commonly listed as relatives consanguines such as grandparents, grandchildren, parents' siblings, parents' siblings' children, parents' parents' siblings, siblings' children, and siblings' children's children. Inclusion of kin types of five or more civil degrees of consanguinity was less common. Eight of the 32 Nisei from whom I obtained kin listings, however, included such a distant consanguine (e.g., first cousin once removed, second cousin, and first cousin twice removed). The common inclusion of consanguines within four civil degrees of removal indicates that kin within this genealogical range are generally considered relatives unless there is a specific personal reason for exclusion. Kin outside this genealogical range are generally excluded from the category of relatives unless there is a specific personal reason for inclusion. The difference between these two sets of genealogical kin types is reflected in the way in which the Nisei listed them. Informants often listed those kin within four civil degrees of removal according to kin type (e.g., "my uncles"), but always listed those of greater genealogical distance with reference to a specific person (e.g., "Mary S. who is my mother's cousin's daughter").

The affines commonly included as relatives by the Nisei are child's spouse, sibling's spouse, grandchild's spouse, parent's sibling's spouse, niece and nephew's spouse, and first cousin's spouse. All these affinal kin can be included in the category labeled *CA* (ego's consanguine's affines) by Schneider and Cottrell (1975). The reciprocal of *CA* is *AC* (ego's affine's consanguines), in other words, if *X* is a *CA* of *Y*, then *Y* is an *AC* of *X*. Consequently, all the Nisei included *AC* kin as their relatives. This category includes affines such as ego's spouse's parents, spouse's siblings, spouse's grandparents, spouse's sibling's children, spouse's parent's siblings, and spouse's first cousin. A further category of affines commonly included as relatives by the Nisei is that of ego's affine's consanguine's affines (*ACA*). The most common *ACA* kin type listed as a relative is ego's spouse's sibling's spouse. Several Nisei, however, also included additional types of *ACA* kin such as spouse's sibling's child's spouse and spouse's parent's sibling's spouse.

When they discuss *kōden* reciprocity, on the other hand, the Nisei use family units in their determination of who is a relative (Yanagisako 1978). Because the Nisei view *kōden* reciprocity as a Japanese custom governed by Japanese rules, moreover, they say one is expected to give *kōden* regardless of how one feels about a "person" or the character of one's personal relationship with them. The category of relatives to whom the Nisei say one must give *kōden* is made up primarily of conjugal family units to whom ego's natal family or procreative family is connected solely by an affinal tie. These families contain the affinal kin (such as a sibling's spouse's sibling) that only a third of my Nisei informants included in their lists of "relatives." Yet when they discussed *kōden* reciprocity, all Nisei informants claimed these people were "relatives" or "distant relatives" to whom one must give *kōden* (Yanagisako 1978).

"Family" and "Relatives" as Normative Domains

"Family" and "relatives" are both overlapping and discrete categories. On the one hand, any Nisei may include a specific alter in his family in one context, but classify him as a relative in another. If we consider a range of contexts, therefore, the memberships of family and relatives overlap. On the other hand, in any given context, the Nisei draw sharp boundaries between them. When they discussed *kōden* reciprocity, for example, the Nisei clearly distinguished between their "family" (to whom they do not give *kōden*) and their "relatives" (to whom they do). Likewise, when the Nisei drew up lists of their family and their relatives, they made comments such as "I think of people outside the family as relatives," "Well, they're outside the family so they're relatives," and "They aren't relatives, they're family." These statements indicate that, in spite of the variable inclusion of kin types and individuals in these categories, there is a constant difference between them that lies not in a set of genealogical features but in a set of normative features. The first feature is that, despite the invariable inclusion of certain kin as "relatives to whom one must give *kōden*," when Nisei list their "relatives" they make it clear they are deciding whom to include. In contrast, inclusion of people within one's family is not a matter of choice. Parents, siblings, children, and spouses, in particular, are said to be members of one's "family" irrespective of whether one wants to include them or not; according to some, but not all, Nisei, so are other kin such as grandparents, aunts, uncles, nephews, and nieces. Second, and linked with its more voluntary quality, the nature and strength of one's commitment to a relative depends on one's assessment of the "closeness" of the "personal relationship." A Nisei may, for example, say he feels no more commitment to one of his mother's sisters than to invite her to his wedding and to exchange Christmas cards. Yet he may invite another of his mother's sisters to certain family gatherings because he has a close "personal relationship" with her. Likewise, he expects to be invited to the graduation party of a niece or nephew with whom he has such a relationship but not the party of one he feels he "hardly knows."

Whereas relatives are "persons," "family" are nonpersons in the sense that a personal relationship has much less consequence for one's commitment to them. Whether one has seen a lot of a family member recently is less relevant to whether one decides to help her or him financially than it is in the case of a relative. A person's commitment to a family member is not construed as a matter of "personality." As one Nisei man explained: "Outside of the family who you like or dislike is a matter of personality. Within the immediate family you don't have that feeling. You don't love one more than the other, you love them the same. You may treat them differently materially, but feel the same toward them." At the same time, family members should treat each other like "persons" and not take advantage of the unconditional commitment between family members. Yet, because family members have this guarantee, some tend to treat others with less respect than they would people outside the family. A Nisei woman described her sister's tendency to do this in the following terms: "She [my sister] doesn't treat us [myself and my husband] like persons, but like family. To her family is family and she can say anything to them. *Family is not persons* [author's emphasis]. She'll ask us negative questions like 'What are you doing spending money like that?' but she wouldn't treat anybody outside the family that way. She doesn't seem to realize that we're people; and yet I know she means well and she's loyal."

As some of these statements have already implied, the intensity of the emotional relationship among family also differs from that among relatives. Nisei commonly said that a "family" member is "too close to be just a relative." "Relatives" are people one "likes," but "family" are people one "loves." It was not until I recognized that, for the Nisei, "love" pertains to "family" and "like" to relatives that the following statement by an informant became intelligible. In response to my question as to whether she considered her husband a relative, this woman said: "If you like your husband as well as love him, then he's your relative [in addition to being a family member]." "Love" and "like" differ not only in intensity but also in contingency and duration. The more casual, light affection one feels for a relative may change as the relationship changes. The more intense, deeper affection among family members, in comparison, is not contingent upon any such "personal" relationship. Husbands and wives can get divorced, of course, and families can break up, but otherwise family members have an enduring commitment to each other, a commitment referred to as "love."

The noncontingency of love gives the family a durability that renders it a unit of long-term reciprocity. There is no rush to balance the accounts. One can borrow items freely from someone inside the family without being anxious about breaking them or returning them immediately in perfect condition, because eventually the exchange will balance out. With a relative, however, one should not be so casual. A favor from a relative requires an immediate return of some kind lest one seem ungrateful or greedy. Short-term, balanced reciprocity is therefore the normative order of exchange among relatives.

Finally, the contrast between "family" and "relatives" is a contrast between shared identity and separate identity. "Family" is an extension of the self, as evinced in such statements by Nisei as "Because they are my family they are a part of me, so they're not relatives," and "You don't call your right hand your relative." Whatever unit is referred to as a "family," moreover, has a set of attributes and a social history—in short, a reputation. Nisei say of their and other people's families that they are "smart," "ambitious," "successful," "have always been leaders in the community," or "have been in the community for a long time." "Relatives" do not share such characteristics, neither do they have a common biography.

That the family is a unit of shared identity means not only that its members, through their actions, have an impact on each other's current reputation in the community, but that those actions are evidence of the members' shared past, that is, of qualities transmitted through past generations. These qualities—attitudes, motivations, and personality styles—are not only genetically inherited (through "blood") but socially transmitted (through "upbringing"). Thus, an individual who achieves a prestigious occupation or who becomes a community leader simultaneously affirms both his own and his family's worth. If the rest of his siblings remain in much less prestigious occupations, it is chiefly his own intelligence and ambition that are affirmed. But a professional whose siblings are also professionals affirms these qualities as transmitted through the family.

The combined achievements and deeds of individual members of a family, therefore, create a reputation and a history for it that extend farther into the past than anyone's knowledge of its ancestors. Present character is interpreted as evidence of past character. Good conduct is proof of good blood as well as good upbringing. A family with a reputation has a common interest in guarding and enhancing that reputation. Hence, any family may have secrets that are kept inside it. These secrets include mostly information that would make it or any of its members look bad in the eyes of the community.[10] Conflicts and tensions among members, financial transactions, the incomes of members, divorce, extramarital affairs, premarital pregnancies, abortions, certain illnesses, and what the Nisei call "anything embarrassing" should not be revealed "outside the family." If a woman's sister gets pregnant before she is married or her siblings are embroiled in an inheritance dispute, she should not discuss it even with a best friend. If a couple are in serious financial straits, either of them may talk about it with other family members, but not with anyone else.

The boundaries of the family within which secrets are contained, of course, vary just as the composition of the family varies from one context to another. So, for example, if a man's parents are quarreling, he should not reveal it to his wife's parents or even to his mother's sister, for in this context they are "outside the family." But if a man's mother is quarreling with her brother, he is free to discuss it with his mother's sister because in this context she is "part of the family." In the same way that the boundaries within which secrets are contained define the boundaries of "family" in any context, so who argues freely with whom in front of whom else defines the boundaries of "family" in any context. Because they are all "family," parents will argue with an adult child in front of other adult children and even their spouses. And they will argue with each other in front of their children and their spouses. But they would never argue with each other or with their children in the presence of a child's spouse's parents or a child's spouse's siblings.

Because family boundaries change from one quarrel to another, one secret to another, and one crisis to another, people must be careful to avoid infringing on the privacy of a "family" they may, in another context, be members of. If they are aware of the secret, they should feign ignorance or at least lack of interest, even if members of that family absentmindedly mention it in their presence. To enter into a discussion of a problem or secret which resides inside a family of which one is not at that moment a member is to risk being thought of as meddling in other people's business.

[10] A family may have secrets of other kinds too. However, the only such secret the Nisei ever mentioned to me was the location where they hunted for the highly desired *matsutake* (pine mushroom). Some families were said to have maps pinpointing the spots in the Olympic Peninsula forests where they had found *matsutake*. As only "family" are shown these maps, I never saw one.

SIBLINGS AND FAMILIES: CONTINUITY AND INDEPENDENCE

By now it should be clear why the Nisei conception of siblinghood cannot be understood apart from the Nisei construct of family. The sibling relationship, as we have seen, is located between the normative domains of "family" and "relatives." Even after they marry and have their own families, siblings are thought of as "too close to be just relatives." Yet, despite their inclusion in a familial domain in which "personality" is deemed irrelevant to the quality of commitment, the Nisei interpret and explain the character of their sibling relationships in terms of the "personal relationship" between two unique individuals—that is, "persons." It is not surprising, therefore, that my Nisei informant's complaint about being treated like "family" rather than like "persons" was prompted by, or at least addressed to, a sibling's behavior. Given their placement in the murky area where the norms governing relations between persons merge with the norms governing relations between non-persons (i.e., "family"), siblings are perhaps more vulnerable than other kin to being accused of inappropriate behavior. Likewise, the Nisei uneasiness with the term "obligation" in reference to a sibling relationship is balanced by their assertion that one does have "responsibilities" toward siblings. Again, when we consider the contrast between the long-term, asymmetrical exchanges deemed appropriate to family and the short-term, symmetrical exchanges expected of relatives, siblings fall somewhere in between. Finally, siblings both do and do not share their social identities with other family members such as their parents and children. What a sibling does is, in one sense, "his own business." Yet Nisei siblings are members of a family that has a biography, a reputation, and relations with other families. Thus, in the continuing flow of *kōden*, a flow that reaffirms and recreates the kinship and friendship web of the community, adult siblings are interchangeable as givers and receivers because of their identity as members of the same family.

FROM KAZOKU TO "FAMILY"

Unlike Issei siblings, Nisei siblings do not become "strangers" or *shinrui*. Instead, they provide the basis for the social continuity of families that are radically different from the *kazoku* of the Issei. It is the sibling relation that, as I will show, enables "the family" to continue even after its junior members have formed conjugal families of their own. One consequence is that, given Nisei gender constructs, sisters are "closer" than brothers. No doubt the tensions and resentments resulting from their unequal treatment by parents have helped to make Nisei brothers less close. Yet it is more than past and present inequity that has made brothers poor candidates for coordinating the activities and transactions upon which family continuity depends. In the analysis of Nisei marriage and gender domains, we saw that the Nisei view men as the leaders of (conjugal) families and as providers of the income that ensures its proper independence from all other families, conjugal and otherwise. Given their status as the heads of conjugal families, men must remain independent of, and therefore distant from, their brothers and fathers. For brothers to cooperate closely in promoting family unity could only threaten the symbolic independence of conjugal families. Their sisters are under no such constraint. Again it is not merely that Nisei sisterhood is unblemished by past or present asymmetries and resentments, nor that sisters are so much like each other in tastes and opinions. More importantly, women are neither the leaders in marriage nor the heads of conjugal families. Hence they can cooperate and negotiate to unify "the family" without appearing to threaten the independence of their own and their brothers' conjugal families.

The change from a stem-family system, in which the perpetuation of households demanded the separation of siblings, to a conjugal family system, in which the continuity of "families" demands the cooperation of siblings, has been accompanied by a change in the character of family constructs. By this I mean not that the genealogical composition of *kazoku* and "family" differ, because, as I have shown, neither of these terms has a constant genealogical referent. Rather, I mean that the Issei construct of *kazoku*, which matched a bounded social group with a normative domain, has been replaced among the Nisei by the construct of "family," which defines a normative domain through which different sets of people—parents, siblings, children, grandchildren, cousins, aunts, brothers-in-law, etc.—flow depending on the occasion. For the Issei, the boundaries of *kazoku* have always been clear as regards both its normative prescriptions and its personnel. In Chapter 7 I argued that, in spite of the changing genealogical composition and functions of the units that the Issei identify as their past and present *kazoku*, the core meaning of *kazoku* has not changed for them. It continues to refer to the group of people upon whom one can, or should be able to, depend for enduring, unconditional loyalty and support. Furthermore, even though the composition of one's *kazoku* changes over time and with one's stage in the life cycle, at any point in time one's *kazoku* consists of a single group of people. Whether one is a widow living with a married daughter, so that one's primary claims and loyalties reside with her conjugal family, or whether one lives apart from the children and their conjugal families that one includes within that domain of primary claims, *kazoku* membership does not change from one context to the next. Although it does not refer to an exclusive group (some members of one's own *kazoku* are members of other *kazoku*), neither does it refer to an occasional group like the Nisei's "family."

For the Nisei, as I have just shown, the constant referent of "family" is a normative domain that, in different contexts, applies to different sets of people. Of all the people who move in and out of this domain, siblings are the most transient and hover closest to its boundaries. Consequently, the conjugal families of married siblings can be simultaneously independent of and subsumed within "the family."

If the latter bears any similarity to those amorphous forms commonly referred to in the literature on kinship in industrial society as "extended families," they can by no means be traced to the so-called traditional family patterns they are so often assumed to perpetuate in "modern" times. To the contrary, I have shown that behind these larger Japanese American families are not traditional family values, but *transformed* family values.

CHAPTER 9

Conclusion: Transforming the Past

TRADITION, Raymond Williams (1977, 115) has noted, is "always more than an inert historicized segment." Rather, it is an "intentionally selective version of a shaping past and a preshaped present" that offers "a historical and cultural ratification of contemporary order" (ibid , 117). In the case at hand, Japanese Americans have constructed a selective version not only of a traditional Japanese past but of a modern American present. In placing what they conceive as Japanese culture and American culture in symbolic opposition, the Issei and even more so the Nisei have reinterpreted symbols, norms, and forms of action from each culture as the opposites of those from the other. In doing so, they have created a new system of meanings in which the elements of the "American" present are as much a product of this dialectic of reinterpretation as are the elements attached to the "Japanese" past.

Because Japanese Americans construe their history as a history of cultural change, explication of their folk model of culture and history has been central to my analysis of kinship change. I have been concerned with the categories by which Issei and Nisei connect their contemporary kinship relations with past ones because it is through this symbolic process that Japanese Americans have reinterpreted and modified their kinship relations. In this final chapter, I consider the ways in which Japanese Americans' conception of such connections at once differentiates them from other Americans and yet renders them the same. After reviewing the pertinent core symbols, I describe the process through which Japanese Americans metaphorically construct a model of Japanese American kinship from models of the "Japanese" past and the "American" present. I then consider some other studies in anthropology that, like mine, bring folk models of history into the analysis of historical processes. Finally, recognition that such folk models are central to both ethnicity and cultural change leads me to propose a solution to the riddle of the unity and diversity of American kinship.

CULTURAL SYMBOLS AND KINSHIP CHANGE

My main method of studying the construction of Japanese American kinship has been to analyze the meanings that cultural symbols such as "family," "work," "duty," "love," "Japanese," and "American" have for the two generations in the context of their social history. In Part I, my comparison of the gender domain metaphors used by Issei and Nisei revealed that more had changed over two generations of marriage than the manner in which spouses were selected, the extent of male authority, and the conjugal division of labor. The Issei gender metaphor of sociospatial opposition, which assigned women to an "inside" domain encompassed by a male "outside" one, had been supplanted by the Nisei labor-specialization metaphor, which assigned to women the reproductive function of "family" and "home," and to men the productive function of income-earning "work." This shift, from a conception of gender domains that carried with it an inherent structure of authority to one that did not, entailed a change in people's ideas about what determines the power relations between spouses. For the Issei, the power relation in any particular marriage was a product of the social resources that the spouses derived from their respective positions in society. Thus Issei wives whose parents were successful entrepreneurs in Seattle were advantaged over those whose parents were tenant farmers in Japan.

The same cultural logic lay behind the association between Issei conjugal power relations and the successor or nonsuccessor status of Issei marriage: the greater degree of male control over a number of spheres in successor marriages was made possible by successor sons' claims to the headship of established households in their natal communities in Japan. For the Nisei, in contrast, men's authority and power in marriage were considered the consequence, not of their location in a hierarchy of sociospatial domains, but of the material resources they acquire through their income-producing work. Hence, although the Nisei gender domain metaphor did not dictate a fixed structure of male authority over women, related notions about the social prerogatives of earning an income endowed Nisei husbands with greater power in a world where men were the primary breadwinners. Moreover, the metaphor helped to explain why Nisei wives, who exhibited different rates of employment in their initial years of marriage, ended up with rates that were much the same, and also why, unlike their Issei counterparts, Nisei wives of self-employed businessmen were no more likely to work during their childbearing years than Nisei wives of salaried husbands.

The Nisei gender domain metaphor was also seen to organize the distribution of filial obligations among siblings. At the same time, my exploration of how the Nisei have differentiated the formerly unified successor-son role revealed inheritance to be a central symbol of filial transmission in the dialogue through which Issei and Nisei negotiate their filial relations. The fact that many Issei die intestate and decline to articulate rules for inheritance, while the Nisei insist upon the moral justice of equal inheritance among siblings, speaks of the different meanings the two generations attach to inheritance. For both Issei and Nisei, inheritance symbolizes whatever it is that is transmitted between parents and children. But, for the Issei, the core of what parents transmit to children, and of what children should later return to parents, is a social identity and the claim to a respectable place in the social world. For the Nisei, the core of parental transmission is the "love" that makes for emotionally complete individuals who are capable of returning it later to their parents in the form of care and support. Although the Issei were only too ready to expound the "rules" of what they perceived as Japanese filial relations, they were unwilling to articulate any such rules for inheritance or any other aspect of filial relations in contemporary American society. This apparent discrepancy became comprehensible once it was recognized that the Issei were caught between two meanings of equal inheritance. What for them symbolized the division and demise of a social identity for the Nisei symbolized the equal and just division of parental love. Likewise, the Issei hesitated to broadcast their desires and hopes for one child, preferably a son, to take on all the components of the successor role, for they were well aware that for the Nisei this was an uncaring practice that divided the sibling group and threatened to destroy the love holding the family together.

In addition to their conceptions of gender, Nisei conceptions of "love," "equality," and what is "practical" and "natural" were found to underlie their normative differentiation of the successor role and its distribution among siblings. The meanings of coresidence, inheritance, and other components of the formerly fused role of successor were transformed as the Nisei responded to the ambiguities in filial relations generated by the disruptions of World War II. Before the war, for example, coresidence of a married couple with one of the spouse's parents had signaled unequivocably the former's status as successor to the latter. After the war, however, coresidence no longer represented succession and the perpetuation of a social identity but nurturance and the reciprocation of filial love. The increasing power of the Nisei to define the meaning of coresidence and its gender connotations explained the postwar rise in uxorilocal postmarital residence and the corresponding decline in virilocal postmarital residence.

In Part III, consideration of the sibling relation showed it to be a boundary issue both in the reproduction of stem families and in the independence and continuity of conjugal families. For this reason, movement from a stem-family system to a conjugal family system necessitated a change in the conception of siblings. The relative poverty of exegesis on siblinghood by the Issei reflected their classification of siblings as *shinrui* and thus placement of them outside the *kazoku* and the domain of primary obligations. What unified the diverse sibling histories of the Issei recounted in Chapter 7 was the Issei notion of siblinghood as a relation born of the *kazoku*, but that moved inexorably outside it to the domain where *shinrui* joined neighbors, *kenjin*, and friends as variations on the same theme of secondary relations. It was not surprising, therefore, that the many cooperative business ventures among Issei brothers, their coresidence in Seattle, and their mutual aid in young adulthood were experienced as, and so became, transitory arrangements.

With the replacement of the Issei concept of *kazoku*, which matched a bounded social group with a normative domain, by the Nisei concept of "family," which defines a normative domain through which different sets of people flow depending on the occasion, the location of siblings was changed. Siblings now hovered around the interstitial area between the domain of family and the domain of relatives, rendering married siblings at once members of different families and members of the same family. Thus the changing concept of siblinghood, and its relation to the categories into which people divided the cultural universe of kin, provided a key to understanding how the Nisei had moved from a stem-family system to a conjugal family system while claiming to perpetuate "Japanese family tradition."

Nisei notions of siblinghood and gender, moreover, were shown to underlie the women-centered character of Japanese American kin networks. Cooperation among siblings enabled inclusive conjugal families to maintain their social identity in the community even after their junior members had married and formed conjugal families of their own.

As heads of what were supposed to be independent families, however, men had to maintain distance from brothers and fathers, while relations between sisters and between mothers and daughters were under no such constraints because they did not threaten the symbolic independence of such families. Women's centrality in kin networks and their effort to maintain the identity of their natal families was perceived by the Nisei as a continuation of supposedly traditional family values. Likewise, the Nisei construed the large size and complex genealogical composition of Japanese American family gatherings as a link with the intensely familial Japanese past. Yet, here again, the family units being affirmed in these gatherings were not the products of the hypothetical traditional Japanese family system that the Nisei had symbolically constructed, but rather of a transformed family system in which married siblings and their families constituted the core of a different kind of enduring family.

RETHINKING TRADITION: THE JAPANESE AMERICAN MODEL OF CULTURE AND KINSHIP

Japanese American notions of how and why their kinship relations take their present form are aspects of a more general folk model of history and culture that shapes a good deal of Japanese American social life. Like Japanese American personality and identity, the Japanese American family is viewed by Japanese Americans as the product of a history of substitutions and compromises between the cultural orders symbolized by "Japanese" and "American." These cultural orders, which constitute contrasting hierarchies of values, psychological tendencies, interactional styles, and modes for the determination of action are summarized in Table 23.

This is not to say that the Issei and Nisei have manufactured false symbols, norms, or actions in order to construct a mythical "traditional Japanese" past or an idealized "modern American" present. Instead, they have transformed the symbols, norms, and actions of the past by attributing to them meanings that make sense of current experience and that speak to current dilemmas and issues. Conversely, they interpret and act upon the present in light of their models of the past. In Chapter 7, for example, I showed how the Issei utilize both individuals and households as the units of *shinrui* relations. So do the Nisei. The latter, however, order their varying usage of these units according to a Japanese/American opposition, viewing individuals as the appropriate units vis-à-vis relatives in "American" contexts and families (rather than households) as the appropriate units vis-à-vis relatives in "Japanese"

TABLE 23

Two Cultural Orders as Viewed by Japanese Americans

"Japanese"	"American"
Precedence of *giri* (duty) over feelings:	Precedence of feelings over duty:
Marriage is rooted in *giri*	Marriage is based on "love"
Obligations to jural parents take precedence over ones to biological parents	Biological parents are one's "real" parents
Emotional restraint; absence of displays of affection	Emotional expressiveness; public displays of affection
Social groups are the units of social action:	Individuals are the units of social action:
Families are the units of *kōden* exchange	Persons are the units in determining who is a relative
Families are self-sufficient and independent units	Individuals are self-sufficient and independent units
Action is governed by rules:	Individuals choose a course of action by considering a multiplicity of factors:
Filial relations are governed by unambiguous rules	Filial relations are shaped by competing values, desires and feelings, "practicality" and the specific situation
Marriage is not a matter of choice	One chooses to marry and chooses one's own spouse
Sexual division of labor is rigid	Sexual division of labor is flexible
Hierarchical social relations:	Egalitarian social relations:
Male dominance	Greater sexual equality
Unquestioned obedience of children to parents, strict discipline	Parental authority based on "reason," relaxed discipline
Siblings ranked by birth order and gender	Sibling equality

contexts. The Nisei, therefore, endow these units with meanings that did not underlie their usage in Japan or among non-Japanese Americans in the United States. By eliminating individuals as units in their version of Japanese kinship, moreover, the Nisei construct a model of Japanese social relations that, like most models of culture, is both simpler and more consistent than reality. They do the same by eliminating families as units in "American" kinship. The Nisei conception of *giri* provides another example of the decontextualization of a symbol and the transformation of its meaning. In the cultural system articulated by the Issei, both *giri* (duty) and *ninjo* (feeling) were present as contrastive motives and values. However, the normative priority placed on *giri* in the Japanese cultural system, contrasted with the relatively greater emphasis on feeling in the American system, appears to have moved the Nisei to select only one element as representative of each culture. Consequently, *giri* came to represent the Japanese system and feeling the American one. Necessary or not, this decontextualization enabled the Nisei to reduce complex systems of meaning to simple elements.

These examples show the Nisei to have engaged in a practice that, were they anthropologists, they could be faulted for. The Japanese concept of *giri*, after all, is not the symbolic opposite of the American concept of individual feelings, for opposites can exist only in the same system of meaning, not in different ones. The Nisei, of course, fashioned their ethnotheory of culture not to further the goals of ethnology, but to guide their actions and interpretations of actions in daily life. The decontextualization of cultural elements, which for an anthropologist would be an act of misinterpretation, is for the Nisei an act of reinterpretation in the creation of a new system of meanings and new normative expectations.

Throughout the book I have shown how Japanese American norms for kinship relations are formed out of elements extracted from either of the contrastive cultural orders or from both of them, depending on the perceived context. If an event, practice, or setting is perceived to be "American," as in the case of listing one's relatives or choosing one's spouse, then "American" values, social units, and modes of action are called for. If an event, practice, or setting is perceived as "Japanese," as in the case of *kōden* exchange, then "Japanese" values, social units, and modes of action are called for. A balanced compromise or synthesis of elements from both cultural orders is appropriate in contexts construed as "Japanese American." Being Japanese American entails being able to alternate between these contrastive cultural orders and, above all, to integrate opposed elements within oneself. Dominance of elements from either order threatens a Nisei's identity as a Japanese American, since too much emphasis on American elements renders one indistinguishable from a *hakujin* (white) and too much emphasis on Japanese elements makes one too "Japanesey" and "old-fashioned."

Japanese American kinship norms, therefore, are metaphorically constructed from Japanese American folk models of Japanese and American culture. What is defined as Japanese American in any context is not so much a compromise between what people have observed of kinship relations in Japan and America as compromise between these two models. For example, the Nisei think that, since Japanese

American sibling relations should be such a compromise, they should incorporate the emphasis on duty found in Japanese culture but also the emphasis on choice and feeling found in American culture. They formulate these norms by drawing upon the models. They do the same in formulating their norms for Japanese American marriage, filial relations, and family gatherings. From this we can see how, for example, the Nisei can attribute the closeness and enduring cooperation between Nisei sisters to their "Japanese heritage." As Chapter 7 showed, Issei siblings experienced the growing distance expected of siblings in the Japanese stem-family system. Neither Issei sisters nor Issei brothers had relations over time that resembled the Nisei image of an intensely familial past. The Nisei image was not derived from an observed history of sibling relations among Japanese, but rather from their notion of what Japanese siblinghood must have been like given their model of Japanese culture.

Thus in my analysis, the tension between Japanese American conceptions of their supposedly Japanese kinship traditions and my reconstruction of their kinship history has brought to light processes of change overlooked by a cultural pluralist perspective. In the latter, kinship differences among ethnic groups in complex societies such as the United States are attributed to the maintenance of so-called cultural traditions. Whether this type of analysis admits some degree of acculturation or emphasizes cultural retention in any particular instance, it fails to elucidate the historically situated symbolic processes through which symbols and meanings, and hence culture, are transformed. This failure issues from a naive view of tradition as the inert aggregate of beliefs, values, norms, and practices whose meanings and relations are forever ascribed by culture. In such a model of culture, people can choose only between fixed alternatives rather than act to transform the alternatives. Hence, it is rather easy for someone who accepts the model to mistake what people identify as "tradition" as evidence of cultural continuity, and to overlook the possibility that symbols, norms, and practices that are superficially similar may have decidedly different social meanings and social consequences.

Treating tradition as a folk concept, in addition, encourages us to reevaluate the common assumption that the learning of tradition goes on inside families while the learning of new ideas takes place outside them. We have long recognized that people learn about families from outside agents and institutions. Hence, we have no difficulty in apprehending that the Issei learned the "rules" of Japanese familial relations as students in a Japanese national school system, as well as from their experience as children in Japanese households. Nor would we overlook the fact that the Nisei learned their metaphor of gender domains and the meaning of inheritance in American schools and from the popular media rather than from their Japanese parents. Yet there remains a strong tendency (as shown, for example, in Greeley and McCready 1975) to equate what is learned inside families with tradition and what is learned outside them with change. Thus, when the Nisei cite the absence of physical affection and the paucity of verbal communication between their parents as features of "Japanese" marriage, it is tempting to oppose a "tradition" of marriage learned inside families with a "modern" American one learned outside them. But that is to fail to understand that the Nisei's perception of their parents' conjugal relationships and the meaning that "Japanese marriage" holds for them is as much a product of what people outside their family and community said about love, marriage, and tradition as it is a product of what their parents said or did.

My point is that people do not simply learn a traditional system of ideals, symbols, metaphors, and norms about family and kinship from conservative agents of cultural transmission inside the family and a modern system from progressive agents of cultural transmission outside it, but rather that they construct notions of "traditional" and "modern" from what they are told by all agents of cultural transmission and what they experience both inside and outside families. Just as the Nisei's model of traditional Japanese marriage is shaped by experiences and ideas confronted outside families, so their model of modern American marriage is shaped by experiences and ideas confronted inside those same "traditional families." When the Nisei balance American marriage and Japanese marriage to create a Japanese American synthesis, therefore, they do not choose between a type of marriage they learned outside the family and one they learned inside the family, but rather between models they have fashioned from what they learned inside and outside families.

A cultural analysis of tradition, finally, keeps us from misconstruing the Issei as the embodiment of a Japanese baseline from which the Nisei have moved. The succession of generations has been a key mechanism of social change among Japanese Americans as it has been among other groups, but to treat the Issei as the "conservative" upholders of a Japanese kinship and the Nisei as its "progressive" modifiers is to confuse what the Issei symbolize with what they do. Just because the Issei are viewed and view themselves as the representatives of Japanese culture, does not mean they have remained unchanged. The Issei as much as the Nisei have altered their actions and norms in kinship relations in response to problems of action and meaning encountered over the years. Their kinship relations, transformed by their experience as immigrants, are as much Japanese American as the Nisei's. They have been just as active participants, moreover, in the intergenerational dialogue and negotiation about what constitutes Japanese American identity and kinship.

FOLK MODELS AND THE ANALYSIS OF CULTURE CHANGE

In making a folk model central to my analysis, I join the authors of not a few recent ethnographic studies that have benefited from a like approach. In an era of growing dissatisfaction with synchronic studies, a focus on historical process appears to offer the greatest promise of helping anthropology break free of the opposition between structure and history that has proven a major limitation of structuralist approaches, whether of the British (Radcliffe-Brown 1952), American (Parsons and Bales 1955), or French (Lévi-Strauss 1967) varieties. At the same time, a growing appreciation of the importance of the symbolic underpinnings of social action has led to a concern for the way history is made by individuals. Among the cultural constructs that guide their actions are their conceptions of history and culture. In other words, folk conceptions of how their present experience and orientations are to be understood in relation to their past and future ones, of how some things remain the same and some things change, are now being recognized as playing an important role in shaping the historical process.

Three monographs in particular together display the impact of widely differing folk conceptions of history on the course of social change and present-day social relations. Marshall Sahlins's (1981) analysis of the early post-contact period of Hawaiian history, for one, argues that we cannot understand why the Hawaiians responded as they did to the Europeans and the subsequent radical changes in Hawaiian institutions without understanding the Hawaiian theory of the European presence and, more broadly, the Hawaiian conception of history. In particular, the Hawaiians' interpretation of the incidents surrounding the arrival and killing of Captain Cook was steeped in their conception of history as myth repeating itself (Sahlins 1981, 9). Exploration of the historical perceptions of the Ilongot of northern Luzon by Renato Rosaldo (1980) reveals a radically different historical consciousness from the Hawaiian one. The Ilongot sense of history as improvised and unpredictable rather than rule-governed yields an un derstanding of "what Ilongot social life is most significantly about" (1980, 23), for it displays the cultural idiom that reflects past experiences and guides present actions. At the same time that he destroys the illusion of a timeless social structure among so-called primitive societies, Rosaldo shows how the Ilongot construct of history is rooted in their social life—in particular, their marriage practices. For the Ilongot notion of social order "as a number of persons walking single file along paths that shift in direction" (1980, 57) reflects marriage practices in which children, who generally do not marry the close kin of either parent, must seek their spouses in other directions (ibid., 59). Among the Merina of Madagascar, conceptions of culture and history that Maurice Bloch (1971) places at the core of their social life are, in turn, of another sort—in this case, somewhat closer to that of Japanese Americans. The Merina believe themselves to be a people faced with choosing between two totally different principles of life, one the "good" life of the "Malagasy past" and the other the compromised life of the present that has followed the arrival of foreigners. All Merina actions are interpreted in terms of these cultural-historical categories, and the ultimate compromise and atonement of a Merina for deviating from the ways of the ancestors is burial in the tomb of his ancestral kin group, often after a temporary burial in the location where he lived.

If hill-dwelling Ilongot, nineteenth-century Hawaiians, and people of Madagascar seem a far stretch of the anthropological imagination from Japanese Americans, the conceptions of culture and history that Karen Blu (1980) ascribes to the Lumbee of North Carolina bring us closer to home. Moreover, they suggest a way to connect up analyses of so-called acculturation among recognized ethnic groups with studies of culture change in general. What makes the Lumbee so interesting a case of American ethnicity is that they lack a formally recognized, recorded history of links to an ancestral Indian tribe, an Indian language, any peculiarly Indian customs, and even explicit membership criteria (ibid., 1-2). Instead what constitute Lumbee identity and hold them together are their shared ideas about themselves as a people. The most well-formulated aspect of these is the Lumbee "history" of their beginnings in the intermarriage of members of the Roanoke lost colony with friendly Indians—an account that is particularly appealing to southern whites with their love of histories and genealogies. Yet, at the same time that they play to a southern white audience, the Lumbee's notion of what differentiates them as a people from both whites and blacks draws not upon the racial symbolism prevalent in the American South but rather upon what Blu labels "ethnic symbolism" (ibid., 169). Blu differentiates the folk concept of race, which is based on notions about current biological differences between sets of people, from the folk concept of ethnicity, which is based on notions about their "heritage" or "background." Cast in Lévi-Straussian structuralist terms, her argument is that race as a folk construct is about the division between people "in nature," whereas ethnicity is about the division of people "in culture" (ibid., 205).

Blu hypothesizes that the progressive replacement of racial symbolism in American society by the symbolism of ethnicity signals the rejection of the symbolic domination of WASP culture and its associated institutions. I am less concerned here with the validity of this hypothesis than with a further implication Blu derives from it, namely, that the increased emphasis on ethnicity necessarily brings an increased concern with historical matters, for this suggests a connection between ethnicity and folk constructs of history.

"History, as perceived by both insiders and outsiders," Blu notes, "is at the core of ethnic identification." It is not a frill, but rather lies "at the heart of a symbolic structure of ethnicity in the United States" (ibid., 215). Members of an ethnic group are concerned not only with their own past but with the pasts of other groups with whom they interact. A wide range of symbols from many domains, including food, music, kinship, language, religion, and even race, can represent ethnic diversity. But all of them, rightly or wrongly, are deemed to share a link with a group's past.

In construing their present as the outcome of their past, the members of ethnic groups merge with a larger category of folk whose conceptions of history are central to their formulation of social action and their interpretation of its meaning. In addition, they interpret their contemporary relations with members of other ethnic groups in light of their perceptions of their ancestors' relations with those groups in the past. Yet this in itself does not endow them with a peculiar symbolic system. Others for whom an ethnic identity is less salient in social life and even those who disclaim having an ethnic identity also commonly interpret their present experience in light of their perceptions of their ancestral past. I am not claiming that all people everywhere and for all time have understood their present situation in terms of a perceived ancestral past, or that they have done so in the same manner. Rather, the point is that members of recognized ethnic groups are not unique in making history central to their notion of who they are and why. By placing Lumbee and Japanese Americans alongside Ilongot, Hawaiians, and Merina, we blur the boundaries of the phenomenon of ethnicity in order to consider a broader category of people for whom folk models of history and culture have a significant impact on the shape of social life and processes of change. In the final section of this chapter, I suggest how seeing ethnicity in this light offers a useful way to understand the unity and diversity of American kinship. For family and kinship in America are inextricably bound up with folk models of history and culture.

UNITY AND DIVERSITY IN AMERICAN KINSHIP

Intrasocietal diversity poses a formidable challenge to anthropology not merely because we now study "complex" societies as well as "simple" ones, but because we now adhere to less naive and less monolithic models of culture. American kinship poses the conundrum of how the members of an ethnically heterogeneous, class-stratified society can at once have different norms and ideas about kinship and yet share the same culture.

Japanese American kinship today is, at all levels of analysis, both similar to and different from what has been described as the kinship system of white, middle-class Americans. At the level of observable patterns of action, for example, the household composition of Japanese Americans does not differ significantly from that of their white neighbors. But the composition of Japanese American family gatherings and life-cycle celebrations is decidedly larger and genealogically more extended than those generally reported for the white middle class. As regards normative expectations, the filial responsibilities of Nisei sons and daughters appear more sharply defined and more differentiated by gender than the filial responsibilities articulated by middle-class whites. Certainly, the assignment of the role of representative of the sibling group to the eldest brother is not common among other Americans. Yet the Nisei's expectation that siblings are equal and should inherit equally is shared by the rest of the middle class (Cumming and Schneider 1961). So too are Nisei norms for the roles of husbands and wives.

As for the definition of kinship categories, Japanese Americans appear to both agree and disagree with other Americans. According to Schneider's (1968, 30) middle-class Chicago informants, "my family" or "the immediate family" refers to a unit that contains a husband and wife and their children. For the Nisei, however, these terms signify both conjugal families (a husband and wife and their children) and inclusive conjugal families (a husband and wife, their children, their children's spouses, and their grandchildren). In some contexts, the Nisei use "my family" to refer to even more genealogically inclusive units. Likewise, in other contexts the Nisei agree with Schneider that the "decision as to who is a relative is made by and about a person" (ibid., 82). In other contexts, however, the Nisei decision as to who is a relative is made by and about families rather than persons. Finally, the Nisei both confirm and disconfirm Schneider's claim that at the cultural level kinship is structured by the same system of symbols and meanings for all Americans. According to Schneider, the distinctive features defining the cultural universe of relatives are relationship as natural substance (blood) and relationship as code for conduct. These features, in turn, represent the two major cultural orders that provide the core symbolic structure of American kinship: the order of nature and the order of law or culture. Some of the statements the Nisei make about "relatives" and about "nature," "blood," and gender might well be generated by a symbolic opposition between nature and law. Yet, just because the Nisei and Schneider's informants attach similar meanings to cultural units such as "person," "family," and "relative" in some contexts, it does not follow that they do so in all contexts. For the Nisei, after all, in many contexts "family" represents a "Japanese" social unit while "person" represents an "American" one. Thus, the meanings of these units, like the meanings of "duty," "love," "equality," and "rules," are structured for Japanese Americans by an opposition between "Japanese" and "American." It is not that the symbolic opposition between nature and law or culture is irrelevant to Nisei kinship, but it is not a fundamental problem of meaning as the integration of the opposition between Japanese and American is.

This opposition represents for the Nisei and Issei not the opposition between nature and culture, but the opposition between culture and culture—that is, between two fundamentally different ways of life. Because Japanese Americans view biogenetic substance ("blood") as the basis of their racial identity as Japanese, it might appear that for them the symbolic opposition between Japanese and American is but a surface transformation of a more fundamental opposition between nature and culture. According to Japanese Americans, what makes an individual who is "Japanese" by birth (nature) an "American" are learned values and styles of behavior (culture). Yet other symbolic alignments preclude the reduction of the contrast between Japanese and American to an opposition between nature and culture. For both generations, as I have shown, "Japanese" symbolizes rules and constraints that exist outside people, while "American" symbolizes the feelings and desires arising from inside one's self and so from natural impulses. Thus "Japanese" has some cultural connotations just as "American" has some natural ones.

Why, then, are Japanese Americans more concerned with integrating the symbolic opposition between Japanese and American than the opposition between nature and law? The answer to this question, I suggest, is to be found in the connection between the troubled political and social history of Japanese in the United States and the symbolic categories through which they interpret and formulate their kinship relations. If this is so, then it seems likely that a significant part of the variation in American kinship may be traced to the particular problems of meaning that members of different sectors of American society perceive to arise out of their particular cultural histories. It also suggests a solution to the conundrum of American kinship.

Japanese American kinship is at all levels of analysis both the same and different from kinship in these other sectors because Japanese Americans and other Americans both share the same folk model of the relation between their history and their culture and have different models of their respective cultural histories. That is, they are participating in a shared cultural process and in separate ones at the same time. The shared cultural process is one in which they construct a model for kinship relations out of two other models: one of their own perceived kinship past, and one of contemporary family and kinship relations among typical and hypothetical Americans. This process does not rest upon systematic empirical observation of the family relations of actual people considered to be typical Americans, nor upon systematic reconstruction of ancestors' kinship relations. Neither does it entail the adoption of a hegemonic model of the morally correct form of the family promulgated by cultural elites who are viewed (and who view themselves) as transcending the parochialism of any particular ethnic identity other than perhaps a plain old (or an old colonial) American one.

Instead, this model of modern American family and kinship attributed to a nonexistent, hypothetical sector of Americans—most commonly conceived to be white and middle-class—is constructed from bits and pieces of information and the more substantial cultural stories and dramas transmitted through schools, newspapers, television, novels, and other forms of mass culture. In the early twentieth century this model of the American family probably was attached to a hypothetical category of white, middle-class Americans who were thought to reside in a medium-sized town. Today these hypothetical Americans, while still white and middle-class, are most often thought of as living in a suburb. They may even have a tinge of ethnic flavor. Regardless of where they live, whether or not they are thought by now to have experienced divorce, or to have edged more toward the upper levels of the middle class—the class that for most Americans includes the majority of the population—their family and kinship relations are continually being rethought and so modified by Americans. For, like the Japanese Americans in my study, Americans in all sectors of society are engaged in assembling bits and pieces of cultural information along with preassembled packages of cultural dramas and scenarios and constructing from them a more or less coherent model of kinship that is practiced by no one. The so-called modern American family is a folk model, a Weberian ideal type, that describes no one's behavior, nor anyone's normative system—other than, of course, that of a hypothetical category of Americans.

The folk model of the traditional past is likewise an ideal type constructed from bits and pieces of information and the more substantial cultural stories and family histories transmitted by those who claim knowledge of the ancestral past. While parents and grandparents are among the claimants, they are far from unique. For information about the traditional past of the ancestors also comes from the popular media, schools, and academic accounts. In addition, because the traditional past and the modern present are construed as contrasting cultural orders, they mutually shape each other's characters in a continuing process of symbolic opposition. This latter aspect of the process is crucial because it explains how Americans have both the same and different models of the modern American family. The similarities derive from their being the recipients of a mass culture that transmits images, facts, and statistics out of which models of the modern family can be constructed. The differences derive from their interpreting these images, facts, and statistics as forming a contrast with their models of their perceived traditional past.

What holds Japanese American kinship together and differentiates it from kinship among other Americans is Japanese Americans' shared model of their cultural history. The model is at the same time a charter for what Japanese American social life should continue to be and how it might change. Other Americans do not share this charter even though they may share many of its provisions, for other Americans do not conceptualize their kinship relations in terms of their connections with an ancestral Japanese past and the experience of Japanese immigrants to America. What many other Americans do share with Japanese Americans, however, is the notion that the historical experience of their ancestors, whether they were immigrants or not, has shaped their contemporary kinship relations. They may not agree with the Nisei that the ideal family is one that is a balanced compromise between a traditional past and a modern present. Rather, they may believe it is one that discards the tyranny of an oppressive past to freely explore the options of a liberating present. Or, conversely, they may believe the best family is one that faithfully reproduces the past and protects it from a corrupting present. But whatever normative conclusions they draw from their models of past and present, a good many Americans think about family and kinship relations in terms of cultural-historical categories.

Because for Americans kinship is rooted in biogenetic links among people, both living and dead, it inescapably connects them with an ancestral past. Ancestors, moreover, are thought to transmit more than genes and biogenetic substance to the living. Like Japanese Americans, most other Americans believe that their ancestors' experiences as well as their values and forms of relationships are transmitted across generations through a series of parent-child links. If they did not hold this belief, the traditional past of their ancestors would be no more relevant to their present model of kinship than the traditional past of someone else's ancestors. Nor would the perceived cultural history that connects them with that past explain for them how and why their families take their current form.

To say that folk concepts of history are central to both ethnic identity and kinship in America—that, in other words, both are about tradition—is merely to affirm Schneider's point that kinship is not a distinct symbolic domain in American culture. Instead, it merges with other domains, including those of religion and nationality. Schneider (1976), however, has focused on the fundamental symbolic opposition between nature and culture that structures this larger galaxy of meaning. In contrast, I have been concerned to show that a folk model of culture and history also structures meaning and actions in kinship relations.

This folk model of history, culture, and kinship, which I propose is shared by most if not all Americans, at the same time generates different symbolic categories through which particular groups interpret and fashion their kinship relations. As different Americans conceive of themselves as the biological descendants of different ancestors, they interpret their current kinship relations in terms of different perceived cultural histories. Even if they have apparently similar norms regarding, for example, the conjugal relationship, Americans conceptualize these norms in the light of different folk histories. Thus, some Americans say that to understand the authority of men over women in their family today you must understand the cultural tradition of their southern Italian ancestors, others that you must understand the cultural tradition of their Russian Jewish ancestors, and still others that you must understand the cultural tradition of their Japanese ancestors. Yet the different cultural traditions offered to explain rather similar forms of gender inequality among a variety of Americans are not merely empty symbols. In referring to a traditional past of male dominance in the family, Americans are talking about both the same thing and different things. The same thing is the general folk model about the historical transmission of cultural experience from one generation to the next. The different things are the particular cultural histories with which different Americans identify, and that make for varying meanings of tradition.

Blu (1980, 217) has suggested that given the centrality of the perceived past to ethnic identity in the United States, the kind of past the members of a group see themselves as having, and that others attribute to them, will make a difference for their present view of themselves. The same is true, I propose, of kinship in the United States. Like Japanese Americans, other Americans interpret their particular cultural histories in ways that generate particular issues of meaning and symbolic categories that in turn structure their kinship norms. These issues and categories are not ones that groups of people create themselves in isolation from the rest of American society. Rather, like the dilemma of how one could be both "Japanese" and "American" at the same time, people meet with them through experience both in their smaller communities (whether these are ethnic, regional, or religious) and in the larger society. It was not only Japanese, after all, who wondered whether "Japanese" and "American" or "Oriental" and "American" were mutually exclusive categories. The well-documented history of anti-Japanese discrimination and legislation on the West Coast attests to the strength and persistence of that concern outside the Japanese American community.

If, as I believe, folk models of cultural history are central for kinship in America, then we will better understand both the unity and the diversity of American kinship if we explore the dimensions of such folk models among different sectors of American society. We might ask, for example, how black Americans explain aspects of their family and kinship relations in light of their cultural history. Just as anthropologists and sociologists have attributed aspects of the black family to various elements in their and their ancestors' experiences, so, I expect, do black

Americans themselves interpret their present model of kinship in historical terms. Given black Americans' experience of slavery and of racial and economic oppression in America, we might expect issues of race, power, and social class to be central to their dialectical construction of their own kinship tradition in opposition to a white one. A cultural analysis that attended to the symbolic categories through which black Americans link their familial present with the past would enrich our understanding of the black family, which has tended to be viewed primarily from an acultural utilitarian perspective or in terms of simple models of cultural domination or resistance.

Nor is it only people with a distinctive ethnic identity whose kinship relations could be better understood in this way. For conceptions of tradition are central to the construction of kinship among Americans whose ethnic identity is less important to them than a regional or a religious one. Such folk too formulate their kinship norms through symbolic processes that transform the past and present in a dialectic of reinterpretation. Once we have examined the cultural histories and symbolic categories through which Americans with a variety of ethnic, regional, and religious identities order their kinship relations, we will better understand the shared symbolic process that has given birth to so many family traditions.

REFERENCE MATTER

Sampling Procedures and Representativeness of the Sample

In 1973, I collaborated with two graduate students in physical anthropology, Donna L. Leonetti and Jay McGough, to collect survey data on the demographic and social characteristics of the Seattle Japanese American population. From the beginning of our research, we were interested in what we called the "nuclear population" of Seattle Japanese Americans whose families shared a historical experience rather than mere inclusion in a racial or ethnic category. We included in the definition of the Seattle Japanese American nuclear population the following groups:

1. Japanese (Issei) who immigrated to the United States before 1925, settled in Seattle prior to World War II, were incarcerated in relocation camps during World War II, and resettled in Seattle prior to 1950.

2. The American-born children (Nisei) of the above immigrants who lived with their parents in Seattle prior to World War II, resettled in Seattle after the war, and currently reside in Seattle. Incarceration in relocation camps during World War II is not a criterion for Nisei, since a number who were outside the Pacific coastal zone at the time were not imprisoned. Most of these were college students at midwestern or eastern universities, males in the armed forces, or Nisei attending schools and universities in Japan at the outbreak of the war. The latter, known as Kibei (a category including all Nisei educated in Japan), are included in the nuclear population and classified as Nisei if they resided in Seattle for at least fifteen years prior to World War II and returned to Seattle no later than 1950. Nisei born and raised in other U.S. Japanese communities prior to World War II but who married Seattle Nisei and have lived in Seattle since their marriage (for at least twenty years) are also included in the nuclear population as in-marrying spouses.

3. The American-born children (Sansei) of the Seattle Nisei who presently reside in Seattle. Seattle is defined to include the greater Seattle metropolitan area, including the suburbs of Mercer Island, Bellevue, Kirkland, and Renton.

In 1967 and 1971 my dissertation adviser, Professor Laura Newell-Morris, had initiated two pilot studies of families in the nuclear population. As these families had been contacted through third-generation (Sansei) students at the University of Washington, however, we could not assume they were representative of the nuclear population even though national surveys report that as many as 88 percent of Sansei have had some college training (Levine and Montero 1973, 15). Because the pilot studies were conducted in 1967 and 1971, moreover, they were limited to Nisei parents with children born in a restricted time period (approximately 1944 to 1953), one that tended to exclude Nisei from early and late marriage cohorts.

To counterbalance this bias, we developed a procedure for sampling a wider range of what we defined as the Seattle Japanese American nuclear population. In late 1942 the U.S. War Relocation Authority (WRA), which was charged with administering the camps in which Japanese Americans were imprisoned, had conducted a survey of all internees. WRA Form 26 contains information on each internee, including name, age, educational status, preinternment address, occupation, place of birth, camp household composition, marital status, height, weight, and health condition. From this 1942 enumeration of the imprisoned Japanese American population, we selected every tenth camp household that included members with a Seattle address from before incarceration. The 1973 Seattle Japanese American Community Directory, which lists the addresses and telephone numbers of all persons with Japanese surnames in the Seattle area telephone directory, was used to locate Nisei members of the selected households. From July 1973 to February 1974, 17 such Nisei were interviewed in addition to 27 other Nisei to whom they referred us. Of the 54 Nisei contacted, all but 1 was married. Among the 53 married Nisei, 3 were married to Issei, 1 to a Sansei, and 1 to a postwar bride from Japan. Combined with the 10 Nisei interviews from the pilot study these interviews yielded demographic, educational, occupational, residential, and genealogical information on 102 Nisei, hereafter referred to as the Nisei survey sample. More detailed kinship histories were collected on 48 of the Nisei married couples in this survey sample. These 48 couples are referred to as the Nisei marriage sample. I also interviewed 30 Issei (12 of them randomly selected from the WRA list and 18 suggested by other informants), which gave me an Issei marriage sample of 24 couples.

COMPARISON WITH OTHER SOURCES

The three sample groups from which the data for this study are derived can be compared with other sources of data on Japanese Americans in general and those in Seattle in particular. It must be kept in mind, however, that U.S. census data and immigration records, even when they are specific to the Seattle Japanese American population, do not accurately reflect the characteristics of the Seattle Japanese American *nuclear* population. On the one hand, such figures before World War II include a large proportion of Issei who returned to Japan.

Not only were these returned immigrants absent from the post–World War II nuclear population, but they generally did not leave children in Seattle and so contribute to that population's second generation. Between 1911 and 1920, for example, eighty-seven thousand Japanese immigrants were admitted to the continental United States, but seventy thousand departed—a net gain of only seventeen thousand (Ichihashi 1932, 62). Unfortunately, we do not know what percentage of those entering in any year were doing so for the first time, nor what percentage of those departing would never return to the United States. After 1924, when new immigrants could not enter from Japan, the number of Japanese aliens departing from the continental United States exceeded the number returning. In 1925, for example, just over three thousand Japanese aliens entered the United States, while just over seven thousand returned to Japan (Thomas 1952, 573). Given the fluidity of the Japanese population in Seattle and other communities before World War II, we do not know how stable were the populations enumerated from one census to another. Nor do we know whether those immigrants who returned to Japan differed significantly in age, occupation, marital status, or any of a number of other characteristics from those who remained in Seattle and produced the next generation of Japanese Americans. On the other hand, U.S. census data after World War II—in particular, after the 1950 census—lump together all persons of Japanese parentage and so include recent Japanese immigrants who, as I explained in Chapter 1, do not share the history or characteristics of the nuclear population, as well as Japanese Americans who have migrated to Seattle from other communities. When I compare my sample with census figures after World War II, therefore, it must be remembered that the latter enumerate an ethnic category while the former samples an ethnic community.

The Nisei Survey Sample

The characteristics of the Nisei survey sample ($N = 102$) are extensively documented in Yanagisako 1975a (297-305), where they are also compared with other sources of data on the Seattle Japanese American population (ibid., 322-27). There it is shown that the Nisei survey sample represents well the range of Nisei in the Seattle Japanese American nuclear population. For example, with respect to age distribution, the sample displays a proportionate representation of the Nisei birth cohorts in the 1940 census (ibid., 325). In addition, comparison of the birth cohorts of these Nisei's parents with the age structure of Seattle Issei in the 1940 census reveals a similar age distribution (ibid., 326). As the Nisei survey sample is not relied upon greatly in the present monograph, I refer the reader to my earlier documentation of its characteristics and representativeness.

The Nisei Marriage Sample

The age distribution of the Nisei marriage sample reveals a proportionate representation of Nisei birth cohorts. Table A.1 compares the birth cohorts of the marriage sample with those reported for "native-born" (i.e., American-

TABLE A.1

Comparison of Birth Cohorts of Nisei Marriage Sample with
American-born Japanese in Seattle, 1940 Census

Birth cohort	1940 U.S. census		Nisei marriage sample	
	Number	Percent	Number	Percent
Before 1901	39	1%	0	0%
1901-10	179	4	4	4
1911-20	1,219	30	33	36
1921-30	1,939	47	43	47
1931-40	732	18	12	13
TOTAL	4,108	100%	92	100%

NOTE: 1940 census figures are from U.S. Bureau of the Census 1943b, table 33, "Japanese Population by Age, Nativity, and Sex for Selected States, Urban and Rural, and for Selected Cities, 1940."

born) Japanese in Seattle in the 1940 census. That census provides the best source for certain characteristics of the nuclear populations. For one, the distinction made between foreign-born and native-born Japanese allows us to differentiate Nisei and Issei characteristics, because there were few Sansei at the time. Secondly, in 1940 there were no recent Japanese immigrants, so the census population is identical to the nuclear population. The only drawback of the 1940 U.S. census is that it enumerates a prewar population—one-third of which would not return to constitute the postwar nuclear population. Aside from a slight overrepresentation of the 1911-20 birth cohort and an even smaller underrepresentation of the 1931-40 birth cohort, the marriage sample and the 1940 census population are very similar.

The representativeness of the Nisei marriage samples as regards occupational status is more difficult to assess because the 1940 census is useless for this purpose and the 1970 U.S. census tables on the occupational status of the Seattle Japanese population do not differentiate Issei, Nisei, and Sansei. Although the Nisei constituted the bulk of the employed persons in that population who were enumerated in the 1970 census, working Issei, Sansei, and recently arrived Japanese were numerous enough to affect the census figures. Table A.2 compares the occupational distribution of the Nisei men and women in the marriage sample with the 1970 census report of all employed Japanese sixteen years and older in Seattle. The Nisei marriage sample has a noticeably larger proportion of men in professional, managerial, and administrative positions and a smaller proportion of men in laboring and service positions. Likewise, a larger percentage of women in the Nisei marriage sample are found in higher-level occupations, although the percentage in sales and clerical work is close to that reported by the 1970 census. The extent to which the census's inclusion of Issei and Sansei, a larger proportion of whom were in laboring and service occupations in 1970, accounts for the larger proportion of blue-collar workers is unknown.

When compared to the national sample of the UCLA Japanese American

TABLE A.2

*Comparison of Occupational Status of Nisei
in Marriage Sample with All Persons (16 Years and Older)
Employed in Japanese Population of Seattle, 1970 U.S. Census*

	Males		Females	
Occupation	1970 census (N = 2,798)	Nisei marriage sample (N = 47)	1970 census (N = 2,286)	Nisei marriage sample (N = 34)[a]
Professional, technical, and kindred workers	20%	28%	14%	21%
Managers and administrators (nonfarm)	14	34	5	9
Sales, clerical, and kindred workers	19	17	39	44
Craftsmen, foremen, and operatives	23	19	21	14
Laborers (nonfarm)	10	0	2	3
Farmers, farm managers, laborers, and foremen	1	0	1	0
Private household and service workers	13	2	18	9
TOTAL	100%	100%	100%	100%

NOTE: 1970 census figures are from U.S. Bureau of the Census 1973, table 14, "Family Income, Poverty Status, Weeks Worked, and Occupation of the Japanese Population for Selected Standard Metropolitan Statistical Areas and Cities, 1970."

[a] Excludes nine women who were housewives at the time of the study.

TABLE A.3

*Comparison of Occupational Status of Nisei Men in Marriage Sample and
UCLA Japanese American Research Project National Survey*

Occupation	JARP national survey[a] (N = 1,998)	Nisei marriage sample (N = 47)
Professional, technical, and kindred workers	32%	28%
Managers and administrators (nonfarm)	20	34
Sales, clerical, and kindred workers	11	17
Craftsmen, foremen, and operatives	12	19
Farmers, farm managers, laborers, and foremen	14	0
Service workers and laborers (nonfarm)	11	2
TOTAL	100%	100%

[a] Taken from Bonacich and Modell 1980, 121.

TABLE A.4

Comparison of Educational Attainment of Nisei Men in Marriage Sample and UCLA Japanese American Research Project National Survey

	JARP national survey[a] (N = 1,903)		Nisei marriage sample (N = 45)	
Years of education	Number	Percent	Number	Percent
0-12	809	43%	15	33%
13-15	480	25	10	22
16	304	16	16	36
17+	310	16	4	9
TOTAL	1,903	100%	45	100%

[a]Taken from Bonacich and Modell 1980, 144.

Research Project (Bonacich and Modell 1980), however, the Nisei marriage sample does not appear to overrepresent Nisei men in higher occupational categories (see Table A.3). As the JARP survey includes Nisei from both urban and rural areas of the continental United States, it has greater numbers of farmers and fewer nonfarm managers and administrators than would be found in Seattle. But the percentage of Nisei men in professions in that sample is similar to that in my Nisei marriage sample. Unfortunately, there are no comparative figures on women's occupational distribution.

Finally, as regards educational attainment, my Nisei marriage sample has a higher proportion of men with college degrees than the JARP sample, although it has a smaller percentage of men with postgraduate educations (Table A.4). As the JARP sample is itself probably a little biased toward better-educated Nisei, it would appear that the Nisei marriage sample also overrepresents those with higher educations.

Issei Marriage Sample

As a representative of all Issei who ever lived in Seattle the Issei marriage sample quite obviously suffers from a serious bias, namely, that of survivorship. Because it does not include Issei marriages in which both spouses died before 1973, it is biased toward the younger members of the total population of immigrants who remained in Seattle and produced the next generation of Japanese Americans. The existence of this bias is confirmed when one compares the birth cohorts of Issei in the marriage sample both with the foreign-born Japanese in Seattle in the 1940 census and with the parents of the Seattle Nisei survey sample. Table A.5 shows that the women in the Issei marriage sample underrepresent the pre-1890 birth cohorts of the Issei women in the 1940 census just as they underrepresent the mothers of the Nisei survey sample, although they overrepresent the 1891-1900 and 1901-10 birth cohorts. The overrepresentation of younger birth cohorts is not as great, however, for the men in the Issei marriage sample, who come close to representing the proportions in the

TABLE A.5

Comparison of Birth Cohorts of Foreign-born Japanese in Seattle in 1940 Census with Parents of Nisei in Survey Sample and Issei Marriage Sample

	Males			Females		
Birth cohorts	1940 census ($N=1,645$)	Parents of Nisei survey sample ($N=78$)	Issei marriage sample ($N=24$)	1940 census ($N=1,222$)	Parents of Nisei survey sample ($N=77$)	Issei marriage sample ($N=24$)
Before 1881	19%	23%	21%	13%	3%	0%
1881-90	44	53	38	34	30	13
1891-1900	20	20	38	32	48	54
1901-10	12	5	4	15	20	33
1911-40	5	0	0	6	0	0
TOTAL	100%	100%	100%	100%	100%	100%

NOTE: 1940 census figures are from U.S. Bureau of the Census 1943b, table 33, "Japanese Population by Age, Nativity, and Sex for Selected States, Urban and Rural, and for Selected Cities, 1940."

pre-1881 and 1881-90 cohorts reflected in the 1940 census. But, like their wives, the men in the Issei marriage sample overrepresent the 1891-1900 cohort. Their tendency not to overrepresent the more recent birth cohorts can be attributed to the fact that information on seventeen of the twenty-four Issei marriages was obtained from surviving Issei widows whose husbands were consequently included in the Issei marriage sample despite their death (and earlier birth dates).

Given the underrepresentation of older Issei, the Issei marriage sample also is biased toward later-arriving immigrants. Table A.6 compares the immigration dates of the Issei marriage sample with those of all Japanese immigrants to the continental United States, and with the parents of the Nisei survey sample. Although the latter do not differ significantly from the total immigration figures as regards year of immigration, the Issei marriage sample itself clearly underrepresents those who immigrated before 1911 and overrepresents those who immigrated after 1911. This is not surprising, as we would expect the surviving Issei to be relatively younger ones who immigrated in later periods. Given a mean age at migration of twenty-one, the Issei who came before 1911 would have been eighty-four and older by the time I began my research in 1973. In spite of the age and immigration-year bias of the Issei marriage sample, it appears to represent well the occupational and educational characteristics of the Seattle Issei. The occupations of the Issei in the marriage sample at the outbreak of World War II match closely Miyamoto's (1939) report of Seattle Issei occupations in 1935. Seventy-five percent of the men in the marriage sample (18 of 24) were self-employed in 1940, as compared to the 77 percent of Issei men Miyamoto (1939, 71) classified as engaged in "trade" and "domestic and personal services." Since the latter category was composed overwhelming-

TABLE A.6

Comparison of Immigration Records, Parents of Nisei Survey Sample,
and Issei Marriage Sample on Year of Entry to the Continental United States

Period of immigration	Immigration records[a]		Issei parents of Nisei in survey sample		Issei marriage sample	
	Number	Percent	Number	Percent	Number	Percent
1891-99	15,356	7%	8	7%	3	7%
1900-1910	71,711	34	44	40	11	26
1911-20	87,581	41	48	43	21	50
1921-24	39,237	18	11	10	7	17
TOTAL	213,885	100%	111	100%	42	100%

[a]These figures are derived from immigration records as cited by Thomas 1952, 573. They include all Japanese aliens admitted each year and, therefore, those who were arriving for the first time as well as those returning.

ly of hotels, restaurants, barber shops, and laundries, Miyamoto justifiably lumped them with the occupations (such as grocery stores and grocery stands) classified as "trades" in a category of the "small shop." The majority (58 percent) of the Issei in the marriage sample came from farming households in rural villages, but almost a third (32 percent) had fathers who were self-employed businessmen or craftsmen (storekeeper, silk wholesaler, textile mill operator, importer, soy sauce manufacturer, bookstore owner, hotel operator, cleaning shop operator, and tailor). Finally, a small number (10 percent) had fathers who were employed in salaried or wage-earning occupations (village official, professor, and laborer).

Finally, the educational backgrounds of the Issei in the marriage sample were similar to those reported for the Issei as a whole. Mean years of education were slightly higher for men (9.2 years) than for women (8.0 years). This was close to the mean number of years of education (8.6 for men and 7.6 for women) reported for the Issei in California before the war (Strong 1933, 186). It was also comparable to the combined rate for male and female Issei respondents, 64 percent of whom had completed 8 or fewer years of schooling in Japan and 36 percent of whom had gone beyond that, in the JARP sample (Levine and Montero 1973). Although the Issei had more formal education than most other immigrants arriving in the United States at the turn of the century, they were by no means above the average for Japan, where 8 years of compulsory education had been the law since the 1870's (Dore 1958, 194).

Works Cited

Alexander, Jack (1976). "A Study of the Cultural Domain of 'Relatives.'" *Am. Ethnol.* 3: 17-38.

Anderson, Michael (1971). *Family Structure in Nineteenth Century Lancashire.* Cambridge, U.K.

Barth, Frederick (1966). *Models of Social Organization.* Royal Anthropological Institute Occasional Paper, no. 23. London.

Batteau, Alan (1978). "Class and Status in an Egalitarian Community: A Study of the Structure of American Society." Ph.D. diss., University of Chicago.

Beardsley, Richard K., John W. Hall, and Robert F. Ward (1959). *Village Japan.* Chicago.

Befu, Harumi (1963). "Patrilineal Descent and Personal Kindred in Japan." *Am. Anthropol.* 65: 1328-41.

——— (1971). *Japan: An Anthropological Introduction.* San Francisco.

Bloch, Maurice (1971). *Placing the Dead: Tombs, Ancestral Villages and Kinship Organization in Madagascar.* London.

——— (1975). "Property and the End of Affinity." In *Marxist Analyses and Social Anthropology,* ed. Maurice Bloch, 203-22. New York.

——— (1977). "The Past and the Present in the Present." *Man* 12: 278-92.

Bloom, Leonard [Leonard Broom] (1943). "Familial Adjustments of Japanese-Americans to Relocation: First Phase." *Am. Soc. Rev.* 8: 551-60.

——— (1947). "Transitional Adjustments of Japanese-American Families to Relocation." *Am. Soc. Rev.* 12: 201-9.

Blu, Karen (1980). *The Lumbee Problem.* New York.

Bonacich, Edna, and John Modell (1980). *The Economic Basis of Ethnic Solidarity: Small Business in the Japanese American Community.* Berkeley, Calif.

Bott, Elizabeth (1957). *Family and Social Network: Roles, Norms, and External Relationships in Ordinary Urban Families.* London.

Bourdieu, Pierre (1977). *Outline of a Theory of Practice.* Trans. Richard Nice. Cambridge, U.K.

Broom, Leonard, and John I. Kitsuse (1973). *The Managed Casualty: The Japanese-American Family in World War II*. Berkeley, Calif. Reprint (1956).

Broom, Leonard, and Ruth Riemer (1949). *Removal and Return: The Socio-Economic Effects of the War on Japanese-Americans*. Berkeley, Calif.

Brown, Keith (1966). "*Dōzoku* and the Ideology of Descent in Rural Japan." *Am. Anthropol.* 68(5): 1129-51.

―――― (1968). "The Content of *Dōzoku* Relationships in Japan." *Ethnology* 7: 113-38.

Buell, Raymond L. (1924). *Japanese Immigration*. Boston.

Cancian, Francesca M., Louis Wolf Goodman, and Peter H. Smith (1978). "Capitalism, Industrialization, and Kinship in Latin America: Major Issues." *J. Family Hist.* 3(4): 319-36.

Carroll, Vern, ed. (1970). *Adoption in Eastern Oceania*. ASAO Monograph, no. 1. Honolulu.

Chock, Phyllis P. (1974). "Time, Nature and Spirit: A Symbolic Analysis of Greek-American Spiritual Kinship." *Am. Ethnol.* 1: 33-46.

―――― (1976). "Kinship in Greek American Ethnic Identities: Rethinking Ethnicity." Paper presented at the 75th Annual Meeting of the American Anthropological Association. Washington, D.C.

Connor, John W. (1977). *Tradition and Change in Three Generations of Japanese-Americans*. Chicago.

Cottrell, Calvert B., and David M. Schneider (1963). "Some Aspects of American Genealogy." Paper presented at the 62nd Annual Meeting of the American Anthropological Association. San Francisco.

Cumming, Elaine, and David M. Schneider (1961). "Sibling Solidarity: A Property of American Kinship." *Am. Anthropol.* 63: 498-507.

Daniels, Roger (1962). *The Politics of Prejudice: The Anti-Japanese Movement in California and the Struggle for Japanese Exclusion*. Berkeley, Calif.

―――― (1971). *Concentration Camps USA: Japanese-Americans and World War II*. New York.

DeVos, George (1955). "A Quantitative Rorschach Assessment of Maladjustment and Rigidity in Acculturating Japanese Americans." *Genetic Psychol. Mon.* 52: 51-87.

di Leonardo, Micaela (1984). *The Varieties of Ethnic Experience: Kinship, Class, and Gender among California Italian-Americans*. Ithaca, N.Y.

Dore, Ronald P. (1958). *City Life in Japan: A Study of a Tokyo Ward*. Berkeley, Calif.

Drummond, Lee (1978). "The Transatlantic Nanny: Notes on a Comparative Semiotics of the Family in English-speaking Societies." *Am. Ethnol.* 5(1): 30-43.

―――― (1980). "The Cultural Continuum: A Theory of Intersystems." *Man* 15: 352-74.

Eggan, Fred (1966). *The American Indian: Perspectives for the Study of Social Change*. Chicago.

Embree, John (1939). *Suye Mura: A Japanese Village*. Chicago.

Evans-Pritchard, E. E. (1940). *The Nuer*. Oxford, U.K.

Firth, Raymond (1951). *Elements of Social Organization*. London.

Firth, Raymond W., J. Hubert, and A. Forge (1969). *Families and Their Relatives: Kinship in a Middle-Class Sector of London—an Anthropological Study*. London.

Forde, C. Darryl (1934). *Habitat, Economy, and Society: A Geographic Introduction to Ethnology*. New York.

Fortes, Meyer (1949). *The Web of Kinship Among the Tallensi*. London.

——— (1969). *Kinship and the Social Order: The Legacy of Lewis Henry Morgan*. Chicago.

Fox, Robin (1967). *Kinship and Marriage*. Harmondsworth, U.K.

Fukutake, Tadashi (1967). *Japanese Rural Society*. Trans. R. P. Dore. Ithaca, N.Y.

Gans, Herbert H. (1962). *The Urban Villagers*. Glencoe, Ill.

Geertz, Clifford (1957). "Ritual and Social Change: A Javanese Example." *Am. Anthropol.* 59: 32-54.

——— (1973). *The Interpretation of Cultures*. New York.

Geertz, Hildred, and Clifford Geertz (1975). *Kinship in Bali*. Chicago.

Glenn, Evelyn Nakano (1980). "The Dialectics of Wage Work: Japanese-American Women and Domestic Service, 1905-1940." *Feminist Studies* 6(3): 432-71.

Godelier, Maurice (1975). "Modes of Production, Kinship and Demographic Structures," In *Marxist Anthropology*, ed. Maurice Bloch, 3-27. New York.

Goody, Jack (1972). "The Evolution of the Family." In *Household and Family in Past Time*, ed. Peter Laslett and Richard Wall, 103-24. London.

——— (1976). *Production and Reproduction: A Comparative Study of the Domestic Domain*. Cambridge Studies in Social Anthropology, no. 17. Cambridge, U.K.

Greeley, Andrew M., and William C. McCready (1975). "The Transmission of Cultural Heritages: The Case of the Irish and the Italians." In *Ethnicity: Theory and Experience*, ed. Nathan Glazer and Daniel P. Moynihan, 209-35. Cambridge, Mass.

Gutman, Herbert G. (1976). *The Black Family in Slavery and Freedom, 1750-1925*. New York.

Hareven, Tamara (1978). "The Dynamics of Kin in an Industrial Community." *Am. J. Soc.* 84 (supp.): S151-82.

Ichihashi, Yamato (1913). *Japanese Immigration: Its Status*. San Francisco.

——— (1932). *Japanese in the United States*. Stanford, Calif.

Ichioka, Yuji (1980). "*Amerika Nadeshiko*: Japanese Immigrant Women in the U.S., 1900-1924." *Pac. Hist. Rev.*, May 1980, 339-57.

Inden, Ronald B., and Ralph W. Nicholas (1977). *Kinship in Bengali Culture*. Chicago.

Ito, Kazuo (1973). *Issei: A History of Japanese Immigrants in North America*. Trans. Shinichiro Nakamura and Jean S. Gerard. Seattle.

Johnson, Colleen L. (1973). "The Japanese-American Family and Community in Honolulu: Generational Continuities in Ethnic Affiliation." Ph.D. diss., Syracuse University.

——— (1974). "Gift Giving and Reciprocity Among the Japanese Americans in Honolulu." *Am. Ethnol.* 1: 295-308.

———— (1978). "Authority and Power in Japanese-American Marriage." In *Power in Families*, ed. Ronald E. Cromwell and David H. Olsen, 182-96. Beverly Hills, Calif.

Kapferer, Bruce, ed. (1976). *Transaction and Meaning: Directions in the Anthropology of Exchange and Symbolic Behavior.* Philadelphia.

Kashima, Tetsuden (1977). *Buddhism in America: The Social Organization of an Ethnic Religious Institution.* London.

Kennedy, Theodore R. (1980). *You Gotta Deal with It: Black Family Relations in a Southern Community.* New York.

Kiefer, Christie W. (1974). *Changing Cultures, Changing Lives.* San Francisco.

Kikuchi, Charles (1973). *The Kikuchi Diary: Chronicle from an American Concentration Camp.* Ed. John Modell. Urbana, Ill.

Kitagawa, Daisuke (1967). *Issei and Nisei: The Internment Years.* New York.

Kitano, Harry H. (1976). *Japanese-Americans: The Evolution of a Subculture.* 2d ed. Englewood Cliffs, N.J.

Kitano, Harry H., and Akemi Kikumura (1976). "The Japanese American Family." In *Ethnic Families in America: Patterns and Variations*, ed. Charles H. Mindel and Robert W. Habenstein, 41-60. New York.

Kitano, Seiichi (1962). "*Dōzoku* and *Ie* in Japan: The Meaning of Family Genealogical Relationships." In *Japanese Culture: Its Development and Characteristics*, ed. R. J. Smith and R. K. Beardsley, 42-46. Chicago.

Kourvetaris, George A. (1976). "The Greek American Family." In *Ethnic Families in America: Patterns and Variations*, ed. Charles H. Mindel and Robert W. Habenstein, 168-91. New York.

Lamphere, Louise, Filomena M. Silva, and John P. Sousa (1980). "Kin Networks and Family Strategies: Working-Class Portuguese Families in New England." In *The Versatility of Kinship*, ed. Linda S. Cordell and Stephen Beckerman, 219-49. New York.

Laslett, Peter (1972). "Introduction: The History of the Family." In *Household and Family in Past Time*, ed. Peter Laslett and Richard Wall, 1-90. London.

LaViolette, F. E. (1946). *Americans of Japanese Ancestry: A Study of Assimilation in the American Community.* Toronto.

Leach, Edmund R. (1954). *Political Systems of Highland Burma.* Cambridge, Mass.

Leonetti, Donna L. (1976). "Fertility in Transition: An Analysis of the Reproductive Experience of an Urban Japanese-American Population." Ph.D. diss., University of Washington, Seattle.

Leonetti, Donna Lockwood, and Laura Newell-Morris (1982). "Exogamy and Change in the Biosocial Structure of a Modern Urban Population." *Am. Anthropol.* 84: 19-36.

Levine, Gene N., and Darrel Montero (1973). "Socioeconomic Mobility Among Three Generations of Japanese Americans." *J. Social Issues* 29 (2): 33-48.

Lévi-Strauss, Claude (1967). *Structural Anthropology.* Trans. Claire Jacobson and Brooke Grundfest Schoepf. Garden City, N.Y.

——— (1969). *Elementary Structures of Kinship*. Rev. ed. Trans. James Harle Bell, John Richard von Sturmer, and Rodney Needham [ed.]. Boston.

Light, Ivan H. (1972). *Ethnic Enterprise in America—Business and Welfare Among Chinese, Japanese and Blacks*. Los Angeles.

Litwak, Eugene (1960). "Geographic Mobility and Extended Family Cohesion." *Am. Soc. Rev.* 25(3): 385-94.

Macfarlane, Alan (1978). *The Origins of English Individualism*. New York.

Malinowski, Bronislaw (1963). *The Family Among the Australian Aborigines: A Sociological Study*. New York.

Mannheim, Karl (1952). "The Problem of Generations." In *Essays on the Sociology of Knowledge*, ed. Paul Kecskemeti, 276-320. 2d ed. London.

Maykovich, Minako K. (1972). *Japanese American Identity Dilemma*. Tokyo.

Meillasoux, Claude (1972). "From Reproduction to Production." *Economy and Society* 1: 93-105.

Mindel, Charles H., and Robert W. Habenstein, eds. (1976). *Ethnic Families in America: Patterns and Variations*. New York.

Mitchell, William E. (1978). *Mishpokhe: A Study of New York City Jewish Family Clubs*. New York.

Miyamoto, Frank Shotaro (1939). *Social Solidarity Among the Japanese in Seattle*. Seattle.

Miyamoto, S. F., and R. W. O'Brien (1947). "A Survey of Some Changes in the Seattle Japanese Community since Evacuation." *Research Studies of the State College of Washington* 15: 147-54. Pullman, Wash.

Modell, John (1968). "The Japanese American Family: A Perspective for Future Investigations." *Pac. Hist. Rev.* 37: 67-82.

——— (1969). "The Japanese of Los Angeles: A Study in Growth and Accommodation, 1900-1946." Ph.D. diss., Columbia University.

——— (1971). "Tradition and Opportunity: The Japanese Immigrant in America." *Pac. Hist. Rev.* 40(2): 163-82.

Mullins, William Henry (1973). "San Francisco and Seattle During the Hoover Years of the Depression: 1929-1933." Ph.D. diss., University of Washington, Seattle.

Nakane, Chie (1967). *Kinship and Economic Organization in Rural Japan*. London.

Netting, R. McC. (1968). *Hill Farmers of Nigeria: Cultural Ecology of the Kofyar of the Jos Plateau*. Seattle.

Nimkoff, Meyer F., and Russell Middleton (1968). "Types of Family and Types of Economy." In *Man in Adaptation: The Cultural Present*, ed. Yehudi Cohen, 384-93. Chicago.

The North American Times Year Book of 1928. Seattle.

Ortner, Sherry (1973). "On Key Symbols." *Am. Anthropol.* 75: 1338-46.

Parsons, Talcott (1943). "The Kinship System of the Contemporary United States." *Am. Anthropol.* 45: 22-38.

——— (1949). "The Social Structure of the Family." In *The Family: Its Function and Destiny*, ed. Ruth Anshen, 241-74. New York.

Parsons, Talcott, and Robert F. Bales, eds. (1955). *Family, Socialization, and Inter-action Process.* New York.

Pasternak, Burton, Carol R. Ember, and Melvin Ember (1976). "On the Conditions Favoring Extended Family Households." *J. Anthrop. Res.* 32: 109-23.

Petersen, William (1971). *Japanese Americans: Oppression and Success.* New York.

Platt, Joan (1969). "Some Problems in Measuring the Jointness of Conjugal Role-Relationships." *Sociology* 3: 287-97.

Radcliffe-Brown, A. R. (1950). "Introduction." In *African Systems of Kinship and Marriage,* ed. A. R. Radcliffe-Brown and Daryll Forde, 1-85. London.

——— (1952). *Structure and Function in Primitive Society.* London.

Rapp, Rayna (1978). "Family and Class in Contemporary America: Notes Toward an Understanding of Ideology." *Science and Society* 42: 278-300.

Reiter, Rayna R. (1975). "Men and Women in the South of France: Public and Private Domains." In *Toward an Anthropology of Women,* ed. Rayna R. Reiter, 252-82. New York.

Rosaldo, Michelle Z. (1974). "Woman, Culture, and Society: A Theoretical Overview." In *Woman, Culture and Society,* ed. Michelle Z. Rosaldo and Louise Lamphere, 17-42. Stanford, Calif.

——— (1980). "The Use and Abuse of Anthropology: Reflections on Feminism and Cross-Cultural Understanding." *Signs* 5: 389-417.

Rosaldo, Renato (1980). *Ilongot Headhunting, 1883-1974: A Study in Society and History.* Stanford, Calif.

Ryder, Norman (1965). "The Cohort as a Concept in the Study of Social Change." *Am. Soc. Rev.* 30: 843-61.

Sahlins, Marshall (1981). *Historical Metaphors and Mythical Realities: Structure in the Early History of the Sandwich Islands Kingdom.* Ann Arbor.

Scheffler, Harold W. (1976). "The 'Meaning' of Kinship in American Culture: Another View." In *Meaning in Anthropology,* ed. Keith H. Basso and Henry A. Selby, 57-91. Albuquerque.

Schneider, David M. (1968). *American Kinship: A Cultural Account.* Englewood Cliffs, N.J.

——— (1972). "What is Kinship All About?" In *Kinship Studies in the Morgan Centennial Year,* ed. Priscilla Reining, 32-63. Washington, D.C.

——— (1976). "Notes Toward a Theory of Culture." In *Meaning in Anthropology,* ed. Keith H. Basso and Henry A. Selby, 197-220. Albuquerque.

——— (1980). "Twelve Years Later." Afterword in *American Kinship: A Cultural Account.* 2d ed., 118-37. Chicago.

Schneider, David M., and Calvert B. Cottrell (1975). *The American Kin Universe: A Genealogical Study.* University of Chicago Studies in Anthropology, Series in Social, Cultural, and Linguistic Anthropology, no. 3. Chicago.

Schneider, David M., and Raymond T. Smith (1973). *Class Differences and Sex Roles in American Kinship and Family Structure.* Englewood Cliffs, N.J.

Seattle Japanese-American Community Study (1978). "Progress Report to National Institutes of Health." Dept. of Anthropology, University of Washington, Seattle.

Silverman, Martin G. (1971). *Disconcerting Issue: Meaning and Struggle in a Reset-tled Pacific Community.* Chicago.

Smith, Anthony B. (1973). *The Concept of Social Change: A Critique of the Functionalist Theory of Social Change.* Boston.

Smith, Raymond T. (1978). "The Family and the Modern World System: Some Observations from the Caribbean." *J. Family Hist.* 3(4): 337-60.

Smith, Raymond T., and Larissa Adler Lomnitz (1980). "Theoretical Problems in Latin American Kinship Studies." Paper presented at Conference on Theoretical Problems in Latin American Kinship Studies, sponsored by the Social Science Research Council and the American Council of Learned Societies. New York.

Smith, Thomas C. (1959). *The Agrarian Origins of Modern Japan.* Stanford, Calif.

———— (1977). *Nakahara: Family Farming and Population in a Japanese Village, 1717-1830.* Stanford, Calif.

Spicer, Edward H., Asael T. Hansen, Katherine Luomala, and Marvin K. Opler (1969). *Impounded People: Japanese-Americans in the Relocation Centers.* Tucson.

Stack, Carol B. (1974). *All Our Kin: Strategies for Survival in a Black Community.* New York.

Steward, Julian, Robert A. Manners, Eric R. Wolf, Elena Padilla Seda, Sidney W. Mintz, and Raymond L. Scheele (1956). *The People of Puerto Rico.* Urbana, Ill.

Strathern, Andrew (1973). "Kinship, Descent, and Locality: Some New Guinea Examples." In *The Character of Kinship,* ed. J. R. Goody, 21-34. London.

Strathern, Marilyn (1981). *Kinship at the Core: An Anthropology of Elmdon, a Village in Northwest Essex in the Nineteen-Sixties.* Cambridge, U.K.

Strong, Edward (1933). *Japanese in California.* Stanford, Calif.

Sussman, Marvin B., and Lee Burchinal (1962). "Kin Family Network: Unheralded Structure in Current Conceptualizations of Family Functioning." *Marriage and Family Living* 24(3): 231-40.

Thomas, Dorothy Swaine (1950). "Some Social Aspects of Japanese-American Demography." *Proc. Am. Philosoph. Soc.* 94: 459-80.

———— (1952). *The Salvage: Japanese-American Evacuation and Resettlement.* Berkeley, Calif.

Thomas, Dorothy Swaine, and Richard S. Nishimoto (1946). *The Spoilage: Japanese-American Evacuation and Resettlement.* Berkeley, Calif.

U.S. Bureau of the Census (1932). *Reports by States, Showing the Composition and Characteristics of the Population for Counties, Cities, and Townships or Other Minor Civil Divisions.* Fifteenth Census of the United States: 1930, Population. Vol. 3, pt. 2. Washington, D.C.

———— (1943a). *Characteristics of the Population.* Sixteenth Census of the Population: 1940, Population. Vol. 2, pt. 7. Washington, D.C.

———— (1943b). *Characteristics of the Non-white Population by Race.* Sixteenth Census of the Population: 1940. Washington, D.C.

———— (1972). *General Social and Economic Characteristics.* U.S. Census of Population: 1970. Final report, PC(1)-C49. Washington, D.C.

——— (1973). *Japanese, Chinese, and Filipinos in the United States*. U.S. Census of Population: 1970, Subject Reports. Final report, PC(2)-1G. Washington, D.C.

Wallace, Anthony F. C. (1969). "Review of American Kinship: A Cultural Account." *Am. Anthropol.* 71: 100-106.

Watanabe, Theresa (1977). *A Report from the Japanese-American Community Study*. Dept. of Anthropology, University of Washington. Seattle.

Williams, Raymond (1977). *Marxism and Literature*. Oxford, U.K.

Witherspoon, Gary (1975). *Navaho Kinship and Marriage*. Chicago.

Yanagisako, Sylvia Junko (1975a). "Social and Cultural Change in Japanese-American Kinship." Ph.D. diss., University of Washington. Seattle.

——— (1975b). "Two Processes of Change in Japanese-American Kinship." *J. Anthrop. Res.* 31: 196-224.

——— (1977). "Women-centered Kin Networks in Urban Bilateral Kinship." *Am. Ethnol.* 4: 207-26.

——— (1978). "Variance in American Kinship: Implications for Cultural Analysis." *Am. Ethnol.* 5(1): 15-29.

——— (1979). "Family and Household: The Analysis of Domestic Groups." *Ann. Rev. Anthrop.* 8: 161-205.

Young, Michael, and Peter Willmott (1957). *Family and Kinship in East London*. London.

Index

Adachi, Denkichi and Fumiyo, 52f, 56, 60, 139, 196, 199, 206

Adoption, 164; as successor, 35-36, 38, 137ff, 162ff, of sons-in-law as successor, 35-36, 138ff, 148, 164-65, and sons' birth order, 36n; annulled, 141; Nisei view of, 173

Aotanis, 53, 56

Arashi, Masaru and Grace (Nisei couple), 109, 114, 121, 157

Arashis (Issei couple), 43f, 101-2

Baishakunin (go-between), 70, 81, 148, 149

Birth order, Issei: of adopted sons and sons-in-law, 36n; and marriage, 37; and succession, 38; and immigration, 38n

Birth order, Nisei: and parental control of marriage, 69, 72; and wedding expenses, 71; and differential parental treatment, 147, 172, 180, 186; and postmarital residence, 149-50; and filial relations, 171-72, 174f

Blood relationship (*chi*), 162, 164, 256

Brothers, Issei: involvement in sister's marriage, 198, 200; mutual help with employment, 198-99; joint businesses, 198-99; maintain separate accounts, 199; and sibling relationships, 200-202, 204-5

Brothers, Nisei: frequency of contact, 215-16; contact with sisters, 216-17; role in family gatherings, 226-27; role

of eldest in *koden* obligations, 228; social distance between, 229-30, 231

Bunke (branch house), 138ff, 208-9

Capitalism, petty: incidence among Issei, 41-42; types of businesses, 42; participation of wives in, 42-43, 46-48; occupational trend toward, 43-45; reasons for high incidence of, 45; help of prefectural associations and credit societies, 45-46; capital needs, 46; wife's labor in, 49-50; among Nisei in prewar cohort, 71-72, 82-83; among Nisei in wartime cohort, 75. *See also* Entrepreneurship

Capitalist-industrial society: theory of kinship in, 9

Chicago: Japanese Americans in, 76n

Child care and rearing, Issei: and business activities, 47-48; role of wives in, 48-49; as aspect of female domain, 100-102, 126-127

Child care and rearing, Nisei: role of wives in, 89, 112-13; as aspect of female domain, 127, 129

Children, of Issei: sent to Japan, 40-41, 147, 196; control over, as aspect of conjugal power relations, 52ff, 55; control over, in successor vs. nonsuccessor households, 59-61; differing attitudes of Issei and Nisei women toward, 126

Children, of Nisei: priority of conjugal re-

Library of Congress Cataloging in Publication Data

Yanagisako, Sylvia Junko, 1945-
  Transforming the past.

  Bibliography: p.
  Includes index.
  1. Japanese American families—Case studies.
2. Kinship—United States—Case studies.
3. Japanese American families—Washington (State)—
Seattle.   4. Kinship—Washington (State)—Seattle.
5. Seattle (Wash.)—Social conditions.   I. Title.
E184.J3Y36   1985   306.8'089956073   83-42541
ISBN 0-8047-1199-2 (cloth)
ISBN 0-8047-2017-7 (pbk.)